READING HISTORY

General Editor: Michael Biddiss
Professor of History, University of Reading

D1100474

THE RISE OF LABOUR

The British Labour Party 1890–1979

KEITH LAYBOURN
Senior Lecturer in History, Huddersfield Polytechnic

Edward Arnold
A division of Hodder & Stoughton
LONDON   BALTIMORE   MELBOURNE   AUCKLAND

© 1988 Keith Laybourn

First published in Great Britain 1988

British Library Cataloguing Publication Data

Laybourn, Keith
    The rise of Labour : the British Labour party
    1890–1979.——(Reading history).
    1. Great Britain. Political parties : Labour
    party (Great Britain), to 1979
    I. Title   II. Series
    324.24107'09

    ISBN 0–7131–6524–3

Typeset in 10/11pt Linotron Times by Northern Phototypesetting Co,
Bolton
Printed and bound in Great Britain for Edward Arnold, the
educational, academic and medical publishing division of Hodder and
Stoughton Limited, 41 Bedford Square, London WC1B 3DQ by
Biddles Limited, Guildford and London

CONTENTS

GENERAL EDITOR'S PREFACE

The aim of this series is to provide for students, especially at undergraduate level, a number of volumes devoted to major historical issues. Each of the selected topics is of such importance and complexity as to have produced the kind of scholarly controversy which not only sharpens our understanding of the particular problem in hand but also illuminates more generally the nature of history as a developing discipline. The authors have certainly been asked to examine the present state of knowledge and debate in their chosen fields, and to outline and justify their own current interpretations. But they have also been set two other important objectives. One has been that of quite explicitly alerting readers to the nature, range, and variety of the primary sources most germane to their topics, and to the kind of difficulties (about, say, the completeness, authenticity, or reliability of such materials) which the scholar then faces in using them as evidence. The second task has been to indicate how and why, even before our own time, the course of the particular scholarly controversy at issue actually developed in the way that it did – through, for example, enlargements in the scale of the available primary sources, or changes in historical philosophy or technique, or alterations in the social and political environment within which the debaters have been structuring their questions and devising their answers. Each author in the series has been left to determine the specific framework by means of which such aims might best be fulfilled within any single volume. However, all of us involved in 'Reading History' are united in our hope that the resulting books will be widely welcomed as up-to-date accounts worthy of recommendation to students who need not only reliable introductory guides to the subjects chosen but also texts that will help to enhance their more general appreciation of the contribution which historical scholarship and debate can make towards the strengthening of a critical and sceptical habit of mind.

MICHAEL BIDDISS

Professor of History
University of Reading

PREFACE

During almost two decades of teaching British Labour history I have never failed to be surprised at the limited knowledge and understanding displayed by many students who should have had a much greater awareness of this subject. Although they may have been conversant with the major published works they frequently displayed little more than rudimentary knowledge of the immense amount of literature contained in journals. Lacking an overview of the recent debates they often failed to appreciate fully the basic issues being discussed; their knowledge stopping short of the incisive cutting edge of current research. Most detailed research thus fails to reach many students in higher education and in sixth forms. It is with the intention of rectifying this situation that I have written this book, which seeks to examine the key issues which dominated the history of the British Labour party from 1893, when the Independent Labour party was formed, up to Jim Callaghan's miscalculation in holding a general election in 1979, after the 'winter of discontent' in industrial relations.

There are, of course, other books which have attempted to offer a similar type of coverage. James Hinton's, *Labour and Socialism: A History of the British Labour Movement 1867–1974* provides a very useful outline of British Labour history, though it makes no pretence of offering historiography and tends to focus upon the fringe Labour movements rather than the more substantial Labour party. Ralph Miliband, Henry Pelling and others have offered their own partial approaches (see Suggestions for Further Reading). The distinctive features of the book I offer are two; that it attempts an historiography of the debates which have convulsed the study of the Labour party and that its findings are partly rooted in regional research. The focus of the work is not confined to 'high politics' but draws widely upon the 'low politics' of rank and file Labour members and their provincial organizations. On any major political issue which faced the Labour party it is important to examine the reactions of the rank and file and to perceive how they transmitted their views to the national party, and with what effect. It is also important not to enter the terrain of Labour history with too many preconceptions. Certain factors, such as working-class support and trade unionism, are obviously central to any explanation of Labour's rise and fall. Nevertheless, the history of the British Labour party does not follow any clearly defined trajectory, and one should not expect to find one. Polemical history is fine for the converted, but it often loses its credibility in the cold light of research.

Naturally I owe a great debt to many fellow historians who have qualified and tempered my views and stimulated my interest in the history of the Labour party. I am also deeply indebted to David Clark, David James, Tony Jowitt, John Halstead, Elvira Willmott and David Wright who, over many years, have been generous with their advice. But pride of place must go to Jack Reynolds, who first revealed the existence of the Independent Labour party to me more than 20 years ago when, as a student, I took his special-subject course. Since then he has remained a seminal force in my education and research.

Keith Laybourn

Pudsey, January 1988

ABBREVIATIONS

AUEW   Amalgamated Union of Engineering Workers
ILP   Independent Labour Party
LRC   Labour Representation Committee
NAC   National Administrative Council (of the ILP)
NATO   North Atlantic Treaty Organization
NEC   National Executive Committee (of the Labour Party)
NHS   National Health Service
PLP   Parliamentary Labour Party
SEATO   South East Asian Treaty Organization
WEC   War Emergency Committee
WEWNC   War Emergency: Workers' National Committee

LIST OF TABLES

1 ISSUES IN LABOUR HISTORY

The rise of the Labour party and its development over almost ninety years are events of more than usual significance for our time. The early years of the twentieth century saw the Labour party replacing the Liberal party as the progressive party in British politics, lifting it alongside the Conservative party as one of the two major parties in British parliamentary politics. Yet by the 1980s there has been a degeneration of this arrangement to such an extent that Labour's political position has appeared to be seriously threatened by the Liberal–SDP alliance. Indeed, at the 1983 General Election it seemed that Labour's days as the second party of the state were numbered. Although the situation now seems less serious than it did then, Labour's poor election performance sensitized Labour politicians to examine the reasons for its decline and fuelled debate amongst historians of Labour history. In the 'eye of the storm' they have reflected upon two major factors, neither of which augur well for the Labour party. In the first place, there is substantial evidence that the traditional two-party system is less dominant than it used to be: in the early 1950s the two major political parties took about 96 per cent of parliamentary votes but this had fallen to 80 per cent by 1979 and 72 per cent in 1983. There was, however, a small increase to about 76 per cent in 1987. Secondly, the industrial working class, the basis of Labour's rapid growth in the 1920s, is fast declining as a major sector in the British workforce to be replaced by an expanding white-collar sector whose political voting behaviour remains far from clear. In addition, although the official trade-union movement remains loyal to the Labour party it has been estimated that up to half of trade unionists voted Conservative in the 1983 General Election: Labour no longer holds the monopoly on the trade-union vote. It may well be that the factors which helped to make the Labour party are those which are now threatening its very existence; and Labour may well have to change and diversify if it is to survive as a major political party.

Of course, it is true that the Labour party has never enjoyed the generally high level of political support won by the Conservatives. The two inter-war Labour governments were minority administrations and the Wilson and Callaghan governments of 1964–66 and 1974–79 often had a most tenuous hold on power. Indeed it is only the two Attlee administrations, between 1945 and 1951, and the Wilson government of 1966–70 which have seen the party hold any significant majority in Parliament. This relatively limited parliamentary success has perplexed Labour supporters who have often divided between those who feel that the Labour party has never been socialist enough to win more widespread electoral support and those who feel that too much emphasis upon Clause Four and nationalization have inhibited the ability of the party to appeal to the expanding white-collar sector.

These radically different approaches to achieving the Labour party's political success have divided Labour politicians throughout the twentieth century. Ramsay MacDonald, despite his moves to win trade-union support, believed in a party which attracted all the social classes – a conception which was also held by Anthony Crosland and Hugh Gaitskell and, apparently, the present leadership. But between Mac-Donald and Kinnock lies an age when the Labour party became, through the agency of the trade-union movement, the party of the working class. And, in many respects, socialism to the trade unions often came to mean little more than nationalization.

The role, purpose and ideology of the Labour party have naturally dominated its history. Nevertheless, these issues have often been enveloped within several debates which have fascinated historians. There are five major debates currently raging about the history of the Labour party. The first is why did the Labour party emerge and, as a subsidiary, why did the Liberal party decline? This seeks to date the turnover point. Did the Labour party emerge before the First World War or did it emerge as a result of the Asquith–Lloyd George split in 1916? For the inter-war years there are two main debates. One seeks to examine why the Labour party was able to maintain its position as the second party in the British parliamentary system, despite the problems it faced in organizing the local parties and dealing with the difficulties presented by the Communist party and the Independent Labour party. The other seeks to explain why Ramsay MacDonald, Labour's aberrant leader, 'betrayed' the Labour government in August 1931? For the period since 1945 there have been two controversies concerned with the achievements and image of Labour. The Attlee administrations have figured prominently as historians have tried to measure Labour's contribution to the development of the welfare state and the divisive nature of the development and control of the health service. But the main issue at stake has been whether or not Labour's policy was souped-up Liberalism or a genuine attempt to offer economic and social citizenship for all. Since 1951 the major concern has been the conflict within the Labour party on the best way to reverse the dramatic decline in its recent political fortunes and to recapture the vote of those who have abandoned it in recent general elections.

Interpretations

These five debates have been subject to numerous interpretations, though at least four distinct approaches, or 'schools of thought', are evident. Historians of the Liberal party, such as Roy Douglas, T. Wilson, and P. F. Clarke, have questioned the assumption that the Liberal party was losing out to Labour before the First World War and, though they express a considerable range of ideas, conclude that there was nothing inevitable about the 'forward march of Labour' or the decline of Liberalism.[1] The recent revival of Liberal and Alliance fortunes has strengthened them in their conviction that it was the First World War which led to the self-induced division of the Liberal party and that even this had not proved terminal.

A second group of 'Labour' historians, which includes Ross McKibbin and James Cronin, tends to see Labour's growth as being potentially inexorable.[2] This is, in part, a reversion to the ideas put forward by G. D. H. Cole and the Webbs, and maintains that the extension of the franchise to all the working class and the emergence of class voting led to Labour's inter-war growth. By the 1920s the Labour party was the party of the working class. Cronin goes so far as to suggest that the decline of Labour's parliamentary fortunes stems from neglect rather than social change: it has consistently failed to develop policies to deal with the concerns of the growing middle class and women voters since the 1950s, hidebound by the traditional emphasis placed upon nationalization by trade unions. Indeed the formation of the Social Democratic party in 1981, and its appeal to the ex-middle-class Labour party voters, demonstrates this failure. To Cronin, then, a large proportion of the working-class and middle-class electorate want to vote Labour but find that the Labour party has failed to develop the type of policies which would allow their natural inclinations to emerge. In essence, then, Labour developed in the first half of the twentieth century because of class politics and could continue to grow if it recognizes that the traditional working class is disappearing and that it has to be a party of all classes.

Marxist historians provide a third framework through which to view the history of the Labour party. Although there are immense variations between orthodox Marxists, with their emphasis upon the economic substructure determining social relationships, and the 'new' Marxists who place more emphasis upon the political superstructure in class relations, the one dominant theme which emerges is that the Labour party has constantly failed to offer socialism to the British electorate. There is often a touching faith that had it done so then its political success would have been assured, though this view is often tempered by the further assumption that there is nothing to be gained

[1] P. F. Clarke, *Lancashire and the New Liberalism* (Cambridge, CUP, 1971); T. Wilson, *The Downfall of the Liberal Party 1914–1935* (London, Collins, 1966); R. Douglas, 'Labour in Decline 1910–1914', in D. K. Brown, ed., *Essays in Anti-Labour History* (London, Macmillan, 1974).
[2] J. E. Cronin, *Labour and Society in Britain 1918–1979* (London, Batsford, 1984); R. McKibbin, *The Evolution of the Labour Party 1910–1924* (Oxford, OUP, 1974).

from working through the parliamentary system. This strand of thought is also evident in the writings of Ralph Miliband, who has highlighted the Labour party's withdrawal from socialism since 1918 and even in the writings of David Howell, whose reference to 'Ramsay MacKinnock' captures the essential pessimism of some writers towards ever reaching socialism with a British Labour leadership which is prone to compromise.

Marxist historians have, of course, disagreed about the precise course of British Labour history in general and the role of the Labour party in particular. Although the 'peculiarities of the English' debate of the mid-1960s was wider than simply a discussion of the Labour party it had repercussions for attitudes towards it. In the debate Perry Anderson and Tom Nairn rejected E. P. Thompson's romantic and heroic vision of the working class shaping its own history. In its place, they argued that working-class history was determined by the ruling class.[3] Since then the work of Gramsci, on hegemony, has been widely used to suggest that the working class are manipulated by the ruling class. But Gramsci held out hope for socialism for he distinguished between the state and civil society – which was the accumulation of voluntary activities and associations, trade unions, churches, community, political parties and trade unions. In societies such as Britain, where civil society was highly developed, he argued that the advance to socialism consisted of the transformation of civil society, as a basis for the transformation of the state. The implication is clear; the Labour movement could only work within the framework laid down by the ruling class but could achieve socialism, if it wished, through a moral and intellectual crusade in civil society. Indeed, it has been argued that the creation of the welfare state in post-war Britain might be viewed as evidence of the success of building a consensus between a diverse set of social forces in order to transform the state.[4]

A fourth set of opinions, offering an empirical approach, is influenced by the work of R. F. Price, who believed that there is nothing inevitable in the course of Labour history.[5] He maintains that, whether in industrial relations or politics, the Labour process in society has worked through a constant series of accommodations and negotiations, conditioned by the social and economic environment, which as circumstances change may set off a further series of compromises. These arrangements, whether at work or in politics, might strengthen or weaken the position of Labour. For Price, then, it is a normal situation for Labour's forward march to be halted and reversed: there is nothing certain about its growth if the objective conditions change.

---

[3]P. Anderson, 'Origins of the Present Crisis', *New Left Review*, 23 (1964); T. Nairn, 'The English Working Class', *New Left Review*, 24 (1964).
[4]*Marxism Today*, April 1987, Gramsci Supplement.
[5]R. Price, *Labour in British Society* (London, Croom Helm, 1986), p. 12.

Indeed, Price hints that the Thatcher government, faced with Labour's failure to achieve change in industry through the Social Contract, has decided the experiment of undermining the trade unions in order to force Britain to modernize her industry and meet the challenge of foreign competition. In so doing, Thatcher may well be fundamentally altering the balance of forces which has allowed the Labour party to develop throughout the twentieth century.

In sum, then, four approaches have dominated the historiography of the Labour party. To 'Liberal' historians and to some empiricists there is nothing inevitable about the rise of the Labour party. The First World War, and any variety of factors could encourage or delay its growth. To Marxist historians, the Labour party is not likely to achieve socialism, though it might occasionally form a government. Only the McKibbin and Cronin approach exhibits an almost Whiggish belief in the inevitable progress of the Labour party – a progress only impaired by the Labour party's own failure to develop relevant policies.

The Argument

The underlying theme of this book ranges between the attitudes of McKibbin, Cronin and Price. In brief, it maintains that the Labour party's growth in the early twentieth century was inevitable given the social and economic issues of the time, that the association with the working class reached its high-point during the inter-war years but that the post-war years have necessitated that the Labour party meet the changing economic and social environment – and this it has failed to do.

The fluctuating fortunes of the Labour party have been dependent upon three major factors. The first is that, despite the influence of socialist groups, the early years of British Labour politics were dominated by Liberal Radicalism. The early Labour leaders – Keir Hardie, Philip Snowden and Ramsay MacDonald – were raised in the political atmosphere of Liberal Radicalism which committed them to a belief in the inexorable path of progress and made them fervent advocates of Gladstonian economic orthodoxy. It is wise to remember that the Labour party did not adopt a socialist clause until its 1918 Constitution was introduced and that even then Liberal Radicalism prevailed within the Labour leadership and dominated the economic policies of the first two Labour governments in 1924 and 1929–31. It was not until the departure of Philip Snowden and Ramsay MacDonald in 1931 that Liberal Radicalism fully gave way to other forces.

Most importantly, trade unionism became the increasing vital factor in the success of the Labour party. The whole purpose of forming the Labour Representation Committee in 1900 was to win trade-union support from the Liberal party. By 1909, when the Miners' Federation of Great Britain affiliated to the Labour party, this task had been largely accomplished. The trade unions provided the finance and membership for the Labour party and dominated it with their huge affiliated membership. The 1918 Constitution further strengthened the trade-union hold on the party and this was extended through the inter-war years and after. There were obviously advantages for the Labour party in this relationship: its membership increased, its finances improved and trade unionism acted as Labour's *modus vivendi* for obtaining working-class support. The inter-war years saw class politics at its height, largely as a result of this relationship. But there were problems. Local constituency parties began to object at this domination of the trade unions in their politics and tactics. There was also much frustration at the relatively right-wing policies which trade unions exhibited. But most of all, despite their general support for MacDonald and the Labour leadership, trade unionism posed a threat to the vision of a Labour party commanding the support of all the classes – a vision which MacDonald and Philip Snowden strongly supported. This conflict between Labour's Liberal Radicals and Labour's trade unionists, partly explains why the Labour leadership was hesitant in speaking out in favour of the General Strike in 1926 – though trade unions had always attempted to keep workplace problems distant from politics. Above all, it provides at least the background to the crisis of 1931 which saw the departure of MacDonald and Snowden, Labour's class of 1906, from the second Labour government.

It is the increasing domination of the Labour party by the trade-union movement which has presented the party with its third feature and, indeed, its major problem of recent years – its waning political popularity. In the immediate post-war years the Labour party won support for its policies of creating the welfare state and establishing economic citizenship. But since 1951 its policies, which were once so urgent and appealing, have failed to develop and relate to the changing nature of society. The old shibboleths, based upon the trade-union objectives of a fairer treatment for the working class, have been trotted out at general election after general election. Anthony Crosland, Hugh Gaitskell and others, most recently Neil Kinnock and Roy Hattersley, have attempted to diversify Labour party policies, but to little avail. The Labour party is still seen as the party of nationalization rather than as one committed to other measures of social equality and economic growth. The trouble is that the politics of trade-union and working-class loyalty have become less relevant in all general elections since 1951: Labour's proportion of the vote has diminished as fewer of a declining working class vote Labour. But by the 1979 General Election the Labour party, which was gradually expanding its support amongst the lower-middle class, was failing to develop policies to secure that vote. This left the Labour party vulnerable, for any party which offered relevant policies to the lower-middle class and white-collar sector was likely to take away Labour supporters. This partly explains why Labour's middle-class support declined following the formation of the Social Democratic party in 1981. Since the 1950s, then, the problem facing the Labour party has been one of adjusting its trade-union dominated policies to the needs of a changing society. Between the 1950s and 1979, it was failing to register those needs against the background of militant trade unionism and the failure of its governments to fulfil their promises.

This is a surprising failure given the history of the Labour party, which was born out of compromise. There was the alliance with the trade unions in 1900, the Lib-Lab alliance in 1903 and the increasing adjustments to the needs of trade unionism in the 1920s and 1930s. In other words, the growth of the Labour party has often depended upon a sensitivity to change and a strong sense of pragmatism. The problem it now faces is one which Ramsay MacDonald, Philip Snowden and the early Liberal Radicals perceived – the need for the party to make itself the vehicle of social justice for the middle classes as well as the working classes.

National and Local Studies

Many histories of the Labour party have been written from the perspective of 'high politics'. The Webbs, G. D. H. Cole and many other writers of the early twentieth century concentrated upon the national perspective. In recent years, Ross McKibbin, James Hinton, and many others, have followed suit.[6] It is only recently that local and regional histories have begun to emerge to provide the rank and file reactions to the national events. The book which I wrote with Jack Reynolds in 1984, though it had the national title *Liberalism and the Rise of Labour, 1890–1918*, in fact examined the national debates about the embryonic Labour party within the context of a regional study of West Yorkshire – an area famous as an early centre of Independent Labour party and Labour party activity.[7] P. F. Clarke's, *Lancashire and the New Liberalism*, though essentially about the Liberal party offers a similar regional study for Lancashire. Obviously, on national themes such as MacDonald's departure from the second Labour government in 1931, the national perspective is important but it is also useful to be aware of the local and regional research on national events which have shaped the course of British Labour history. It is thus the intention that

[6]McKibbin, *Labour Party;* J. Hinton, *Labour and Socialism: A History of the British Labour Movement 1867–1974* (Brighton, Harvester, 1983).
[7]K. Laybourn and J. Reynolds, *Liberalism and the Rise of Labour 1890–1918* (London, Croom Helm, 1984).

this book will draw upon the regional history of the Labour party, particularly in West Yorkshire, to help to explain the events which have dominated British Labour history.

Final Note

The history of the Labour party is immensely diverse and the issues are intensely controversial, not least because of the polemical nature of much of what has been written. Nevertheless, the increasing availability of a rich seam of papers relating to the ILP and the Labour party now allows for a more up-to-date account of the vital issues which have affected the party. During the last ten or fifteen years Labour party and ILP records have become more readily available through the microfilm and microform production of a variety of primary material, including the LRC correspondence, the minutes and pamphlets of the Labour party, the Francis Johnson collection of ILP correspondence and the records of local Labour party and ILP branches. The Ramsay MacDonald papers have been returned to the PRO and the Cabinet minutes and records of Labour governments up to 1951 are now available. In addition, much can be gained about events since the mid 1950s from the diaries and autobiographies of prominent Labour figures and Cabinet ministers.

In recent years the increasing availability of primary material and the emphasis placed by E. P. Thompson and Asa Briggs on the need for more local studies to examine the rank and file support of the Labour movement and working-class history, in its widest sense, has produced an avalanche of publications many of which need to be drawn into the wider framework of Labour history. The primary aim of this book, as with the series as a whole, is to produce a clear pathway through the forest of detailed research which has appeared on the Labour party in recent years and to reflect upon how the increasing availability of primary sources has begun to change or modify the state of our knowledge.

2 THE RISE OF LABOUR AND THE DECLINE OF LIBERALISM, *c.*1890–1918

From a peak of 400 MPs in the 1906 general election the Liberal party crashed to 40 in 1924. The Labour party had made comparable gains, rising from a mere handful of MPs at the beginning of the century to 191 in 1923 – enough to form a minority government. Even after the general election in 1924, the defeated Labour party had 151 MPs and was clearly the alternative party of government to the Conservatives. In 1929, with 289 MPs, it formed its second minority Labour government.

The voters had clearly abandoned the Liberal party in favour of the Labour and Conservative parties. The problem of historians is to analyse the reasons for the precise timing of the change. Was the shift of support before 1914 decisive or did the Liberal party hold on to the progressive vote until the war? In other words, was class politics decisive in undermining the Liberal party before 1914 or was the Liberal party destroyed by the internal battles between Asquith and Lloyd George in 1916?

Historiography of Debate: Class Politics v. Impact of War

George Dangerfield's, *Strange Death of Liberal England*, written more than half a century ago, announced that the 'death knell of Liberalism was ringing' well before 1914 and after that 1906 the Liberal party was 'no longer the party of the left'.[1] Although Dangerfield's writings are mainly a literary confection of assertions gathered around the view that the Liberal party was incapable of dealing with the challenge of Labour, female suffrage, Ireland and constitutional change they have provided the basis of a debate which still rages today. What he did was to pick up on the ideas of G. D. H. Cole and a number of Fabian historians who had tended to accept an almost Whiggish belief in the continuous and inevitable rise of Labour. Dangerfield merely perpetuated the belief that the Liberal party, amongst other

[1] G. Dangerfield, *The Strange Death of Liberal England* (London, MacGibbon & Kee, 1966 edition), p. 22 and chapter 2.

things, fell victim to the development of class politics as the working class attached itself to the political ambitions of the Labour party.

Dangerfield's work was based almost entirely upon published primary and secondary sources. Living in the USA, he had little opportunity to study his subject at first hand and the accessibility of Labour party and trade union records was still limited. During the next twenty years the LRC and Labour party records became more available, and during the 1950s E. P. Thompson and Asa Briggs began to encourage regional and local studies in order to build up a more accurate picture of British Labour history. It was in this context of an increasing supply of primary resources, the demand for both more national and local research, that Dangerfield's analysis was taken further and modified.

It was almost twenty years before Henry Pelling produced his seminal work, providing evidence of the way in which the ILP, and the Labour party, began to cultivate trade-union support at the expense of the Liberals.[2] More recently Ross McKibbin has been the leading spirit behind this general approach. Examining the history of the Labour party between 1910 and 1924, he has argued that Labour's increasing association with the trade-union movement captured for it the support of the working class: 'Yet the Labour Party was not based upon broadly articulated principles, but rather upon a highly developed class-consciousness and intense class loyalties. The trade-unions cultivated this consciousness and these loyalties . . .'[3] This process of rising working-class attachment to the Labour party was, apparently, well entrenched before the First World War and spelled the decline of the Liberal party.

Since the mid 1960s this class approach to the decline of Liberal party and the rise of Labour has come under attack from historians whose general brief has been to examine the history of the Liberal party. Trevor Wilson, Roy Douglas, P. F. Clarke, Chris Cook, and, more recently, Michael Bentley have attempted to explain the demise of the Liberal party in terms of the cultural and social change brought about by the First World War and the internal conflict within the party resulting from the replacement of Asquith as Prime Minister by Lloyd George in 1916.[4] The 'rampant omnibus of war', not class politics, is thus propounded as the explanation for the inter-war decline of Liberalism for the war initiated a process of disintegration in the

[2]H. Pelling, *The Origins of the Labour Party* (London, Macmillan, 1954).
[3]R. McKibbon, *The Evolution of the Labour Party 1910–1924* (Oxford, OUP, 1974), p. 243.
[4]P. F. Clarke, *Lancashire the New Liberalism* (Cambridge, CUP, 1971); T. Wilson, *The Downfall of the Liberal Party 1914–1935* (London, Collins, 1966); K. D. Brown, *The English Labour Movement* (London, Gill and Macmillan, 1982); K. Burgess, *The Challenge of Labour* (London, Croom Helm, 1980); R. Douglas, 'Labour in Decline 1910–1914', in K. D. Brown, ed., *Essays in Anti-Labour History* (London, Macmillan, 1974).

Liberal party which began in 1916 and was complete by the 1930s – a point stressed more recently by Michael Bentley when he wrote that 'the First World War not only buried the Liberal future but rendered hopeless the past by which Liberals had chartered the course which took them there.'[5]

Given such an explanation, these historians have attempted to prove that the Liberal party was politically healthy in 1914 and that the Labour party was performing badly. This desire has led Clarke to suggest that New Liberalism, with its greater emphasis upon social reform, was the key to the Liberal revival between 1906 and 1914.[6] Others, including K. O. Morgan and A. W. Purdue, have maintained that in some regions of the country the Old Liberalism, with its emphasis upon the shibboleths of peace, retrenchment and free trade and its roots in Nonconformity, was surviving well.[7] Yet others have questioned the success of the pre-war Labour party. K. D. Brown has recently questioned the extent of pre-war working-class support for Labour and reminded us of Philip Snowden's reflection that labour representation in Parliament, in 1913, was there 'mainly by the good-will of the Liberals'.[8] Roy Douglas's article, 'Labour in Decline 1910–1914', stresses that whilst indications of Labour's standing on the eve of war are mixed that its parliamentary by-election results were poor and that it did not seem to be making progress.[9]

The sharp lines of demarcation are obvious – was it class politics or the First World War which accounted for the failure of the Liberal party? However, the broad debate has spawned a number of sub-debates – the most important concerning the issues of the franchise, the New-Liberal ideology and local developments.

The issue of the impact of the pre-war parliamentary franchise has become extremely complex in recent years, and is now studded with speculative calculations about the proportions and numbers of middle-class and working-class males excluded from the parliamentary vote before 1914. Matthew, McKibbin and Kay have argued that if the four million or so, largely working-class, men who did not have the vote in 1914 been enfranchised as they were under the 1918 Franchise Act then the Labour party would have presented a more serious political challenge to Liberalism than was apparent in its pre-war parliamentary

[5]Wilson, *Downfall*, p. 23; M. Bentley, *The Climax of Liberal Politics: British Liberalism in Theory and Practice 1868–1918* (London, Edward Arnold, 1987), p. 152.
[6]Clarke, *Lancashire*, pp. 1–14.
[7]K. O. Morgan, 'The New Liberalism and the Challenge of Labour: The Welsh Experience, 1885–1929', in Brown, ed., *Essays in Anti-Labour History;* A. W. Purdue, 'The Liberal and Labour Party in North East Politics', *International Review of Social History*, I (1981).
[8]*Labour Leader*, 26 June 1913.
[9]Douglas, 'Decline', pp. 116–19.

representation.[10] P. F. Clarke, M. Hart and Duncan Tanner disagree, their views being represented by the statement that 'The war caused the Liberal party to break up intellectually, in the constituencies (especially after the election), and in Parliament.'[11] Furthermore, they argue that the pre-war franchise imposed random inequality and denied the vote to male members of both the middle and working classes. Indeed, contrary to the impression given by McKibbin, and others, that it was only the working-class males who were disfranchised, Duncan Tanner has estimated that at least '350,000 single middle-class men must have been either voteless or registered under some other heading', due to the vagaries of a franchise which did not guarantee the vote to lodgers.[12] In addition, it is further contended that it is simply nonsense to assume that nearly all those male voters who were disfranchised before 1914 would have voted Labour if they had had the opportunity.

Less speculative and more contentious is the debate surrounding the impact of New Liberalism. It was L. T. Hobhouse, J. A. Hobson and David Lloyd George who, attempting to retain working-class support within the Liberal party at a time when organized Labour was demanding a bigger say in the economic and political structure of the nation, offered a variety of 'social reforms' and compromises to the working class which have become known as New Liberalism.[13] Their prime concern was to reconcile the demands of labour with the need for Liberal party unity, an equation which was never going to be easily arranged given the party's reliance upon industrial and capitalist wealth. They offered industrial conciliation as a solution to industrial conflict, public ownership when efficiency would be served and communal responsibility over sectional interests.[14] The distinctive feature of these, and other New Liberal, policies was that they offered a framework whereby harmony rather than class or sectional, conflict would be promoted. Indeed, Lloyd George stated to the National Reform Union in 1914 that 'it is better that you should have a party which combines every section and every shade of opinion, taken from all classes of the community, rather than a party which represents one shade of opinion alone or one class of community alone'.[15] On another

[10]H. C. Matthew, R. I. McKibbin and J. A. Kay, 'The franchise factor in the rise of the Labour party', *English Historical Review*, XCI (1976).

[11]M. Hart, 'The Liberals, the War, and the Franchise', *English Historical Review*, XCVII (1982), p. 381.

[12]D. Tanner, 'The Parliamentary Electoral System, the "Fourth Reform Act" and the Rise of Labour in England and Wales', *Bulletin of the Institute of Historical Research*, LVI (1983).

[13]D. Powell, 'The New Liberalism and the Rise of Labour, 1886–1906', *Historical Journal*, 29, 2 (1986).

[14]*Op. cit.*, pp. 376, 379, 382.

[15]*Manchester Guardian*, 7 November 1904, quoted in Powell, 'New Liberalism', p. 391. Also see C. Wrigley, *David Lloyd George and the Labour Movement* (Hassocks, Harvester, 1976).

occasion he added that 'Liberals are against anything in the nature of class representation and I think it was a mistake for the Labour Party to go in for anything like independent class representation. They will realize that sooner or later'.[16] Community, compromise and agreement were thus seen as the alternatives to a socialist-type Labour party committed to changing society in favour of the working class. New Liberalism was to be the referee in British society not the harbinger of class interest.

P. F. Clarke has been the clearest exponent of the view that this New Liberalism was responsible for the Liberal revival before the First World War. His classic regional study of Lancashire suggests that the changing fortunes of the Liberal party in that county were very largely a product of the new Liberal ideas which were offered to the electorate by C. P. Scott, editor of the *Manchester Guardian*, Winston Churchill and Lloyd George. The difficulty for Clarke is that he asserts that Lancashire was the cockpit of Edwardian politics and that the factors which were important in Lancashire were evident elsewhere.[17] The fact is that there is little supporting evidence for his viewpoint, even from those who maintain that the Liberal party was performing well up to 1914. Welsh Liberalism was, apparently, successful because of Old Liberalism, with its traditional commitment to free trade, peace, retrenchment, Nonconformity and Welsh Nationalism: 'new Liberalism barely existed. It with with virtually no discussion in the Welsh language press'.[18] There is little to suggest that New Liberalism, rather than old Liberalism, was responsible for the Liberal party's political successes in the nonconformist North East nor that there was a significant input of New Liberalism into other regions such as the West Riding of Yorkshire and London. Indeed, Paul Thompson, in his classic study of London politics between the 1880s and the First World War, has suggested that the London Liberal party recovered in the Edwardian period due to a variety of fortunate factors, including the advantages it gained from the electoral pact with the LRC. However, once Labour was separately organized it appears that the 'ultimate outlook for Liberalism was bleak'.[19] It was precisely because the Liberals did not have to offer a programme designed to appeal to the Labour vote in 1906 and 1910 that the Liberal party was successful. The issues of free trade in 1906 and the actions of the House of Lords in 1910 made New Liberal policies unnecessary. In contrast those who reject the view that the Liberal party was well placed on the eve of war

---

[16]*Carnarvon Herald*, 21 October 1904, quoted in Powell, 'New Liberalism', p. 391.
[17]Clarke, *Lancashire*, p. vii.
[18]Morgan, 'Welsh Experience', p. 164.
[19]Purdue, 'North East Politics'; K. Laybourn and J. Reynolds, *Liberalism and the Rise of Labour 1890–1918* (London, Croom Helm, 1984), P. Thompson, *Socialists, Liberals and Labour: The Struggle for London 1885–1914* (London Routledge & Kegan Paul, 1967), p. 170.

have stressed that in areas as diverse as Norfolk and West Yorkshire it was Old Liberal sentiments which survived to push the party into its suicidal conflict with Labour.[20]

Criticism has been taken further by David Powell who feels that New Liberalism might have been the right response to the industrial conflicts of the 1890s and early 1900s but that its very neutrality in rejecting the sectional interests threatened the trade-union movement and the Labour party.[21] In the final analysis, he has argued that, New Liberalism was not sufficiently committed to the type of change that trade unions and the emergent Labour movement wanted. It failed to reconcile the demands of organized Labour with those of capitalism and did not halt the aspirations of the politically active members of the working class: 'Once the Labour party had come into existence, it rapidly acquired an identity and a momentum of its own and was able to present itself as a credible alternative focus for working-class loyalties'.[22]

Whatever occurred in Lancashire, it appears that New Liberalism had little to do with the survival and recovery of the Liberal party in other areas.[23] Moreover, Kenneth Morgan makes a telling point about Lloyd George, one of the chief architects of New Liberalism: 'After 1908, he was a Liberal in England and an Old Liberal in Wales'.[24] In the end regional demands counted for more than the personal desires of even the most eminent politician. Also, it is questionable whether the Liberal social reforms of 1906 to 1914 carried much political weight amongst the working class and with organized labour. Pat Thane has recently argued convincingly that Labour job security, fair wages, and trade-union wage rates, were greater priorities than social welfare legislation and that the Labour party did not simply offer passive support for government-initiated reforms.[25] Perhaps one should not subsume the Labour vote into the wider progressive vote for New Liberalism, as Clarke does for Lancashire.

The franchise issue and New Liberalism are, of course, central themes to any analysis of the regional and local political scene throughout Britain. But it is immediately evident that Clarke stands almost alone in suggesting that Lancashire, as the cockpit of British politics, was representative of what was going on in British politics between 1906 and 1914.[26] The fact is that most regional and local

[20]A. Howkins, 'Edwardian Liberalism and Industrial unrest', *History Workshop*, 4 (1977).
[21]Powell, 'New Liberalism', pp. 381, 384, 393.
[22]*Op. cit.*, p. 383.
[23]Clarke, *Lancashire*, preface, nevertheless maintains that the argument is less over Lancashire than a 'general theory which can subsume Lancashire'.
[24]Morgan, 'Welsh Experience', p. 170.
[25]P. Thane, 'The Labour Party and State "Welfare" ', in K. D. Brown, ed., *The First Labour Party 1906–1914* (London, Croom Helm, 1985).
[26]Clarke, *Lancashire*, preface.

surveys based primarily on local records and the press have demonstrated a variety of experiences. Welsh, North East and Yorkshire Liberalism survived on Old Liberal values and support. In some towns, such as Bradford, Halifax and Leicester, the ILP and the Labour party had made significant inroads into areas where Liberalism had once been omnipotent. The patchwork of experience is not open to easy interpretation but one thing is clear – New Liberalism may have been vital in Lancashire but it failed to sustain Liberalism elsewhere.

One problem in interpreting the local and regional evidence is that most attention is still focused upon parliamentary politics. On this basis even the strongest of Labour areas would appear to have presented a limited challenge to an entrenched Liberal party. In West Yorkshire, for instance, the Labour party held only three or four parliamentary seats at any one time between 1906 and 1914 whilst the Liberal party normally gained the other nineteen, except for the 1895 and 1900 general elections when it won only fourteen.[27] Concentration upon the results of parliamentary by-elections lead to a similar conclusion, as is evident in Roy Douglas's article 'Labour in Decline 1910–1914' and Michael Bentley's book on *The Climax of Liberal Politics*. The trouble is that such pre-occupation with parliamentary results alone hides the substantial evidence of Labour's growth which emanates from municipal and local election results, the annual indicators of change. Recent research indicates that Labour's success in local contests cannot be lightly dismissed as representing 'no more than the natural result of increased intervention'.[28] By the same token, it could be argued that Labour's failure to intervene in parliamentary elections, because of limited finance, obviously meant that Labour's political strength would be under-represented in Parliament.

The fact is that there is now sufficient reason to consider that Parliamentary performances are not an adequate basis for analysing the changing appeal of the political parties. The limited franchise, at a time when the Labour party had few full-time agents to represent its supporters at the registration courts, may well have blighted Labour's political performance. But above all, parliamentary elections normally occur only every four or five years and, as Clarke and others have suggested of the First World War, the climate of opinion might well have changed in that period. The local and municipal election results on the eve of war suggest that this was the case and that the Labour party was capturing a substantial local vote between 1910 and 1914.

Though there is, as yet, no fully detailed survey of Labour's political challenge in local and municipal politics, one recent survey of municipal election contests in England and Wales has suggested that the Labour party was making significant inroads into Liberal support from

---

[27]K. Laybourn and J. Reynolds, *Liberalism and the Rise of Labour, 1890–1918* (London, Croom Helm, 1984), p. 127.
[28]Douglas, 'Labour in Decline', p. 123.

about 1909 onwards and that 'this material casts grave doubt on the notions that both Labour and Liberalism may be "subsumed in progressivism"; Labour "fared abysmally" in all contests with the Liberals from December 1910 to the outbreak of war; or that it was "in decline" '.[29] This evidence is supported by some regional research which, whilst indicating the volatility of the local electorate, suggests that the Labour party was making significant political gains on the eve of war.[30] Some of this evidence is presented in Table 2.1.

Table 2.1 Labour's local and municipal success, 1901–13

Year	Municipal victories in England and Wales	West Yorkshire	
		Municipal representatives	*All local representatives
1901	31	26	68
1902	56	26	69
1903	82	27	72
1904	90	37	86
1905	136	41	81
1906	91	47	89
1907	80	51	89
1908	87	44	107
1909	82	47	121
1910	95	44	128
1911	135	61	154
1912	101	70	162
1913	171	85	188

*This figure includes municipal, County Council, urban district council, rural district council, parish council, board of guardian and school board representatives.

Moreover, those who have detected Labour's breakthrough at a number of towns and constituencies, in both local and parliamentary election results, have often been consumed by the question – why did Labour emerge to undermine Liberal hegemony? Some have argued that the crucial factor was that trade union support flowed from Liberalism to Labour. The clearest exponents of this viewpoint have been Henry Pelling and Ross McKibbin, though, more recently, there has been a spate of publications by James Hinton, Keith Laybourn and

[29]M. G. Sheppard and John L. Halstead, 'Labour's Municipal Election Performance in Provincial England and Wales 1901–13', *Bulletin of the Society for the Study of Labour History*, 39 (1979), p. 42.
[30]Sheppard and Halstead, 'Municipal Election', p. 43; Laybourn and Reynolds, *Liberalism and Labour*, pp. 109, 149.

Jack Reynolds which have explored this point further.[31] The argument tends to be that rising industrial conflict, resulting from the speeding up of machinery, exposed the fact that the majority of the Liberal middle class were opposed to trade unions in industrial disputes and that this become overt in the actions they were prepared to support against trade unionists. Others have suggested that the strong ethical appeal of socialism counted for more, especially in areas where trade unionism was weak. David Clark had argued that the Labour party in Colne Valley was successful because 'As trade unionism was particularly weak in the area, the collectivist instinct of their Socialism was based upon the clubs, and divorced from the strictures of trade unionism, the ethical nature of their Socialism became dominant. This was reinforced by the itinerant "preachers" of the "Gospel of Socialism" who became such a feature of the Labour clubs'.[32] David James has painted a similar picture of Keighley.[33] However, whatever their differences, these historians are united together in their implacable belief that the pre-war Liberal party was failing to meet the challenge of Labour.

From these three sub-debates, it becomes clear that unifying strategies divide these two groups or schools of historians. Those who maintain that the Labour party was rising rapidly before the war invoke the class conflict of pre-war years, the formation of the Labour party and the political attachment to it by trade unionism as evidence of the failure of Liberalism. They argued that the inequalities of the franchise meant that Labour underperformed in parliamentary elections and that it was this factor, not New Liberalism nor Old Liberalism, which confined the pre-war Labour party to limited parliamentary success and fitful, though significant, advances in local elections. In sharp contrast, those who stress that the resilient pre-war Liberal party was destroyed by the First World War assume that the random inequalities of the franchise meant that the Liberal party was just as disadvantaged as the Labour party and that it was New Liberalism or Old Liberalism, or a combination of the two, which explain the healthy state of Liberalism on the eve of war. Lacking common ground the two 'schools of thought' have been trenchant and bitter in debate. They rarely perceive the weakness of their own presumptions nor do they allow for the evidence of their opponents.

[31]J. Hinton, *Labour and Socialism: A History of the Labour Movement 1967–1974* (Brighton, Harvester, 1983); J. Reynolds and K. Laybourn, 'The Emergence of the Independent Labour Party in Bradford', *International Review of Social History*, XX (1975); J. Hill, 'Manchester and Salford Politics and the Early Development of the Independent Labour Party', *International Review of Social History*, XXVI (1981).
[32]D. Clark, *Colne Valley: Radicalism to Socialism* (London, Longman, 1981), p. 126.
[33]D. James, 'The Keighley ILP 1892–1900: Realising the Kingdom of Heaven', in J. A. Jowitt and R. K. S. Taylor, eds., *Bradford 1890–1914: The Cradle of the ILP* (Bradford, Occasional Papers University of Leeds, 1980).

A more balanced approach is necessary which accepts that the First World War was responsible for significant political and social change. Nevertheless, there is no doubting that the Liberal party was finding great difficulty in containing the challenge of Labour before the war. Its problems were largely a product of the development of trade unionism before the war and its own inability to absorb the organized working class within the caucus system which it had developed in the 1860s and the 1870s. In the end, the lack of a positive response from the Liberal party drove the working man to look towards the Labour party not for socialism so much as for the representation of its own sectional interests.

Trade Unionism and Working-Class Support

What happened to working-class and trade-union support for political parties between 1890 and 1914? This is the crunch question in our debate, for if it can be shown that the trade-union movement, and its membership, transferred its allegiance from the Liberal party to the Labour party well before 1914 then the central tenet of the Pelling–McKibbin school of thought, the 'Labour school', is established.

Even as late as 1890 the Labour movement was a weak vehicle for the political aspirations of the working class. Trade unionism was patchy and trades councils were only just beginning to emerge in many areas. In truth, the Liberal party had little to worry about and was confident in its estimation that at least two-thirds of the working-class voters would continue to vote Liberal in the future. It was the almost endemic weakness of organized Labour which deluded the Liberal party into thinking that it could stand still in the face of the 'little breezes' of discontent that occasionally emerged. What the national Liberal party, and its local organizations, failed to appreciate was the seething discontent which had erupted among trade unionists from the late 1880s onwards. This neglect combined with working-class anger and frustration to produce an independent Labour movement.

Few historians seem to doubt the importance of industrial conflict in creating the climate for independent political action by the working classes. E. P. Thompson noted this in his seminal article 'Homage to Tom Maguire' and many more of the 'Labour school' have concurred.[34] Even the 'Liberal school' have accepted this point. K. D. Brown and Keith Burgess, in their general surveys of British Labour history, have made much the same point.[35] Consequently detailed accounts of the new unionism and the industrial disputes of the late 1880s and early

---

[34] E. P. Thompson, 'Homage to Tom Maguire', in A. Briggs and J. Saville, eds., *Essays in Labour History* (London, Macmillan, 1960).
[35] Brown, *English Labour*, chapters 5 and 6; Burgess, *Challenge of Labour*, pp. 81–95.

1890s have been rife. These disputes, indeed, were significant.

The strike amongst the girls at the Bryant and May match factory in 1888, partly led by Annie Besant, and the London Dock Strike of 1889, which shot Tom Mann and Benn Tillett to fame, were, indeed, seminal. The Dock Strike, in particular, demonstrated that relatively unskilled workers, in badly paid occupations, could secure industrial victories if the economic conditions were propitious and their organization effective. This was amply demonstrated by the gas workers. Will Thorne had organized the London gasworkers in 1888 and, following victories against the South Metropolitan Gasworks, there was a spate of gas strikes throughout the provinces,in 1889 and 1890 – which temporarily won the eight-hour day in place of the normal twelve-hour shift worked by the gas stokers.

In the textile district of West Yorkshire the impact of the 'new unionism' and industrial conflict was immediately felt. In Keighley, normally the most sedate of towns, the engineering strikes of August and September 1889 united skilled, semi-skilled and unskilled engineering workers together in the demand for a wage increase. This dispute exposed the genuine grievances of the working classes in Keighley who had been unfairly treated under the old system. A speaker at a strike meeting reflected the new, less compliant spirit of the workforce:

> Keighley was known throughout the country for two things. In the first place it was famous for science and art and technical education, and in the second place . . . it was notorious, not famous, for low wages. He wanted to put the two together and he wanted to ask them seriously what was the benefit of science and art and technical education unless they put more money in their pockets.[36]

In the wake of this dispute a Trades Council was formed, which was closely identified with the Keighley ILP in the early 1890s.

Of more lasting and pervasive influence was the Manningham Mills strike of 1890 and 1891. It was the product of the attempt by Samuel Cunliffe Lister and the shareholders of Manningham Mills to reduce the wages of their silk and plush weavers by amounts varying from 15 per cent to 33 per cent. During the course of the dispute the entire workforce, of several thousands, struck or were forced out of work, the Weavers' Association became embroiled in the dispute, the issue of free speech was raised, violence occurred and the riot act was read.[37] This dispute has been scrutinized by many historians, most notably E. P. Thompson.[38] They have demonstrated how vital it was to

---

[36] *Keighley News*, 7 September 1889.
[37] Laybourn and Reynolds, *Liberalism and Labour*, pp. 41–2.
[38] Thompson, 'Maguire'.

the political education of the working classes of West Yorkshire. Much contemporary evidence, the many recent interpretations, have stressed the way in which the political consensus between the Liberals and the working classes was destroyed and replaced by a sense of deep injustice amongst a significant proportion of the working classes in Bradford and West Yorkshire. The *Bradford Observer* reported that 'The struggle took on the character of a general dispute between capital and labour since it is well known that a large number of prominent Bradford employers agreed with the action Mr Lister had taken'.[39] The strike evoked a remarkable display of local working-class solidarity, so much so that the *Yorkshire Factory Times*, the weekly newspaper which served the textile workers, announced the end of the strike with the prophetic statement that 'Labour has so associated itself that even defeat must be victory'.[40]

E. P. Thompson, Laybourn and Reynolds, and others, have seen the Manningham Mills strike as a catalyst for many trade unionists and individuals who had begun to doubt both the impartiality of the Liberal party and its willingness to represent their interests. The *Yorkshire Factory Times* was correct in its estimation of the impact of the strike for the process of disengagement from Liberalism had already begun before the end of the dispute. In April 1891, at a strike meeting at Peckover Walks, a famous open-air meeting place in Bradford, speaker after speaker pinpointed the lessons of the strike. Charlie Glyde summed up the frustrations of many when he reflected that 'We have had two parties in the past, the can'ts and the won'ts and it is time that we had a party that will'.[41]

The 'party that will' was officially formed at the end of May 1891 at Firth's Temperance Hotel, formerly Laycock's, in East Parade, Bradford. It presaged the rapid formation of similar bodies throughout the provinces, and particularly in Lancashire and Yorkshire. This surge of activity culminated in the formation of the Independent Labour Party at its inaugural conference at Bradford in January 1893. At that stage, the new party already had a representative in James Keir Hardie, who had won one of the West Ham seats in 1892, and it very quickly mounted a local and parliamentary challenge to the Liberal and Conservative parties. By 1895 there were 305 ILP branches throughout the country, 105 of them in Yorkshire, 73 in Lancashire and Cheshire, 41 in Scotland, 29 in London, 23 in the Midlands, 18 in the North East, eight in Kent, four in the Eastern Counties, three in Ireland, three in Southern England and one in Wales.[42] Within five years, following a disastrous general election performance in 1895, the ILP had pushed

[39] *Bradford Observer*, 28 April 1981.
[40] *Yorkshire Factory Times*, 1 May 1891.
[41] *Bradford Observer Budget*, 25 April 1891.
[42] A. W. Roberts, 'The Liberal Party in West Yorkshire, 1885–1895', unpublished PhD, University of Leeds (1979), p. 256.

for the formation of the Labour Representation Committee, the early Labour party, whose objective was to secure more trade-union support.

Though most historians accept that industrial conflict engendered demands for political independence amongst part of the original working class they differ over the extent of that support. The 'Labour school' maintain that from the 1890s to the First World War, the trade-union movement was providing increasing support for the Labour party. This was, according to E. P. Thompson, first evidenced in the emergence of a large number of trades councils in the late 1880s and early 1890s whose leadership was not deeply tied up with the Liberal party. Many of these trades councils, and some longer established ones like Bradford, were quickly committed to the Socialist cause. The formation of the Labour Representation Committee was seen as an affirmation of that alliance and the capture of the political support of the Miners' Federation of Great Britain in May 1908 confirmed the success of the Labour party's attempt to win trade-union support. By that time the Labour party had increased its trade-union membership of 353,700 in 1901 to well over one million.[43] On the other hand, the 'Liberal school', feel that the trade-union support for Labour did not necessarily imply the support of their membership. The gist of their argument is best presented by K. D. Brown who wrote that

> Max Weber has argued that the bulk of everyday actions are a matter of almost automatic responses to habitual stimuli. This perhaps explains why political allegiances, once formed, are very hard to shift, unless some major interruption in the stimuli pattern occurs. Viewed in this light, therefore, it could be argued that supporting socialism, even voting Labour, in the late nineteenth century was tantamount to an aberration in political behaviour, a breaking of habits long moulded by economic, family and working circumstances.[44]

Some, including H. A. Clegg and Roy Douglas, would argue that this was also very true of the voting behaviour of working men in the early twentieth century.[45] Indeed a large proportion of the Miners' Federation membership were still opposed to supporting Labour in 1908.

Clearly, there were many trade unionists and working men still

---

[43]Pelling, *Origins*, pp. 244–5.
[44]Brown, *English Labour*, p. 189.
[45]Douglas, 'Decline', pp. 106–7; H. A. Clegg, *A History of British Trade Unions since 1889: Vol. II 1911–1983* (Oxford, Clarendon Press, 1985), p. 13; H. Clegg, A. Fox, A. F. Thompson, *A History of British Trade Unions since 1889* Vol. I 1911–1933 (Oxford, Clarendon Press, 1964); E. H. Phelps Brown, *The Growth of British Industrial Relations: a study from the standpoint of 1906–14* (London, Macmillan, 1959); C. Wrigley (ed.), *A History of British Industrial Relations, 1875–1914* (Hassocks, Harvester Press, 1982).

committed to the Liberal party. It had not, by any means, lost all of its working-class support. Nevertheless, there is strong evidence to suggest that it was not able to effectively represent the working-class voter. Once the Labour party had come into existence it offered an alternative focus for working-class loyalties. Even the emergence of a loosely based Lib-Lab arrangement in Edwardian politics distanced the Liberal party from the trade unions, since their influence on trade unions was to be increasingly directed through the LRC/Labour party. In addition, the very formulation of the Lib–Lab pact in 1903, whereby the two parties agreed to leave certain seats free for Liberal and Labour candidates to fight Conservative candidates alone, was anathema to the New Liberal idea of a harmony of interests operating within the Liberal party – its very existence was a recognition of the distinctions which were growing and the increasing popularity of the LRC. But above all, it was rapidly becoming clear that the Liberal party could not embrace trade unionism after 1900 and that by 1914 British trade unionism was firmly identified with the Labour party.

David Powell noted the Liberal party's loss of trade-union support in his article on New Liberalism.[46] To be fair, of course, New Liberalism did not stand a chance of offering industrial harmony to trade unions in a climate of debate poisoned by events such as the Taff Vale case.

In 1901 the House of Lords upheld the claim made by the Taff Vale Railway Company against the Amalgamated Society of Railway Servants for financial damages incurred by its members during a strike. The decision exposed all union funds to similar claims. In this, and other similar cases, the House of Lords had stripped away the financial impunity of the trade unions. With one fell swoop, the Lords had given added impetus to the demand for independent parliamentary representation for the working classes and strengthened the case of the LRC. As L. T. Hobhouse stated 'that which no Socialist writer or platform orator could achieve was effected by judges'.[47] The LRC promised to work with the TUC to reverse the judgement and, as many historians have noted, the embryonic Labour party was rewarded by a substantial increase in membership; from more than 350,000 in early 1901 to 861,000 by 1903.[48]

Quite clearly, the surge of LRC membership arose from the fact that large unions, including the engineers and Lancashire textile workers decided to affiliate to the LRC. But one must also remember the fact that the Taff Vale judgement gave a spur to trades councils to affiliate. In the West Yorkshire area, the Bradford, Leeds and Todmorden trades councils had affiliated before the judgement. Between 1902 and

[46]Powell, 'New Liberalism', pp. 384–7.
[47]Clarke, *Lancashire*, p. 139.
[48]Brown, *English Labour*, p. 199.

1904 the trades councils at Halifax, Wakefield, Keighley, Dewsbury and Batley, Huddersfield and Shipley also joined.[49] The Trades Disputes Act (1906), which nullified the Taff Vale judgement, came too late to staunch this flow of trade-union support to the Labour party. The outburst of industrial conflict between 1910 and 1914, which produced national transport and mining strikes, strengthened and speeded up this process of rising trade-union support for the Labour party, despite the counter claims of support made by a small group of syndicalists led by Tom Mann.

In an article on 'Labour and the Trade Unions', Chris Wrigley has also assembled convincing evidence that the Liberal party could not cope with the demands of trade unions.[50] He acknowledges that the Labour party was not the only mouthpiece of the TUC in 1906, for the TUC also supported the trade-union mining MPs who were Lib-Lab at that time, but suggests that it rapidly became so. Many trade unionists were still suspicious of socialists and both Liberal and Conservative parties vied for trade-union support despite the fact that many trade unions paid political funds to Labour; but the Osborne Judgement put the matter beyond doubt.

Walter Osborne was a determinedly non-Labour party trade unionist who extolled the virtues of trade unionism coming to an accommodation with capital, in order to achieve industrial harmony, increased output and improved wages. What he objected to was the socialist type of trade unionism which had emerged to advocate state intervention and the eight-hour day. On an individual basis he campaigned against individual members of trade unions being asked to contribute to the political funds of the Labour party and used the law to uphold his objection in 1908 and 1909. He took legal action to prevent the Amalgamated Society of Railway Servants from levying funds for the Labour party and was supported by the House of Lords. This decision, according to Wrigley, created problems for both the Liberal and Unionist parties. The trade unionists wished for a reversal of the judgement and the Liberals, in particular, were torn between resisting an action which could lead to the strengthening of ties between the trade unions and the Labour party and presenting too hostile a reaction which would alienate trade unionists.

Both Unionists and Liberals were in a quandary and this is reflected by the split within the Liberal party. On the one hand, Herbert Samuel detected that if the Osborne Judgement was not reversed then the result would be 'to increase the separation between Labour and Liberalism' whilst Sir William Robson, a Liberal Attorney General, felt that the conflict between the Liberals and Socialists was inevitable:

[49] Laybourn and Reynolds, *Liberalism and Labour*, p. 107.
[50] C. Wrigley, 'Labour and the Trade Unions', in K. D. Brown, ed., *The First Labour Party 1906–1914* (London, Croom Helm, 1985).

'Nothing can avoid this conflict. It is also unfortunately too clear that the Socialists are in effective command of the Trade Union organization, and if they are at liberty to draw on that organization for funds they may do so up to £80,000 or £100,000 per annum . . .'.[51] To Robson, there were still a majority of trade unionists who objected to the political fund, although it was due to their 'inert assent'.

Lloyd George entered secret negotiations with the Unionists to block a reversal of the Osborne Judgement and the 1913 Trade Union Act did not reverse the Judgement but, rather, permitted unions to hold a secret ballot on the issue. The fact is that neither the Liberal nor the Unionist party felt much compunction to change the Osborne Judgement. In the end it rebounded upon them as union after union, holding secret ballots under the Trade Union Act 1913, voted in favour of Labour representation. Without a shadow of doubt, the Labour party had secured the trade-union vote before 1914. By the beginning of 1914 trade unions with a membership of 1,207,841 had voted on the necessity of establishing political funds for the Labour party. Of more than 420,000 members who voted 298,702 voted in favour and 125,310 against.[52] In other words of the one-third of members who bothered to vote more than 70 per cent favoured the Labour party. The organized trade-union movement and its active rank and file were overwhelmingly committed to the Labour party before the onset of war. As Wrigley suggests: 'These votes ensured Labour's post-First World War electoral finances, and in themselves reflect an element of the explanation for the rise of the Labour party and the decline of the Liberal party in the early twentieth century'.[53] But why was Labour's political performances relatively weak in the pre-war years?

The Franchise

The newly formed LRC performed badly in the general election of 1900 for only two of its fifteen candidates, Richard Bell and James Keir Hardie, had been successful. This number rose gradually through the accretion of parliamentary by-election successes, though the breakthrough in the 1906 general election only raised the figure to 29. Even after the decision of the Miners' Federation of Great Britain to join the Labour party, Labour's parliamentary representation remained disappointingly low at 42 in December 1910. In the fourteen parliamentary by-elections between 1910 and 1914, Labour candidates finished bottom of the poll on all occasions. Such results, presented in a crude and unsophisticated manner, suggest that Labour's parliamentary

[51]*Op. cit.*, p. 142.
[52]*Op. cit.*, p. 152.
[53]*Op. cit.*, p. 151.

gains were steady, though hardly impressive given the trade-union support which it had received. To the 'Liberal school' of thought they illustrate the failure of the Labour party on the eve of war – a party which had made relatively little real headway between 1906 and 1914. Most of this school of writing tend to see the Labour party as an appendage of the Liberal radicals. P. F. Clarke subsumed the twelve Labour MPs returned for Lancashire in the 1906 general election under the title of Liberal progressivism. Roy Douglas has suggested that the constitutional crisis aroused by the People's Budget also tended to relegate the Labour party to a subsidiary role so that even when it struck out against a too close association with the Liberals after 1910, it was unable to make much political impact. The reality was rather different.

The fact is that under the pre-1918 parliamentary franchise political parties required full-time agents if they were to garner their full political strength. The Labour party, unlike its major opponents, had few full-time agents before the war – a mere 17 in 1912, although it sometimes employed solicitors.[54] It was only when the national party provided a grants-in-aid scheme in May 1912, promising to pay 25 per cent of the agents' salaries, that the situation was transformed. By 1918 there were 80 agents and in 1922 the figure reached 133, though it fell to 111 in 1923. Nevertheless, the Labour party had few agents before the war whilst the Liberal party, for instance, seems to have employed nearly 300. The Society of Certificated and Associated Liberal Agents recorded 299 members in December 1915, 357 in June 1920 but only 249 in January 1928.[55] Although prime Labour areas often did have the service of a full-time agent – the Bradford ILP had appointed Sam Hemsley as early as 1897 – most local Labour party organizations relied upon the temporary and infrequent services of part-timers appointed at election time. Thus local party organizations often lacked political continuity.

It was Labour supporters, rather than those of the Liberal and Conservative parties, who were likely to fail to obtain the parliamentary franchise from registration courts simply because they were not represented or put forward. It is also not enough for Duncan Tanner to suggest that 350,000 single middle-class men must have been voteless or registered under some other heading. There were between four and five million disenfranchised males before 1914 and on Tanner's calculations alone at least 90 per cent were working class. Since the middle class represented about 20 per cent of the population it would appear that the inequality of the franchise was far from random. It is clearly impossible to estimate how many of these

[54]McKibbin, *Labour Party*, p. 143.
[55]Minutes of Society of Certificated and Associated Liberal Agents, 1916–1930, Archives Department, Leeds.

disenfranchised adult males would have voted but, given their social position and the rising commitment of the trade-union movement to the Labour party, it would be fair to suggest that at least a majority – if not more – would have voted Labour had they had the opportunity.

There is also the problem that financial position of the Labour party, somewhat reduced by detrimental impact of the Osborne Judgement, meant that it was unable to give many of its enfranchised supporters the opportunity to vote Labour. In the December 1910 General Election, for instance, the Labour party only put forward 58 candidates.

As for the suggestion that the Labour party won no by-elections between 1910 and 1914, this tends to ignore the fact that its share of the vote tended to increase. In West Yorkshire, the Holmfirth by-election of June 1912 saw Labour's proportion of the vote rise from 14.9 per cent in January 1910 to 28.2 per cent. In Keighley the 26.6 per cent of the vote which Labour secured in the 1906 general election rose to 28.9 per cent in the October 1911 by-election and, further, to 29.8 per cent in the November 1913 by-election.[56]

In the final analysis, the parliamentary performance of Labour was hardly indicative of its real appeal throughout the country on the eve of war. The franchise, financial restrictions and the absence of full-time Labour agents in the vast majority of constituencies conspired against Labour's ability to turn its rising trade-union vote to parliamentary effect. A truer measure of Labour's appeal can be seen in the annual round of local elections which, as already, suggested, indicate Labour's surge of popularity from 1909 onwards. This was obviously connected with the rapidly rising level of trade-union support but was also to do with the inability of the Liberal party to offer a credible alternative to what was generally considered to be Labour's socialist policies.

Liberalism and New Liberalism

Locating New Liberalism in regional and local politics is rather more difficult than P. F. Clarke would have us believe. Even in Lancashire, its impact upon Liberal fortunes would appear to be partly the product of subsuming twelve Labour MPs within progressive Liberalism by virtue of the secret Lib-Lab pact of 1903 – the very nature of which is a denial of the harmonizing and unifying qualities of New Liberalism. Elsewhere, even the 'Liberal school' have found it difficult to detect much evidence of active New Liberals or the medicinal powers of New Liberalism. The views of Liberal thinkers and politicians did not always percolate through from Westminster and London to the provinces. This was most obvious in the case of West Yorkshire, which

[56]Laybourn and Reynolds, *Liberalism and Labour*, p. 153.

established its credentials as a Labour stronghold in the 1890s.

West Yorkshire Liberal parties were dominated by a few, intermarried, Non-conformist woollen and worsted manufacturing families – despite the development of the caucus system of politics designed to represent the various sections of Liberal support. These Liberal 'moneybags' resisted the aspirations of the working class and compounded their sins by victimizing some of the leading trade unionists who showed interest in the ILP/Labour party.[57] Liberalism in this area was generally aggressive, abrasive and unwilling to compromise with Labour. Samuel Shaftoe, the secretary of the Bradford Trades Council and one of a small handful of Liberals on the Bradford Liberal Six Hundred, the policy-making body of Bradford and Liberalism as a whole, found himself constantly rejected by official Liberalism in his attempt to gain local political honours. In 1888, the Liberals preferred John Field, a master printer who did not pay trade-union wage rates, for the School Board elections rather than Shaftoe. Given the difficulty of winning the nomination of working-class candidates from the Liberal party it is hardly surprising that many working-class activists drifted into the ILP.

There appears to have been relatively little support for both Lib-Labism and New Liberalism in West Yorkshire. Samuel Shaftoe was active in the national Labour Electoral Association, a body formed in 1887 in order to win more Liberal nominations for working men, but was unable to sustain the movement in the face of obvious Liberal opposition.[58] The more positive social policies of New Liberalism gathered even less support than the electorally based Lib-Lab arrangement.

Martin Pugh has written on New Liberalism in Yorkshire.[59] Unfortunately his work is based upon the fact that Walter Runciman, a pronounced New Liberal, contested the Dewsbury parliamentary by-election in 1902 and not upon any evidence of the growth of New Liberalism in Dewsbury. In fact, Pugh has to admit that Runciman was returned because of Old Liberalism rather than New Liberalism.

Recent local research on Huddersfield has suggested that the Old Liberal party reorganized itself but offered little in the way of New Liberal ideas.[60] The ILP Collection of Letters, the Francis Johnson collection, which has become available on microfilm in recent years suggests that in Leeds the position was not significantly different. Although Herbert Gladstone, the Liberal Chief Whip and party architect of the secret Lib-Lab pact of 1903, was MP for Leeds West there is

[57]*Op. cit.,* pp. 51–2.
[58]Reynolds and Laybourn, 'ILP in Bradford', pp. 324–5.
[59]M. D. Pugh, 'Yorkshire and the New Liberalism?', *Journal of Modern History* (1978).
[60]R. B. Perks, 'Liberalism and the Challenge of Labour in West Yorkshire 1885–1914, with special reference to Huddersfield', unpublished PhD, CNAA through Huddersfield Polytechnic (1985).

little to suggest that New Liberalism and Lib-Labism carried much support.[61] Keighley and other industrial centres reveal little evidence that the new attitudes in Liberalism were percolating into the Liberal heartland of West Yorkshire.

Indeed, there seems to have been only one significant champion of New Liberalism in West Yorkshire – William Pollard Byles – and his fate is indicative of the limited appeal of New Liberalism in the area. Byles's father had been the founder and editor of the *Bradford Observer*, for many years the leading Liberal newspaper in Bradford. His political position thus arose from his own role as editor and owner of that newspaper. Without the constraints of industrial capital, William Pollard Byles felt able to push forward more advanced social policies. True to his New Liberal stance, he tried, unsuccessfully, to bring a speedy and harmonious conclusion to the Manningham Mills strike which convulsed Bradford in 1890 and 1891. At more or less the same time he put himself forward, successfully in the event, as Liberal candidate for Shipley in the face of the Liberal management of Salts of Saltaire, who had hitherto imposed their own candidate upon the Shipley Liberal Association. Despite his narrow victory for the Liberal candidature and the support given to him by the Shipley Trades Council, the bitterness of this conflict ensured that Old Liberalism would remain opposed to him. As a result, although he was successful at Shipley in the 1892 general election, he was narrowly defeated in the 1895 general election when some prominent Old Liberals openly supported his Unionist opponent.[62]

Nevertheless, Byles, throughout his political career, continued to develop both his Lib-Lab and New-Liberal ideas. His election address, published for the 1892 General Election, indicated how progressive a Liberal he was. Whilst he recognized that the main issue of the 1982 General Election was *'the treatment of Ireland'* he regarded the second great issue to be *'the condition of the people'*.[63] Under this second heading he wished to extend the franchise, abolish plural voting and pay MPs, though his main concern was to get the Liberal party to offer a coherent social policy. He referred to the issue of land nationalization and added that 'Beyond these things I hope that it may be found that social reforms will take legislative shape . . . I am ready to support just and reasonable proposals . . . to increase the comfort, the health and leisure, and the education of the people'. Byles's position on these issues had, if anything, hardened by 1895 and once out of Parliament he began to explore the possibilities of working more closely with the ILP.

[61]Laybourn and Reynolds, *Liberalism and Labour*, pp. 129–30.
[62]*Op. cit.,* pp. 82–8
[63]*Mr Byles's Address to the Electors: General Election, 1892, Shipley Parliamentary Division*, Bradford Archives Collection, 40D78/150.

In 1896 he attempted to intervene in the Bradford East parliamentary by-election, hoping to avoid a conflict between Keir Hardie, for the ILP, and a possible Liberal candidate. In one letter to Keir Hardie, which appears in the newly available Francis Johnson collection, he wrote:

> When you say I vacillate between two opinions and do not choose between Liberalism and Labour, you absolutely misunderstand my position. These opinions have led you to disbelieve in the Lib. party as an engine for the reforms you seek, and therefore to leave it and form a separate party. The same opinions have not led me to the same conclusions. Bad and reactionary as many Liberals are, I believe that salvation must come thro the Liberal party wh. still contained more friends of Labour than can be found outside it, and the destruction of which (if it were possible wh. it isn't) would set back the Labour clock a generation.[64]

Despite these views he managed to impose himself upon the Leeds ILP and the LRC as the Labour candidate for Leeds East in the 1900 General Election, though the fact that he never joined the ILP resulted in some trenchant criticism from local Labour activists. But Byles soon returned clearly to the Liberal fold, left Bradford in 1903 and sought his political fortunes in Lancashire, where his New Liberal ideas appear to have won support. His departure, however, prompted an outpouring of bitter recrimination from the *Bradford Daily Telegraph*, the paper of Old Liberalism in Bradford. It maintained of Byles that

> He has affluence, he has leisure, and he has ambition. That other desideratum, 'troops of friends' is denied him, or at least if he has sufficient to be called troops, his enemies are in battalions. Owing to untoward circumstances Mr Byles's political life was so circumscribed here in Bradford that it became intolerable. To find greater breathing space, and ampler air, he has had at the age of 64 to expatriate himself, to leave all his friends and associations, to go to live in Manchester. It is a hard fate but it is necessary if Mr Byles should fulfil the political role to which he is irresistibly drawn.[65]

Perhaps this 'obituary', biased as it is, is accurate. It certainly accords with the views expressed of Byles in one Labour newspaper: 'His Liberalism was not the Liberalism of the Illingworths, and the Illingworth influence is still predominant in Bradford'.[66] Most certainly there is little evidence of any wide-spread support for Byles and

[64] ILP Archive, Francis Johnson collection, 1896/84, letter from Byles to Keir Hardie, dated 21 November 1896.
[65] *Bradford Daily Telegraph*, 31 March 1903.
[66] *Bradford Labour Echo*, 11 February 1899.

New Liberal ideas in West Yorkshire, though this may not have been the case in Lancashire.

The question still arises, however, particularly in view of the peculiar nature of Lancashire politics – how relevant was New Liberalism to British politics in the decade or so before the First World War? In Lancashire the Liberal party needed to change if it was to secure its political revival and overcome a Conservative party which dominated parliamentary politics between the 1880s and 1906. Elsewhere the demand for change was often less pressing, particularly in traditional Liberal strongholds such as West Yorkshire, Wales and the North East. Dr Kenneth Morgan has firmly rejected any suggestion that New Liberalism was responsible for sustaining Liberalism in Wales.[67] Martin Pugh has come to a similar conclusion for Yorkshire in general and Dewsbury in particular: 'in safe Dewsbury . . . Runciman's victories sprang from the unexhausted seam of nineteenth-century Liberalism'.[68] Other research has tended to endorse the view that it was Old, rather than New, Liberalism which was the dominant form in 1914.

Conclusion

In this analysis, the emphasis has been to stress the dangers of over-simplification. The rise of Labour and the decline of Liberalism are not events which are easily susceptible to monocausal explanations. The rise of class politics, as evidenced through the increasing trade-union support for Labour, was just as much a factor in the transformation of progressive politics in Britain as was the First World War. The problem is one of assessing the point at which the process of change became inexorable. In this respect, it is clear that the process of political change was well established before the First World War. Local research, the ILP archive and the LRC minutes and correspondence combine with local evidence to suggest that the Labour party had emerged, had MPs, a rising trade-union membership and increasing financial support. In addition, the Old Liberalism, which was unreceptive to the demands for direct working-class representation, remained the dominant strand in most regions throughout the country. Only in areas where the Liberal party needed to change in order to increase its political support was there much evidence of a New Liberal presence, and even in those areas its influence may have been impaired by the obvious equivocation of its leaders towards reversing the Osborne Judgement in case that action should further encourage the growth of the Labour party. The fact is that the Labour party was a significant political party on the eve of war, though it obviously underperformed

[67]Morgan, 'Welsh Experience', p. 164.
[68]Pugh, 'Yorkshire and New Liberalism', p. D.1154.

in parliamentary elections because of the difficulties of the pre-war franchise. How much difference the 1918 franchise made is still open to speculation but there is no doubt that the Labour party was making significant progress in local elections and in parliamentary by-elections between 1910 and 1914.

On the eve of war the Labour party was well established and threatening the hegemony of the Liberal party in progressive politics, a process which was undoubtedly speeded up by the Asquith–Lloyd George split of 1916. It is difficult to believe, given the pre-war developments, that the war was solely responsible for the decline of the Liberal party or, conversely, that it came 'just in time to save the Labour Alliance'.[69] Nevertheless, it did bring about, and speed up the process of, political change in British society.

[69]Hinton, *Labour and Socialism*, p. 81.

3 THE IMPACT OF WAR, 1914–18

The First World War exerted a major impact upon British politics: it contributed to the growth of state intervention, shaped the Asquith–Lloyd George conflict and accentuated the trade-union base of the Labour party. It has already been established that 'Liberal' historians regard the war as the prime cause of the decline of the Liberal party whilst 'Labour' historians perceive it to be just one, and not the most important, factor in the rise of Labour and the decline of the Liberals. Yet apart from this debate there has been considerable discussion about the precise impact of the war upon the internal workings of the Labour party. Did it force the Labour party to select a socialist policy which would distinguish it from the Liberal party or is the experience of 'war, in itself, an unsatisfactory explanation of the changes in the Labour Party's position in the country'.[1] In other words, did war bring about a dramatic shift in the direction of Labour politics or did it barely affect the pattern of Labour's growth? Was there dichotomy or continuity?

Interpretations

This debate, which has rumbled on in British Labour history for a number of years, through the works of Arthur Marwick, Philip Abrams and Ralph Miliband,[2] was put into sharp focus in 1974 with the publication of two books – J. M. Winter, *Socialism and the Challenge of War: Ideas and Politics in Britain, 1912–18* and R. McKibbin, *The Evolution of the Labour Party 1910–1924*.[3]

It was Winter who offered the orthodox view that the First World War brought about significant changes to British society. Building upon Marwick's numerous studies of the volcanic impact of the First World War upon British values, organization and ideas, Winter argued that the improved incomes and employment prospects of all workers resulted in the blurring of distinctions within the working class

[1] R. McKibbin, 'Labour and Politics: the Great War', *Bulletin of the Society for the Study of Labour History*, 34 (Spring, 1977), p. 3.
[2] A. Marwick, *The Deluge* (London, Macmillan, 1975 edition): P. Abrams, 'The Failure of Social Reform, 1918–1920', *Past and Present* 24 (1963); R. Miliband, *Parliamentary Socialism* (London, Merlin, 1972 edition).
[3] R. McKibbin, *The Evolution of the Labour Party 1910–1924* (Oxford, OUP, 1974); J. M. Winter, *Socialism and the Challenge of War: Ideas and Politics in Britain, 1912–1918* (London, Routledge & Kegan Paul, 1974).

and between classes. The deep involvement of all sections of society in the war effort led to a decline in the deferential attitudes of the working class and the rising prospect of political and social change. In this environment, which Lloyd George described as the 'molten' state of society, Winter believes that Labour leaders were forced to conclude that the reconstruction of the party was essential. This process of rebuilding forced the party leaders to sift through a variety of socialist policies in order to select that which would be most apposite to its post-war growth and distinguish it from the Liberal party. In the final analysis, the wartime conditions favoured the collectivist policies of the Webbs and paved the way for the 1918 Labour Constitution and Clause Four, its clear commitment to a socialist state. The guild socialist policies of G. D. H. Cole and the long-term educational approach of R. H. Tawney did not offer the clarity, immediacy or war-time context which seemed essential to the Labour leaders.

Such an interpretation is, of course, entirely alien to McKibbin who simply rejects the view that the wartime economy made much difference to the potential of Labour politics, cannot believe that the men who drew up the new Labour Constitution, most of whom were in their 50s and 60s, were capable of dramatic conversion or that Clause Four was anything other than an 'uncharacteristic adornment' of that new constitution. To him, the trends in British Labour history were evident before the war and Clause Four was simply a response to the wider electorate which was to be created by the Representation of the People's Act of 1918. He believed that it is inconceivable that this could have been otherwise given that the Labour party was moving to the Right, not the Left, during the war – a fact evidenced by the increased right-wing trade union control of the National Executive Committee of the Labour party under the 1918 Constitution.[4] Thus

> in Britain alone the left wing of the working-class movement did not emerge from the war in some way stronger than it entered it. It is true, certainly, that the unions disliked socialists more than they disliked socialism and it is true also that dislike of socialists' was generated by a highly developed class-consciousness. Were socialists suspect because they were socialists or because they were supposedly not working-class? – it is often hard to tell. But in a way the result was the same, and if the war did not necessarily mean the defeat of socialism in Britain, it did mean the defeat of socialists.[5]

His views are not unlike those expressed by Miliband, who referred to

---

[4] 13 of 23 NEC members were directly elected by trade unionists.
[5] McKibbin, *Labour Party*, pp. 105–6.

Clause Four as a form of Labourism rather than Socialism, and that the party's statement of policy, *Labour and the New Social Order*, was a Fabian blueprint for piecemeal collectivism.[6]

Although both Winter and McKibbin differ on many points, there are only three major issues which divide them. The first is the extent to which the trends evident in the Labour party in 1918 were apparent before the war. The second is whether or not the wartime economy led to the creation of a more homogeneous working-class. The third is the degree to which the Labour party seriously discussed the socialist alternatives: put more bluntly, was the Labour party conscious of the need for a distinguished ideology, concerned with offering a genuine socialist ideology, or simply responding to the political exigencies of the time.

The first sub-debate stems from emphasis which McKibbin has placed upon the growth of the Labour party before the First World War. As far as he is concerned, and the school of 'Labour' historians which he represents, the Labour party was clearly making a determined challenge to Liberalism before 1914. Labour was winning parliamentary and municipal elections and trade unions were increasing their commitment to the Labour party. The growth of class politics augured well for the future of the Labour party and boded ill for the Liberals. Winter, on the other hand, simply presents the Labour party as a growing but rudderless organization. The political situation before the war gave it little choice but to support the Liberals on many parliamentary issues and the trade-union movement, upon which it depended, appeared to be going its own way in the militant strike action which was occuring between 1910 and 1914. As Winter concludes, 'It is important to bear in mind the facts that, both within and outside the pre-war Labour party, there was no consensus about its proper function or even about its future as a political force. The "Labour unrest" brought this problem to the fore and forced many people to reconsider their commitments.'[7]

If there is little agreement about the pre-war trends within the Labour party there is even less about the impact of the wartime economy upon the working class. Underlying Winter's book, and some of his later writings, is the assumption that some of the semi-skilled and unskilled workers tended to fare better than skilled workers through a narrowing of pay differentials. On balance, the life expectancy of the lower classes is supposed to have improved because of a wartime rise in the standard of living.[8] McKibbin simply ignores

[6]Miliband, *Parliamentary Socialism*, pp. 61–2.
[7]Winter, *Socialism and the Challenge of War*, p. 25.
[8]J. Winter, 'Labour Politics in the Great War', *Bulletin of the Society for the Study of Labour History*, 34 (Spring, 1977) p. 4; J. M. Winter, *The Great War and the British People* (London, Macmillan, 1986).

these suggestions in his general refutation of the suggestion that the war had any influence, though in recent years there has been some serious questioning of Winter's assumption of rising living standards by other historians.[9]

According to Winter, the lack of clear Labour party leadership on many issues, forced socialists 'to work out anew political ideas which they hoped would give form and purpose to the growing protests of the labouring population'.[10] This led to discussions about socialist direction in the pre-war Labour party which were clarified by the First World War. The war helped to sift the socialist alternatives and, through the agency of the War Emergency: Workers' National Committee, permitted the gradualist and state-based policies of the Webbs to become dominant in the discussion of the 1918 Constitution of the Labour party and in *Labour and the New Social Order*, Labour's reconstruction programme which was written by Sydney Webb and published in 1918. This interpretation contrasts sharply with McKibbin's view that Clause Four has hogged the limelight of debate to the detriment of the corpus of the 1918 Constitution which 'embodied not an ideology but a system by which power in the Labour Party was distributed'.[11] To McKibbin, it is the practical considerations of the time – Labour in coalition, events in Russia and the 1918 Representation of the People Act – which dominated Labour's approach to the 1918 Constitution. The demands of trade unions were to the fore in the formulating of the new constitution and socialism was very much an afterthought.

Continuity or Change?

When war broke out in August 1914 it exerted an immediate impact upon the objectives of the Labour party. On the eve of war the Labour leaders, and a good proportion of the party in the country, were opposed to conflict and prepared to oppose militarism. There was widespread support for the idea of a 'general stoppage of work' in Britain to coincide with similar anti-war action in other countries.[12] One writer noted, in early 1914, that

> Alone amongst the parties of Britain the Labour party is pledged against militarism . . . We must take up the 'Fiery Cross' and carry it to the remotest hamlet in the country, call every man and woman to the colours. 'Down with militarism'. That is our cry –

[9]Winter, *The Great War*, pp. 103–4.
[10]Winter, *Socialism and the Challenge of War*, p. 25.
[11]McKibbin, *Labour Party*, p. 91.
[12]*Op. cit.*, p. 88.

as it is also the cry of our comrades all over Europe. Blazen it on the banners. Write it on the pavement. Sing it in the streets.[13]

But the outbreak of the war came with startling suddenness and Labour opposition was submerged by the gathering wave of nationalism. Very quickly, the great majority of the Labour party pledged themselves to support the war effort. The party associated itself with the political truce for the duration of the war and eventually joined the two coalition governments formed in May 1915 and December 1916. The TUC supported such fusion politics by declaring an industrial truce and by accepting the Munitions Act, which outlawed strikes on war work, in 1915.

Thus the 'Great War' had deflected the Labour party from its intended path. Patriotism replaced peace and the formal arrangement of coalition replaced the informal association of Labour with the Liberal party. Nevertheless, as far as Labour's party organization was concerned, there were relatively few changes.

It is often suggested that the war, because of the demands it imposed upon the production of armaments, led to a demand for labour, a reduction in unemployment and a rise in trade-union membership. In fact the wartime conditions simply maintained the surge of trade-union membership which had begun in 1910. For the Labour party this meant that trade unionism, which was dominant in 1910, was even more so in 1918. But this was the continuance of a trend, not a break or change in direction.

Table 3.1 British trade union membership, 1910–20

Year	Membership	% Increase
1910	2,565,000	
1911	3,139,000	21.6
1912	3,416,000	8.8
1913	4,135,000	18.0
1914	4,145,000	0.24
1915	4,359,000	4.9
1916	4,644,000	6.0
1917	5,499,000	15.9
1918	6,533,000	15.9
1919	7,926,000	21.3
1920	8,347,000	5.0

Until 1918 the Labour party organization in local constituencies remained much as it had been before the war. It is difficult to get a precise indication of the extent of its constituency organization, even though it had 215 divisional parties and trades councils affiliated to it in

[13] *Bradford Pioneer*, 9 January 1914.

January 1918. Some constituencies were affiliated twice and there was considerable overlapping of responsibilities. Aston division of Birmingham was affiliated to the national party through both the Aston divisional party and the Birmingham Central Labour party. In Bradford it was the ILP which acted as the focus of Labour party organization in the three constituencies until 1918 and the only unifying representative of Labour in the whole area was the Trades Council. In Bradford, constituency organizations were still evolving against a backcloth of rival political groups, all intent upon defending their own interests.

It was not until 1917 and 1918 that this detritus of pre-war Labour politics was quickly absorbed as a more unified Labour party emerged with the re-organization of constituencies, the extension of the franchise and the introduction of a new Labour constitution. As McKibbin has noted, by June 1918 there were 397 affiliated divisional parties and trades councils affiliated with Labour, 400 in 1919 and 626 in 1924.[14]

Recently deposited local Labour party records suggest that most of the West Yorkshire constituency Labour parties transformed their organizations between 1917 and 1920.[15] In Bradford, the process had begun in mid-November 1917, following the decision to divide Bradford into four constituencies in anticipation of the Representation of the People Act. The Bradford Trades and Labour Council called a conference of representatives, trade unions and cooperative societies.[16] A subsequent meeting in September 1918 led the formation of the Bradford Labour party in April 1919 – uniting all Bradford's major Labour organizations into one body for the first time.[17] By 1919, the Bradford Labour movement had a central organization, four constituency parties and 21 ward parties.

This pattern of improved organizational activity was repeated throughout West Yorkshire. The rather amorphous Huddersfield Labour movement was transformed into the more clearly defined Huddersfield Divisional Labour party in the spring and summer of 1918, following meetings between the Trades Council, the ILP and other interested groups.[18] The Colne Valley Divisional Labour party was formed on 9 June 1917 and the Leeds City Labour party reorganized itself in April and May 1918, promoting the formation of six constituency parties for the Leeds divisions.[19]

[14]McKibbin, *Labour Party*, p. 137.
[15]The surviving records of the Leeds City Divisional and War parties, the Huddersfield Labour Party, the Morley Labour Party, the Colne Valley Labour Party and several others were deposited in the appropriate local history, archive and polytechnic libraries from about 1970 onwards.
[16]Bradford Trades and Labour Council, Minutes, 15 November 1918.
[17]*Op. cit.*, 14 September 1918.
[18]Huddersfield Divisional Labour Party, Minutes, 23 July 1918.
[19]Colne Valley Divisional Labour Party, Minutes, 20 January, 1 May and 9 June 1917; *Leeds Weekly Citizen*, 19 April 1918.

The message is clear: the outbreak of the war led to a political truce which gave no encouragement to improve or extend Labour party organization. The impetus for change and improvement did not come until the end of the war and then largely as a result of the Parliamentary Reform Act of 1918 and the decision to redistribute and reorganize parliamentary constituencies. It may be argued that the war helped to extend the franchise but in a substantial work, *Electoral Reform in War and Peace 1906–18*, Martin Pugh has argued that

> Because the 1918 Act, unlike the earlier reform measures, occurred during a war it has often been claimed or dismissed as a product of that situation. This is especially the case with those who study war without also studying the periods before and between wars. Seen in perspective, however, the Great War provided the occasion, rather than the cause of the Reform Act; it was unfinished business. This is emphasized by the fact that in 1917–18 one finds Parliament involved in a prolonged controversy not over the major changes in the franchise, but solely over the reform of the electoral system by proportional representation and the alternative vote. That debate grew directly out of the condition of Edwardian politics: . . .[20]

The fact is that the whole issue of widening the franchise had been frequently debated between 1906 and 1914. The male franchise had not been extended during this period due largely to the fact that the issue of the female franchise divided Liberal opinion. Liberal Cabinets from 1910 onwards harboured a majority of members who were in favour of giving the property qualification to women. Unfortunately they also felt that the majority of the million or so women who would be enfranchised would vote Conservative. Persuaded on the side of caution by Lloyd George and Winston Churchill, these members permitted Asquith's view to prevail – that when the government was ready it would bring in a manhood suffrage bill and allow the House of Commons to introduce a woman's clause if they wished. The intent to extend the franchise to all males and some females was there before 1914; the war simply provided the extra fillip required to get the government to accept a wider franchise, focusing the mind of the Cabinet upon the point that many of those men who were giving their lives at the front did not have the right to vote.

The 1918 Franchise Act, and the attendant legislation to redistribute parliamentary seats arose from issues of Edwardian politics. Labour's improved organization arose from a working through of an old debate, not the emergence of a new factor pushed forward by the war.

Continuity rather than change would appear to have governed the

[20]M. Pugh, *Eelectoral Reform in War and Peace 1906–18* (London, Routledge & Kegan Paul, 1978), pp. ix, 179–80.

evolution of the Labour party organization during the war. Nevertheless, if it can be demonstrated that the wartime conditions did change the structure of the working class it could be argued that the Labour party responded to this challenge by offering new, more collectivist and socialist, policies.

A More Homogeneous Working Class?

Although Winter suggested, more than a decade ago, that the working class became homogeneous during the war[21] it was not until 1986 that he produced detailed evidence for this view in *The Great War and the British People*. His central premiss is that life expectancy improved because of a wartime rise in the standard of living, despite the fact that food supplies were reduced. As a result life expectancy at birth for men rose from 49 to 56 years between 1911 and 1921, substantially greater gains than registered either in the first or third decade of the twentieth century.[22] Offering a wealth of material on morality, infant mortality and maternal mortality, Winter suggests that it was the poorer sections of the working class who were the great beneficiaries of the improvement in the standard of living:

> In Britain during the First World War, underpaid and underemployed labourers were transformed within a few months of the outbreak of hostilities into full working partners in the war effort. (. . . .) Furthermore, when a real challenge to working-class living standards arose in the form of increased rents in early 1915, the government acted with great haste to freeze rents at the pre-war level. What changed in wartime was both an enhancement of the market position of most grades of manual workers as well as the strengthening of the legal and moral entitlement of workers to exchange their labour for a living wage.[23]

As Winter acknowledges, his views run contrary to the received opinion, which is that the reduced levels of consumption in war, the halving of the numbers of doctors due to draftings to the front and the deterioration of housing stock meant that the British population was weakened and incapable of withstanding the influenza epidemic which swept across Europe throughout 1918.

There is no doubt that Winter has offered a controversial interpretation. It is well known that wage rates and earnings tended to lag behind prices for most of the war and that real wages did not rise until 1918 when bonuses, overtime and piece-work rates began to catch up with

[21] Winter, 'Labour Politics and the Great War', p. 4.
[22] Winter, *The Great War*, p. 105.
[23] *Op. cit.*, p. 244.

prices. On the other hand, semi-skilled and unskilled workers tended to fare better than skilled workers through a narrowing of wage differentials. Family incomes at the lower end of the scale were also supplemented by longer hours of work, shift work and remittances from forces pay.

The evidence, however, is inconclusive. Winter relies heavily upon A. L. Bowley's wage data and the official cost-of-living index, both of which are unreliable for detailed analysis. The precise information he offers for the wages of the unskilled are for 1920, which means that they do not relate to the war and may have been thrust upwards by the post-war boom in wages in 1919 and early 1920. The Ministry of Food consumption levels which he offers for the 'average' working class families suggest that there were substantial falls in beef, mutton, sugar, butter and cheese consumption during the war and particularly between October 1917 and March 1918.[24] Flour and potato consumption appear to have remained much the same and the only increase occurred in margarine consumption, which more than doubled upon that of the pre-war years. Such evidence hardly appears to support Winter's contention of rising living standards, nor is it sophisticated enough to shed much light on the changing consumption levels of the poorer sections of the working class.

On balance, Winter's evidence is not very convincing, though it is possible that the standard of living of some working-class groups improved in some regions. Certainly many historians are dubious about his evidence and some, like McKibbin, have shown little or no interest in the issue.[25] Nevertheless, whatever the statistical facts indicate, did the Labour party perceive the emergence of a more unified working class which would provide the party with greater prospects of achieving political power if it could offer the right policies?

The War Emergency: Workers' National Committee and the 1918 Labour Party Constitution

Part of that sense of greater working-class unity, and possible improvements in living standards, may have come from the activities of the War Emergency: Workers' National Committee – the body which Winter feels helped to promote the state socialist ideas of the Webbs within the wider Labour movement and the Labour party. His views are not shared by McKibbin, who simply ignores them, nor by Ralph Miliband, S. H. Beer, or Royden Harrison, who see the structure of power within the Labour party to be more important than the

[24]*Op. cit.*, p. 220.
[25]McKibbin, *Labour Party*, pp. 88–91.

proclamation of socialist intent evident in Clause Four.[26]

The War Emergency Committee was drawn together on 5 August 1914 after Arthur Henderson, as secretary of the Labour party, had written to the NEC to call a special meeting 'to consider what action should be taken in the very serious crisis in Europe and any other business that may arise'.[27] It was formed in the context of a Labour party committed to peace but within the day it was being called to act for a movement which was committed to the war effort. Its prime function became the defence of the rights and interests of the working-class from unreasonable encroachment. It quickly evolved to include not only the NEC of the Labour party but the Co-operative Union and the Co-operative Wholesale Society. Its policy of co-option led to invitations to Ramsay MacDonald, and several individuals, to join it, the absorption of the representatives of many trade unions, the ILP, the British Socialist party, the National Socialist party, the Fabian Society and many other organizations. In short, it soon became the widest representative body in the British Labour movement – incorporating both pro-war and anti-war organizations, although its 'heterogeneous membership – ought not to obscure the fact that it was really an extension of the Labour Party's national office.'[28] Its membership included Sydney Webb, H. M. Hyndman, Ramsay MacDonald, Arthur Henderson, J. S. Middleton, and many other of the leading figures in the formative years of the Labour movement.

Its primary objective was to keep the Labour movement from disintegrating under the impact of war. To achieve this end, the WEC concentrated its efforts on assuming a leading role in defending the living standard of the population. It protested at the 70 per cent inflation that occurred between 1914 and 1916, participated in the trade-union campaign to raise old-age pensions from 5s to 7s 6d, worked for rent restriction in 1915 and worked to ensure that there was an adequate distribution of food supplies. One of its number, R. Smillie the miners' leader, was offered the position of Food Controller in the Lloyd George wartime administration. He refused, pointing out that he would have soon had to resign, for he would have demanded 'plenary powers to deal in my own way with the food profiteers. Some I would be content to send to prison, others I should feel obliged to hang'.[29]

Towards the end of the war, however, the WEC became far more positive in its policies and more aggressive in its approach. The introduction of compulsory military service in 1916 brought about a

[26]*Op. cit.,* Miliband, *Parliamentary Socialism*; R. Harrison, 'The War Emergency: Workers' National Committee, 1914–20', in A. Briggs and J. Saville, eds., *Essays in Labour History* (London, Macmillan, 1971), pp. 211–59.
[27]Winter, *Socialism and the Challenge of War*, p. 184.
[28]*Op. cit.,* pp. 187–8
[29]Harrison, 'War Emergency Committee', pp. 236–7.

fundamental change in strategy. It protested at the Military Service
Act in 1916. Although it could not deflect the Coalition government
from its decision it developed a campaign for the Conscription of
Riches as a *quid pro quo* for Labour's contribution to providing
manpower for the trenches. Evolving from a resolution put forward by
H. M. Hyndman, which was considerably modified by Sydney Webb,
the WEC's policy was essentially one for the 'Conscription of Wealth',
through income tax, supertax, capital tax and sequestration of all
unearned income, and the nationalization of all those industries then
under government control for the duration of the war.[30]

Up to this point there is little disagreement between the various
interpretations of the value and the work of the WEC, if one discounts
McKibbin's total disregard of its work. Both Winter and Harrison
agree that the work of the WEC was important. For Winter it meant
that the Webbian thought was projected forward, for in the wake of
the proposal being formed it was accepted by the Labour party Executive and various other Labour organizations: 'we may see the complete
acceptance of Webbian thought on this measure – the first independent
Labour programme during the First World War'.[31] It followed that,
with Webb's deep involvement in formulating the new Labour party
Constitution, the WEC programme had a direct bearing upon the
formulation of Clause Four. Harrison agrees that Webb was the dominant spirit behind the new policy and that 'In short, the Conscription of
Riches demand led on to clause 4'.[32] But from that point onwards,
there is disagreement. Whilst Winter sees the growing influence of
Webbian socialism as the basis of the new constitution of the Labour
party, Harrison accepts the views of Miliband, and anticipates the
approach of McKibbin, in suggesting that Clause Four has to be seen
within the context of the political pressures being placed upon the
Labour party at this time.

Why did the Labour party commit itself to the socialist goal? Was it
because of the growth of Webbian socialism, thrust forward by the
war, or was it simply a product of political expediency?

There is no doubting that the socialist ideas of the Webbs were
attractive to some sections of the Labour movement. The ILP and the
Fabians had already declared their commitment to vague and broad
resolutions connected with the common ownership of the means of
production. It is also possible, as Winter suggests, that the Russian
revolutions of 1917, and particularly the Bolshevik Revolution which
occurred soon after Arthur Henderson's ill-fated trip to Russia, forced
Labour's leaders to adopt a resolution which would offer a less violent
and more democratic way to socialism. There is also the suggestion

[30]Winter, *Socialism and the Challenge of War*, pp. 214–15.
[31]*Op. cit.*, p. 215.
[32]Harrison, 'War Emergency Committee', p. 256.

that the professional middle class were being drawn to such a policy in the wake of the government collectivization policy. In addition, the Lloyd George Coalition government set up a Ministry of Reconstruction to prepare policies for the post-war years. Of the nine members of the central Advisory Council attached to this Ministry two, Ernest Bevin and J. H. Thomas, were trade unionists and active members of the Labour party. Apart from being in the Coalition, Labour was being drawn into efforts to prepare schemes for housing, health and social welfare in the post-war years on a broader front. It must have appeared that the old *laissez-faire* capitalism was dead and that socialist policies, particularly those of the Webbs, were now more appropriate than ever. To many Labour party activists, it must have appeared that wartime collectivism would not be dismantled, especially after the formation of the Ministry of Reconstruction. Clause Four (or Party Object 'd') ran as follows:

> To secure for the producers by hand or brain the full fruits of their industry by the Common Ownership of the Means of Production and the best obtainable system of popular administration and control of each industry and service.

It was a very imprecise statement of socialist intent, though it was the Labour party's first official commitment to socialism. McKibbin suggests that it was an 'uncharacteristic adornment' of the new Labour party Constitution, not meant to be taken too seriously. That may be so, but presumably it meant something to someone. If it is assumed that it was useful in order to distinguish the Labour party from the Liberal party, to indicate Labour's political independence, then it is fair to assume that this socialist ideology was important to some sections of the Labour party and its supporters. If not, why should it be included at all?

Winter, and other writers, have clearly established a link between the WEC, the Webbs and Clause Four. What they have failed to do is explain how this relates to the ideology of the new class consciousness of the working class. Indeed, there is still no detailed study which examines the evolution of class consciousness in the First World War and explains why it was possible to offer Clause Four in 1918 and not in 1913. McKibbin's suggestion that it was there as a sop to the professional middle class, who had found socialism through the wartime experience, seems unconvincing.[33] One might note that Bernard Barker's attempt to explain why some prominent Liberal MPs, 'the 1918 Liberals', moved over to the Labour party, suggested that they had many motives.[34] Some, like C. P. Trevelyan, were apparently won

---

[33]McKibbin, *Labour Party*, p. 97.
[34]B. Barker, 'The Anatomy of Reform: The Social and Political Ideas of the Labour Leadership in Yorkshire', *International Review of Social History*, XVIII (1973), pp. 1–27.

over to socialism. Others, like Cecil Wilson, hoped to do some good in the party they had joined. All seem to have concluded that the Liberal party was a spent force. Such evidence hardly suggests the attractions of socialism were irresistible but that the new ex-Liberal members were primarily concerned to join a growing party. This might also be the motivation behind the rising level of middle-class support for Labour, though this topic still needs to be examined.

If the Winter explanation is still wanting, then why did Clause Four find its way into Labour's Constitution? It has been suggested that it served a useful purpose in sharpening the divide between the Labour and Liberal parties. McKibbin offers a variety of reasons: the professional middle class were evidently enamoured of socialism, it was of secondary importance to the issue of who controlled the Labour party and the trade unions were not much interested in it, and because its vagueness and lack of rigour permitted it to unite a party where there was otherwise 'little doctrinal agreement'.[35] The first of these suggestions has already been dismissed. The second seems plausible, given that the trade-union movement, with its block vote, was the dominent force in the Labour party and enhanced its control of the NEC under the new Constitution. But it is the third, barely examined by McKibbin, which appears to offer the best answer.

It is the vagueness of Clause Four which permitted it to act as a unifying force within the Labour party. The various Labour and Socialist organizations which accreted to the Labour party exhibited widely different views about socialism and the war. Some favoured a system of workers' control whilst others wished for an extensive programme of nationalization. Many were pro-war but some, like the ILP and the British Socialist party, after 1916, associated with the Peace Campaign of 1917 and were represented at the Workers' and Soldiers' Conference at Leeds. The WEC managed to unite these interests through its defence of living standards and though its 'Conscription of Riches' campaign. Clause Four could be seen as an extension of this approach. As Harrison suggests, 'It is better regarded as a rallying point around which the adherents of different ideologies and representatives of different interests assembled'. (. . . .) The adoption of Clause Four did not imply that the whole membership came to have a common objective, but rather that an objective had been proclaimed which both accommodated and concealed a large diversity of particular concerns'.[36] It was detailed enough to distinguish Labour from the Liberal party but sufficiently vague to avoid serious conflict over the variety of socialist programmes on offer.

Harrison's view is supported by the interest and activities of the Labour movement in West Yorkshire. Here the various Labour

---

[35]McKibbin, *Labour Party*, p. 97.
[36]Harrison, 'War Emergency Committee', p. 259.

organizations were primarily concerned with two issues: the protection of the working-class standard of living and the war. By 1916 the war had fragmented both the ILP and the trade unions. In Bradford the ILP was divided into three major sections. There were those who were pro-war, and it must be remembered that 461 young men out of a membership of 1,473 volunteered to go to the front under the Derby scheme.[37] There was a second section which opposed the war or were pacifists. There was also a third section, undoubtedly the majority, who were equivocal about the war. Whilst they supported peace movements they felt the need to protect Britain and defend Belgium, some even going so far as to suggest that Socialist objectives had to be suspended for the duration of the war. Similar divisions occurred in the Bradford Trades Council, although it has been suggested that the 'militant pacifists' were in control by 1917.[38] It was these issues, alongside reports on the industrial struggle on Clydeside, the Russian revolutions and the Workers' and Soldiers' Council Conference in Leeds, which appear to have attracted the attention of the Local Labour press and the trade-union organizations. The Labour party Constitution appears to have provoked much less interest and there was certainly some attempt to preserve peace between the various Labour organizations. For instance, when the British Socialist party held its annual conference in Leeds in March and April 1918. Though committed to international peace at this stage, and opposed to Labour's involvement with the Coalition government, 86 of the 100 delegates present voted against leaving the Labour party. Councillor Garth of Leeds noted that the BSP was not strong in Leeds but that 'Labour candidates fought on class-conscious lines as Socialists. Not enough emphasis has been placed on the local position, and he hoped no action would be taken which would compromise the relations of the BSP members with the Labour Party'.[39]

Clause Four of the Labour party Constitution appears to have excited little interest either at the national or local level, beyond the recognition of the fact that, by accepting it, the Labour party had formally declared its commitment to socialism. In the end Clause Four proved a useful point of common agreement between socialists of all shades of opinion. But it should not be seen as more than an acceptable flag of convenience.

Conclusion

The First World War obviously disrupted many aspects of British

---

[37] *Bradford Pioneer*, 26 February 1916.
[38] Laybourn and Reynolds, *Liberalism and the Rise of Labour*, p. 190.
[39] *Leeds Weekly Citizen*, 5 April 1918.

society. It undermined the *laissez-faire* capitalism of the pre-war years and extended the role of the state. It removed Britain's dominance in world trade, it enhanced the role of women in British society and it may have contributed to the decline of the Liberal party. It undoubtedly helped to detach the ILP from some of the trade-union support it had enjoyed before the war. But there remains considerable doubt about whether or not it changed the direction of the Labour party. Historians have certainly attempted to explain Clause Four in terms of the impact of wartime experience upon the Labour party. But there is little to suggest that was anything more than a natural development of pre-war trends whereby a Labour leadership, which had openly declared its socialism before the war, took advantage of wartime collectivism to take the party beyond a loose attachment to the working class. More confident in its support from the working class, and faced with a rapidly declining Liberal party the Labour party was striking out alone with a vague commitment to socialism which would, with one stroke, assert its individual identity and yet not offend its socialist and working-class supporters. This became even more important, with the completing of the 'unfinished business' of Edwardian politics, when the Representation of the People Bill became law in 1918.

4 EXPECTATIONS BORN TO DEATH?: THE LABOUR PARTY, 1918–29

The most dramatic domestic development of the inter-war years was the replacement of the Liberal party by the Labour party as the second party in British politics. In 1918 the Liberal party was still the second parliamentary party of the nation – although it was divided between the Asquith-dominated Liberal party and the Lloyd George coalition Liberals, whose presence in Parliament was partly dependent upon the Conservative vote. By 1923 the, by then unified, Liberal party had been overtaken by the Labour party and its political organization was in disarray. In 1929 it was practically dead as a meaningful political organization, unable to arrest the growth of its Labour usurper for the progressive vote. The Labour party's growth appeared almost inexorable. But this vision had been challenged recently by Christopher Howard who has questioned the effectiveness of Labour's organization in the 1920s: 'The image of a vibrant expanding new party was illusion. Labour was fortunate that its opponents were deceived'.[1] Most Labour leaders would not have agreed with this depiction of their party even though the title of Howard's article, which also forms part of the title of this chapter, is drawn from Ramsay MacDonald's comment, written in 1921, that 'the Labour party knocks the heart out of me and expectations are like babies born to death . . .'[2]

Interpretations

Exactly why the Labour party grew so rapidly in the decade after the war has been a matter of considerable debate amongst experts of British political history. Two long-standing interpretations have already been indicated – that Labour's growth was because of the development of its association with trade unions into widespread working-class support and the suggestion that it only grew because of the internecine conflict of the Liberal party during the war. Almost unwittingly, Howard accepts the first of these arguments, for he notes.

[1]C. Howard, 'Expectations born to death: local Labour Party expansion in the 1920s', in J. Winter, ed., *Working Class in Modern British History: Essays in Honour of Henry Pelling* (London, CUP, 1983), p. 81.
[2]*Op. cit.*, p. 65.

that 'Widespread electoral support bore little resemblance to restricted party membership, however, and disappointments were common'.[3] Such a gap could only be explained by class voting which took no note of the party organization and activity, if Howard's assumption of the weakness of Labour's political organization is correct. But the issue is confused by the fact that he also asserts that the Liberals and the Conservatives would have been more successful had they seen through the illusion and perceived the real weakness of the Labour party's organization. Howard doesn't appear to have made his mind up whether it was class politics or the illusion of a rapidly organizing Labour party which accounts for Labour's electoral success in the 1920s.

Nevertheless, the crux of his argument is that Labour's national and constituency activity failed to sustain much active support. The Labour leadership recognized this, Labour failed to win much support in the rural areas, its national and local newspapers were always in a precarious financial position and often collapsed, and even the urban and industrial strongholds lacked faith when the Labour party was unable to deliver the improved society it offered. Even in Aberavon, Ramsay MacDonald's own constituency between 1922 and 1929, one constituent noted, in 1926, that

> with unemployment rising and short-time working now widespread, rank-and-file criticism of the leadership was growing. The future was no longer assured, and at the next election 'J.R.M. will have to work very hard otherwise the seat is lost'.[4]

Howard also adds that

> MacDonald was no doubt relieved to leave all this behind and move to the safer and cheaper seat of Seaham Harbour in 1928. MacDonald may well have said that Aberavon finally asked too much of him, but it might be as well to ask whether the leadership expected too much of the local parties. Despite the heady success of the immediate post-war period, the academic insistence of Barry Hindess and the nostalgic testimony of many who battled through the period, the picture gained from local party records does not suggest that this was the golden age of working-class politics.

A rather different picture is provided by McKibbin and Bernard Barker.[5] They feel that the Labour party was making determined efforts to improve both its national and local organization and that, by

[3]*Op. cit.*, p. 78.
[4]*Op. cit.*, p. 74.
[5]R. McKibbin, *The Evolution of the Labour Party 1910–1924* (Oxford, OUP, 1974); B. Barker, 'Anatomy of Reform, The Social and Political Ideas of Labour Leadership in Yorkshire', *International Review of Social History*, XVIII (1973), pp. 1–27.

and large, despite some obvious difficulties, succeeded in doing so. McKibbin, in particular, acknowledges the strengths and weaknesses of the new constituency and party organizations but stresses the overall general improvements that were achieved. However, to him the overriding developments were the increasing centralization of party organization and the growing union predominance. The party could only go as far as the unions would allow and their influence was apparent at all levels. It was the union organizations in both urban and rural constituencies which guaranteed continuity and finance: 'What emerged was informal, often improvised, but remarkably tough'.[6] In addition, though the party offered its electorate little it was committed to moral ideas and personal liberation to such an extent that it excited passionate enthusiasms. According to McKibbin, the fact is that the Labour party was the vehicle of working-class aspiration by the early 1920s. Since the party was dominated by trade unions accepting it meant accepting an intricate network of loyalties rather than accepting socialism. Idealism was in fact rather less necessary, or sustaining, than loyalty.

The sharp divide of opinions is clear – but which picture is correct? Was the Labour party's growth almost inexorable in the 1920s or was its political development illusory? Did the idealism which won Labour converts fade away when the 1924 Labour government failed to deliver substantial benefits for the working class or was that idealism less important than commitment to a trade-union dominated party? In the final analysis – to what extent was the Labour party well organized and effective in the 1920s?

The 1918 General Election and Party Organization

The 1918 General Election was the first at which the extended franchise and the new constituencies of the 1918 came into use. Since the franchise had been extended to all males above 21 years of age and to all females above 30, the Labour party expected to perform better than it had done in the pre-war general elections. *The Times*, in the light of the Labour party's improving organization between 1916 and 1918, noted that 'it really seems as if the Labour Party were better prepared for the election than any other'[7] and that 'Labour in the early days of the contest threw much more vigour into the campaign than the candidates and workers of any other party'.[8] It therefore came as something of a shock when this much strengthened and potentially

[6]R. McKibbin, *The Evolution of the Labour Party 1910–1924* (Oxford, OUP, 1974), p. 243 and chapter VI, pp. 112–62.
[7]*The Times*, 6 December 1918.
[8]*Op. cit.*, 9 December 1918.

more strongly supported party failed to achieve its target of winning 100 seats. Instead it won 57 seats, 61 with additions on the opening of Parliament. What is more, most of the party leaders – Henderson, MacDonald, Snowden, Anderson and Jowett – lost their seats. This meant that in effect the party in Parliament was, overwhelmingly, dominated by trade unions who sponsored all but eight of the Labour MPs.

The result was most unsatisfactory for the Labour party, though explicable in terms of the 'coupon' nature of the general election and the political arrangements made between some Liberals and the Conservatives. In Leeds there was a particularly squalid compromise whereby the Conservative Coalitionists offered the Liberals a straight run against Labour in four seats in return for a free Conservative run in Leeds North-East division. The offer was too good to resist and, with the unofficial approval of the National Liberal Federation (The Asquithian section of the party) who, according to Alderman Farr, felt that the arrangement 'was to the advantage of the Liberal Party', Asquithian Liberals entered into an arrangement with Conservatives 'so long as Liberal principles were not violated'.[9] The message was clear: the Leeds Liberal Federation was composed of independent Liberals, of the Asquithian type, but had entered into an arrangement with the Conservative coalitionists, thus preserving their parliamentary dominance in Leeds. This was neatly summed up in the Annual Report for 1919:

> Your Executive, during the last years, whilst supporting the coalition in accordance with the understanding at the General Election have preserved the independence and separate identity of the Liberal Party, and they believe that the policy commends itself to Liberals of all shades of opinion.[10]

Such an alliance could not last and the Labour party was determined to improve its organization and propaganda machine. Indeed, its rapid growth was evident at both the national and local level.

The Labour party made extensive advances between the end of the First World War and the 1922 General Election. This began from the centre where the National Executive Committee reorganized its activities, by appointing four standing sub-committees – organization and elections; policy and programme; literature, research and publicity; and finance and general purposes. Egerton Wake became the party's national agent and vigorously pursued the policy of giving direction to the rest of the movement, through the organization of regional and local conferences. Indeed, by 1922 each of the party's nine regions had

[9]Leeds Liberal Federation, Minutes of Executive Committee, 21 November 1918, 4 May 1929, 21 June 1921.
[10]Leeds Liberal Federation, Minutes of E. G., 4 May 1919.

organized at least three regional conferences, many of which were addressed by Wake, Arthur Henderson, the secretary, and a 'star' speaker. Advisory Committees, set up by the NEC on 13 March 1918 in order to help develop the party's policies on a wide range of issues, began to publish reports and statements which added to the corpus of Labour policies. The party also acquired a paper, the *Daily Herald*, whose frequent financial crises had forced it to become dependent upon the party for its existence by 1922. Also, in the wake of the 1918 Franchise Bill, the party formed a Women's Section under Dr Marion Phillips and appointed regional organizers to attract the newly-enfranchised women.

McKibbin rightly points to the deficiencies of the new organization. The party always lacked adequate national finance, the *Daily Herald's* circulation difficulties were a constant draw upon its limited financial resources, the Advisory Committees had to be modified and despite, the efforts of Wake, there were never enough full-time agents – a mere 133 in 1922, falling to 111 in 1923.[11] He rightly suggests that Labour's working-class support transcended such organizational difficulties but it should not be forgotten that considerable improvements were made and that all parties complained of lacking finance and organization at this time.[12] Even the most rudimentary examination of the minutes of the NEC suggests the feverish activity which was occurring in the immediate post-war years and, in these early days, it was to be expected that mistakes would be made and that new directions would be sought. One Labour party circular, issued in June 1923, stressed that

> The results of the [1922] General Election have brought forcibly before us the primary importance both of securing the votes of women electors and of getting a large number of women to take part in an electoral campaign. My Executive Committee is of the opinion that it is essential both for winning and retaining Parliamentary seats that special attention should be given to the whole subject. (. . .)
> The notable results of our methods in organizing women has startled the other parties, who will certainly use their best endeavours to counteract our work. Continual effort between the times of elections will make their attempts futile.[13]

There was certainly no complacency amongst Labour's national leaders, quite the contrary.

[11] R. McKibbin, *The Evolution of the Labour Party 1910–1924* (Oxford, OUP, 1974), p. 143.
[12] Keighley Liberal Association, Minutes, September to December 1924; Leeds Liberal Federation, Cabinet Committee, Minutes, for 1926; Society of Certificated and Associated Liberal Agents, 1916 to 1930 (Leeds Archives).
[13] Archives of Labour Party, NEC, Minutes, June 1923.

The enthusiasm engendered by the national party appears to have lapped over into the local constituencies. Contrary to Howard's vision of effete constituency Labour party organizations rescued by class voting, McKibbin emphasizes their activity and resilience:

> Although there were constant complaints in Labour circles that the enemy had superior forces at his disposal, these complaints came from men who overrated the importance of organization and who found anything less than perfection displeasing. All the evidence, on the contrary, suggests that outside the rural, semi-rural, and overwhelmingly bourgeois constituencies, the enemy was taken aback by the intensity and vigour of Labour's attack.[14]

This is a view strongly supported by the records of the local Labour parties in the textile district of Yorkshire.

At the end of the First World War the Labour party organization in West Yorkshire was little advanced on the chaotic structure of overlapping and competing interests which had existed since the formation of the LRC in 1900. Constituency organization was still evolving against a backcloth of rival political groups, all intent on defending their own interests. Yet the detritus of pre-war Labour politics was quickly absorbed as a more unified Labour party emerged in 1918 with the reorganization of the constituencies, the extension of the franchise and the introduction of a new Labour constitution. The new organization which emerged was never perfect; Labour agents complained as readily as did their Liberal and Conservative counterparts of the shortage of funds and the dependence of the party on a small number of activists. Yet more full-time agents were appointed, funds were increased, and organizational and propaganda work was undertaken.

Throughout 1918 Labour Constituency parties were formed for all four of the Bradford seats and the Bradford Labour party, the city party formally came into existence on 5 April 1919 – uniting the ILP, the Trades Council and the Workers' Municipal Federation into one Labour organization. By 1919, the Bradford Labour movement had a central party organization, four constituency parties and 21 ward parties.[15]

This pattern of improved organizational activity was repeated throughout West Yorkshire. The rather amorphous Huddersfield Labour movement was transformed into the more clearly defined Huddersfield Divisional Labour party in the spring and summer of 1918, following meetings between the Trades Council, the ILP and other interested groups.[16] The Colne Valley Divisional Labour party

---

[14]R. McKibbin, *The Evolution of the Labour Party 1910–1924* (Oxford, OUP, 1974), p. 144.
[15]Bradford Trades and Labour Council, Minutes, 15 November 1918; *Bradford Pioneer*, throughout 1918.
[16]Huddersfield Divisional Labour Party, Minutes, 23 July 1918.

was formed in June 1917 and the Leeds City Labour party reorganized itself in April and May 1918, and promoted the formation of constituency parties in the six divisions which made up Leeds.[17]

Once reorganization was successfully accomplished the main priority of the local parties was to appoint a full-time agent. Such an action was not to be taken lightly for, despite the financial contribution from Head Office, it could impose a crippling financial burden upon even well-funded organizations. Not surprisingly it was the organizations in large towns, such as Bradford, Leeds and Huddersfield, which appointed full-time agents. Most, such as Batley and Morley Divisional Labour party, relied upon part-time agents whose service they paid for during parliamentary contests.[18] Nevertheless, between 1919 and 1922, the NEC of the Labour party approved the appointment of five full-time agents in West Yorkshire: T. Ashworth (City of Bradford), D. B. Foster (Leeds South), J. Lawson (Elland), W. Whiteley (Huddersfield) and T. Myers (Spen Valley).[19]

Lamentably, there was a high turnover of agents and their assistants due to the financial difficulties of the parties. Nonetheless, a few full-time agents became household names in West Yorkshire. D. B. Foster, known affectionately as 'D.B.', dominated the Leeds Labour movement. Tom Myers, whose success at the Spen Valley parliamentary by-election in 1920 had signified the post-war challenge of Labour, became the seminal influence on the Labour movement in the Spen Valley district. There was also the tireless Arthur Gardiner, who replaced W. Whiteley in 1926, who was agent and secretary of the Huddersfield Constituency Labour party until the 1950s.

The prime function of the improved Labour organization was to secure votes. In a period when the life-expectancy of the *Daily Herald* was uncertain and its editorial stance questionable, it was essential for the local Labour parties to have their own papers. The West Yorkshire area was fortunate in this respect. At the end of the First World War it had three established provincial papers, the *Bradford Pioneer*, the *Leeds Weekly Citizen* and the Huddersfield *Worker*. The *Worker* expired in 1920 but the *Huddersfield Citizen* replaced it in 1926 and survived up to the 1960s. In addition there was the *Yorkshire Factory Times*, started in 1889, which acted as the organ of the Yorkshire textile workers until it ceased publication in April 1926. These weekly publications were also supplemented by a whole flotilla of occasional broadsheets, trade-union quarterlies and Labour journals.

In its day the most prestigious of these newspapers was the *Bradford Pioneer*. Amongst its illustrious editors was Joseph Burgess, the journalist whose call led to the formation of the national ILP at

[17]Colne Valley Divisional Labour Party, Minutes, 20 January, 1 May, 9 June 1917, *Leeds Weekly Citizen*, 19 April 1918.
[18]Batley and Morley Divisional Labour Party, Minutes, 1931 to 1933.
[19]Labour Party, NEC, Minutes, June 1918, May 1920, February 1922, March 1922.

Bradford in 1893, Willie Leach, Fred Jowett, the first Labour MP for
Bradford, and Frank Betts, the father of Barbara Castle. Victor
Grayson Feather, later General Secretary of the TUC, was one of its
correspondents and its cartoonist, until he left Bradford in 1926, and
wrote alongside Margaret McMillan, Ramsay MacDonald and Philip
Snowden.

The *Bradford Pioneer* epitomized the propaganda role of these
newspapers when it advised its readers:

> Don't destroy this paper. Become a Pioneer Pusher. Become a
> Pioneer. Persuade your friends and workmates to order it. If
> YOU can sell a few in your workshop let us know and we will
> send them along. New readers means the extension of Labour's
> influence in world politics. 'Nuff said'. Get busy.[20]

The Labour party did 'get busy'. The main focus of its activities was
the winning of members and most Labour organizations oscillated
between stressing the need to organize women's sections and the
broader objective of attracting individual members.

The Labour party had strongly supported the demand for women's
suffrage before the First World War, helped to reorganize the Standing Joint Committee of Industrial Women's Organizations, offered
women two places on the NEC of the Labour Party and appointed Dr
Marion Phillips as Chief Women's Officer in early 1918. As one report
to the NEC indicated: 'Attention was given to Lancashire and
Cheshire, the West Riding of Yorkshire, and the Black Country. (. . .)
Advisory Councils are now in the process of formation in the West
Riding of Yorkshire and the Black Country'.[21] Mrs Anderson Fenn
was appointed to organize the North-East area and was involved in
organizing the West Riding Advisory Council at Leeds in 1919, which
subsequently acted as the focus for various district organizations.

At first, progress was slow – though it speeded up after 1920. In the
spring of 1921, Mrs Fenn visited Bradford to work out a plan of
organization for Bradford's four constituencies, reported on a 'new
section formed at Morley', reflected that Otley was 'largely breaking
new ground' and that Shipley was still in need of work: 'situation here
in organization was very uncertain and practically no effort has been
made to reach the women'.[22] Yet by 1922 many constituencies had
developed a viable women's section and active women's branches.

The centripetal force behind these developments was the Advisory
Council of Labour Women for the West Riding of Yorkshire. It was
formed in 1919 and soon had 303 delegates representing 119 organizations, including 42 local Labour parties, in its ranks. Its work was

[20]*Bradford Pioneer*, 7 March 1919.
[21]Labour Party, NEC, Minutes, 23 June 1919.
[22]*Op. cit.*, 21 July 1921.

most evident in the Leeds and Bradford areas and its leading figure, for many years, was Miss Clara Adams, Assistant Secretary of the Leeds City Labour party for much of the inter-war period. Not surprisingly the Women's Central Committee of Leeds had a thriving membership of 'approximately 500' in 1922.[23]

The 1918 Constitution had permitted individual membership in the Labour party and, by the early 1920s, most constituency parties were making determined attempts to respond to the national Labour party's demands to increase such membership. The Huddersfield Labour party kept its individual membership at between 500 and 600 in the late 1920s and six Leeds constituency parties normally had between 1,500 and 2,000 members for most of the 1920s. There are no accurate figures available for Bradford – though there are indications that it was far in excess of the figure for Leeds.

Underpinning such organizational development was the ubiquitous trade-union movement – whose local branches and trades council were so well represented that they invariably shaped the policies and activities of the local parties. For every individual member of a local Labour party there would be between 10 and 20 affiliated trade-union representatives.

Admittedly, the textile district of the West Riding of Yorkshire was soon to become a 'Labour heartland' but its experience was by no means unusual. A close examination of the records of the Peterborough Labour party, which Howard refers to in his article, would suggest a similar pattern of activity and success in the 1920s. Indeed, it must be remembered that despite the fact that the Peterborough constituency was half urban and half rural, and thus a difficult seat for Labour, it was won by Labour's candidate, J. F. Horrabin, in the May 1929 General Election. Labour's only parliamentary success in Peterborough had come at the end of a decade of feverish activity by Jack Mansfield, Canon. F. L. Donaldson and other local stalwarts. Lancashire, the North East and parts of London also carved out for themselves a political reputation for being Labour strongholds rivalling West Yorkshire in their political success.

Indeed, it was only in rural areas that the Labour party found serious difficulties in developing viable branches. The weak trade-union base, the decline of the farm labourers' union, the opposition of the farmers and the evident lack of sensitivity of many Labour leaders to the need to identify with the dominating influence of the Anglican Church, did not inspire confidence in the party. Rural Labour parties lacked members, finance, full-time agents and the ability to attract funds from the national party. Though Labour was often able to win one-third of the vote at parliamentary elections in counties such as Norfolk and Suffolk, the disquieting fact was that Labour's percentage of the vote

[23]City of Leeds Labour Party, Minutes, 14 September 1921, 18 April 1923.

rarely rose above the level achieved in the 1918 General Election.[24]

Notwithstanding the rural districts, however, the Labour party had made great strides in its organizations between 1918 and 1924. Contrary to the views of Howard, its organization was active and resilient in urban areas, and the political opposition was aware of this. Indeed, the tendency of the Liberals and Conservatives to unite together in 'Anti-Socialist' or 'Citizens' alliances for local elections, even after the end of the Coalition government, indicates how seriously Labour's political opponents took its challenge. And this threat was not an illusion conjured up by Labour politicians in the hope of duping the Conservative and Liberal parties. Local Liberal and Conservative representatives were all too aware of the seriousness of the Labour challenge. In Keighley they discovered this when the alliance collapsed in 1924 and was not revitalized until 1928.[25] As a result of three-way contests Labour's chances improved remarkably in municipal elections. In November 1923 the Council was composed of eight Conservative, 12 Liberals, two Labour, one Irish and two Ratepayers' Association representatives. By 1927 it was composed of seven Conservatives, seven Liberals and 10 Labour representatives.

Anti-Socialist alliances flourished when both parties could see mutual advantages of the arrangement; they declined quickly when one or other party ceased to maintain its position. Nevertheless, an 'Anti-Socialist' alliance operated in most West Yorkshire towns. Only in Leeds, after 1925, did the arrangement come to a permanent end, largely because of the almost total collapse of the Liberal party.[26]

Although the years between 1918 and 1924 were ones of great political volatility, when Liberals and Conservatives might have overestimated the real strength of Labour, there is little doubt that Labour was making rapid political advances. During these years Labour had clearly secured the working-class vote. In 1920 its parliamentary by-election success at Spen Valley had signalled the serious nature of its challenge, even though that seat was regained by the Liberals in 1922. Individual membership was rising quickly, trade unions provided funds for urban parties and in many areas the party was clearly expanding its organization. Liberals and Conservatives did not overestimate their Labour opponents. By 1924 the message was clear: Labour was the party of the working class and had improved its parliamentary position considerably by channelling that support into returning more Labour MPs through its improved organization. McKibbin's relatively optimistic view of the Labour party seems far more accurate than Howard's negative assessment.

[24]Howard, 'Expectations', p. 70.

[25]Keighley Liberal Association, Minutes, 25 September 1924, 21 September 1927, 12 September 1928.

[26]Leeds Liberal Federation, Cabinet Committee, 26 February 1926, 19 July 1926.

The 1924 Labour Government

In 1918 61 Labour MPs were returned to Parliament. This was increased to 142 at the 1922 General Election and to 191 in the December 1923 General Election. Here was proof-positive of Labour's rising appeal and organizational improvements. The party of hope and aspiration had come to office. But, as is well known, its route-way to office was unusual and its real political power severely circumscribed. It could, indeed, be argued that MacDonald should not have formed the first Labour government and observed his own previous advice that it would be suicidal for Labour to take office as a minority government. Certainly, in the light of arguments about Labour's political performance in the 1920s, it is essential to be aware of the consequences of Labour forming a rather ineffectual government in 1924. Did it disillusion the party organization throughout the country because of its failure to deliver social reforms in line with its socialist objectives? What impact did it have upon the symbiotic relationship between the Labour party and the trade unions?

At the beginning of October 1924 Ramsay MacDonald informed the King of the Labour party:

> They have shown the country that they have the capacity to govern in an equal degree with the other Parties in the House . . . and, considering their lack of experience, . . . have acquitted themselves with credit in the House of Commons. [. . .] The Labour Government has also shown the country that patriotism is not a monopoly of any single class or party. Finally, they can justly claim that they have left the international situation in a more favourable position than that which they inherited. They have in fact demonstrated that they, no less than any other party, recognize their duties and responsibilities, and have done much to dispel the fantastic and extravagant belief which at one time found expression that they were nothing but a band of irresponsible revolutionaries intent on wreckage and destruction.[27]

This assessment of Labour's first period in office implies that Labour could achieve little in the way of change at home and that its main purpose in office was to demonstrate its fitness for office. MacDonald claimed not to have been driven by the Socialists but to have met needs of conventional politics.

There were good reasons for his attitude. The Labour party had only

[27]MacDonald to King. October 1924, Geo, V K 1958/26, quoted in M. Cowling, *The Impact of Labour* (London, CUP, 1971), p. 359. The best accounts of the first Labour government appear in R. Lyman, *The First Labour Government 1924* (London, Chapman, 1965); D. Marquard, *Ramsay MacDonald* (London, Jonathan Cape, 1977), chapters 14–16.

come to office because Baldwin had called an election in which tariff reform, the Conservative policy, was rejected by the electorate. The Conservatives won 258 seats but were outnumbered by the free trade parties, for Labour had 191 seats and the Liberals 158. Although there was doubt at what would occur the Labour party eventually assumed office on 21 January 1924, with the general support of the Liberals. Asquith had previously indicated his willingness to give Liberal support to the Labour party since they, the Liberals, would really have control of the situation.

From the start, MacDonald demonstrated his commitment to orthodox politics. He appointed Philip Snowden as Chancellor of the Exchequer. Snowden was a Gladstonian Liberal in his economics, committed to free trade, the return to the gold standard and policies designed to balance the budget. In the early 1920s this meant that he pursued deflationary policies. With Snowden at the economic helm there was little prospect of dramatic government intervention in the economy. Nationalization and major social reforms were to be distant objectives – which could only be financed out of a budget surplus. Most of the other members of the Cabinet were of a similar type. The one exception was John Wheatley, a leading member of the ILP, who became Minister of Housing.

Frankly, the domestic policy of the first Labour Government was disappointing. Snowden's *Housewife's Budget* offered some minor reductions in indirect taxation and then concentrated upon the need to reduce the National Debt before real tax cuts could occur and industrial growth be assured. What is disturbing is that it received the general approval of all sides of the House of Commons. It was praised by the Tories and the Liberals just as much as by Labour politicians. It did not rock the foundations of economic orthodoxy and yet was sufficiently redistributive to satisfy most Labour MPs. One such MP, Thomas Johnston, reflected upon its impact.

> Time was, and that was not too long ago, when Mr Philip Snowden's opposition – unbending and relentless – to all phases of the Bolshevik experiment in Russia . . . created around him such an atmosphere of 'moderation' as was thought in some quarters to betoken a drift towards repudiation of the principles he had spent his life in propagating. But events have again confounded the prophets.[28]

Johnson's quote is in fact rather disturbing and very curious given that the Budget was hardly evidence of Snowden's distance from moderation. It also demonstrates how little was required to attract the loyalty of the party.

The Labour party's only domestic policy of real note was the

[28]*Leeds Weekly Citizen*, 2 May 1924.

Wheatley Housing Act which provided generous housing subsidies to both public and private builders but which stimulated the council house building boom of the 1920s. Other Labour party policies remained in limbo. The government avoided introducing the Capital Levy, to help in the process of redistributing wealth, and seemed almost reactionary when it invoked the Emergency Powers Act against Ernest Bevin's threat to bring out the London underground workers in sympathy with the striking tramwaymen.

The only real achievements were in the field of foreign policy, and much of that success appeared to be personal to MacDonald. At the London Conference of 1924 he discussed the need to compromise on the issue of German reparations, hoping that this would ease relations between Germany and France, although his party was officially committed to abandoning the demand for German reparations. Throughout the summer of 1924 he was deeply involved in negotiating a trade agreement with the Soviet Union along with a general treaty and a third treaty by which Britain would guarantee a loan to Russia. Although this pleased his party it was not popular with the Liberals and Conservatives. Indeed, the Russian treaties united the Liberals and the Conservatives in their determination to remove the Labour government. The pretext, however, was the bungled 'Campbell Case' which arose from the proposed prosecution of J. R. Campbell, a leading Communist, for seditious writing in the *Workers Weekly*. Defeated in the Commons on a vote of confidence, MacDonald resigned and a general election was held in October 1924.

This election was notorious for the publication of the so-called 'Zinoviev Letter', alleged to be evidence of the Communist intention of stirring the masses of workers to revolution with the help of the Anglo-Soviet treaty. This may have damaged Labour's electoral chances, and it has often been suggested that it was a forgery designed to discredit the Labour party. Nevertheless, it could hardly be taken as the reason for Labour's defeat. In fact, it was the collapse of the Liberal party which permitted the return of Baldwin's Conservative administration. The Labour vote increased by more than one million, or about 24 per cent, even though the number of Labour MPs was reduced to 151.

Despite Labour's increased vote it has been argued by James Hinton, and implied by Christopher Howard, that the experience was to prove 'threatening to the unity and coherence of the labour movement'.[29] Most certainly the first Labour government received criticism and censure from within the party. Jimmy Maxton and Clydesiders, George Lansbury and the *Daily Herald*, and Fenner Brockway and the ILP's *New Leader* criticized MacDonald for betraying Labour

[29]Hinton, *Labour and Socialism*, p. 131. Also look at C. Wrigley, *Lloyd George and the Challenge of Labour* (Brighton, Wheatsheaf, 1986).

principles. There was unease within the PLP about the failure to push for at least the nationalization of coal and the trade unions were certainly upset at the use of the Emergency Powers Act to deal with industrial action.[30] But how deep set were these criticisms and did Labour's commitment to progressive rather than socialist policies frustrate its political supporters throughout the country?

If Labour's credibility was impaired then there appears to have been remarkably little evidence of this in the local Labour press and in constituency and local party minutes. Indeed, the contrary appears to have been the case. When Philip Snowden became Chancellor of the Exchequer of the first Labour government 'Colne Valley was honoured' and it was later felt that the chancellorship was a 'position which we believe he is filling with credit to himself and the constituency he represents'.[31] The City of Leeds Labour party reflected upon the educational advances made by the Labour government[32] and, on Snowden's Budget, the *Bradford Pioneer* acknowledged that 'Mr Snowden has obviously and rightly been playing for safety'.[33] Most other local Labour parties in West Yorkshire made little or no mention of Labour's failures to introduce socialist measures. When complaints were levelled they were on relatively trivial matters; the North Leeds Divisional Labour party regretted that the National Party had not 'taken a stand against the silly convention of wearing Court dress'.[34] More criticism, when it came, emerged from the ILP whose York Conference of Easter 1924 was given over to demanding that the Labour government should nationalize land.

Labour's modest achievements in office do not appear to have impaired the enthusiasm for its cause amongst the activists. Again, in West Yorkshire there was substantial organizational effort going on throughout the rest of the 1920s and Labour's municipal strength was improving at a rapid rate. In November 1923 the party had 82 municipal representatives and this figure had increased to 161 by November 1928. Much of this success was due to the sterling efforts of trade unions.

Far from debilitating the Labour party, its period in office appears to have given it a vision of what was possible and inspired the local activists to even greater effort. Willie Leach, a Labour MP for one of the Bradford seats and a junior minister in the first Labour government, certainly expressed the view of many that the experience was essential. Writing on the topic 'Should Labour Refuse Office as a Minority Government', in early 1928, his clear answer was no: 'The

[30]M. Cowling, *The Impact of Labour* (London, CUP, 1971), pp. 378–9.
[31]Colne Valley Divisional Labour Party, Minutes, 29 February 1924.
[32]City of Leeds Labour Party, Minutes, 22 September 1924. Minutes of the Municipal Election Manifesto Committee.
[33]*Bradford Pioneer*, 2 May 1924.
[34]North Leeds Divisional Labour Party, Minutes, 11 April 1924.

hardship of having to water down your proposals to get support, it is true, is vexatious, but is, even so, a great deal better than having your opponents' reactionary proposals forced upon you. . . . Even a minority Labour Government possesses the field all the time it is in office and has previous rights in introducing its proposals'[35]

The failures of the 1924 Labour government neither dampened the idealism of Labour activists nor undermined the trade-union commitment to its political arm. An examination of the records of any party in an urban area with a good Labour tradition will reveal that unions continued to dominate the local party activities, individual membership continued to improve and that the way was paved for even more substantial Labour success. In addition, as Professor Trevor Wilson suggests, the Labour party's rise to office confirmed that it was the Labour party, not the Liberals, which represented the real challenge to the Conservatives.[36] It was the Labour party which benefited from its period in office and the Liberal party which was the real and obvious loser.

Labour in Opposition, 1924 to 1929

Though the Labour party continued its growth in the period between the first and second Labour governments it did face a number of challenges which threatened to throw it off course. The ILP became increasingly difficult and the Communist party proved troublesome, but it was the General Strike which could have been disastrous for Labour.

The General Strike, which lasted for nine days in May 1926, was the confluence of a number of tributary developments in the immediate post-war years. Its immediate cause was the attempt by mineowners to reduce the wages of coal miners, in the wake of Britain's return to the gold standard in 1925 which had made further cost cuts essential if Britain was still to compete in the international markets. Faced with such a situation, the TUC agreed to call out between one and two million workers from essential industries in support of the miners. But it was a long fuse which led to the events of May 1926. Although the Baldwin government's attack upon wages was crucial, the industrial relations of the coal industry and the attitude of the major trade unions also proved vital. In 1921 the miners had been let down by the National Union of Railwaymen and the Dockers' Union, soon to be the Transport and General Workers, who had failed to operate the 'Triple Alliance' when the miners found their wages reduced on the return of coal industry to the coal owners on 1 April 1921. The decision not to

[35] *Leeds Weekly Citizen*, 17 February 1928.
[36] Wilson, *Downfall*, chapters 12 to 16.

support the miners was taken on Friday, 15 April 1921 – the infamous 'Black Friday'. Four years later a contrite trade union movement, increasingly dominated by the General Council of the TUC, was not prepared to permit a repeat of this episode – mindful of the need to expiate the guilt it had felt at 'Black Friday'.[37] When the miners were first threatened with further wage reductions in 1925, the TUC entered the fray, threatened sympathetic strike action and ultimately forced Baldwin to avoid an immediate conflict in mining by proffering a nine-month subsidy to the coal owners and by setting up a Royal Commission under Sir Herbert Samuel. This temporary deal, struck on Friday, 31 July 1925, 'Red Friday', merely delayed the coal lock-out and the General Strike for nine months. When the subsidy expired, and the Samuel Commission failed to offer an acceptable solution, conflict became inevitable. For nine days, the General Strike raged before it was called off, amidst bitter controversy, on 12 May 1926.

The General Strike posed many problems for the Labour party. The reluctance of some Labour leaders, most notably Ramsay MacDonald and Philip Snowden, to be too closely associated with the dispute gave the impression that the Labour party was not fully behind the strikers – although the records of most local Labour parties deny such an impression. The defeat of the strike could also have told disastrously on the confidence of the whole Labour movement. In addition, the General Strike provided the justification for Baldwin's Conservative government to take sweeping action against the whole of the Labour movement. The Trade Union Act of 1927 outlawed 'sympathetic' strike action and replaced the principle of 'contracting out' by 'contracting in', in the clear hope that the apathy of trade unions would reduce political funds for the Labour party. The Conservative government was not disappointed for the number of trade-union affiliated members of the Labour party fell by over one million by the end of 1928, and trades councils began to redefine their precise position with the Labour party.[38]

Nevertheless, there were benefits and compensations for the Labour party. Trade unionists were insensed with the Act and mounted a campaign against it in 1927. Though this did not get very far it confirmed and strengthened the trade-union connection with Labour in much the same way as the Taff Vale judgement had acted as an annealing force between the unions and the LRC. This is reflected in the fact that the trade unions sponsored more Labour candidates in the 1929 General Election than they had done in 1924. It was as though the

[37]G. A. Phillips, *The General Strike; The Politics of Industrial Conflict* (London, Weidenfeld & Nicolson, 1976), pp. 54–5. Also read M. Morris, *The General Strike* (London, Journeyman Press, 1976 and 1980); P. Renshaw, *The General Strike* (London, Eyre Metheun, 1975); J. Skelley, ed., *1926 The General Strike* (London, Lawrence & Wishart, 1976).
[38]Bradford Trades Council, Minutes, for 1928.

failure of industrial action prompted the trade-union movement to throw its full weight behind the political ambitions of the Labour party. MacDonald put it more bluntly: 'Labour could solve mining and similar difficulties through the ballot box'.[39]

The galvanizing of the relationship between the unions and the Labour party, which was soon apparent in the rising importance of Ernest Bevin in the latter, served to reduce the importance of the other political disputes which divided the party. This was particularly true of divisions provoked by the Communist party.

Between 1920 and 1928, the Communist party of Great Britain had attempted to affiliate with the Labour party. This caused some consternation within the Labour party which, whilst rejecting the Communist application at successive annual conferences, found it impossible to exclude individual members of the Communist party from its annual proceedings. The problem was that trade unions could send Communist delegates to the Labour party annual conferences. Faced with its own version of 'the enemy within', the Labour party sought to remove the offending delegates. At the 1922 Edinburgh Conference, the Labour party agreed that every delegate should have individually accepted the constitution and principles of the party. Trade-union opposition to this made the policy unworkable. But after the 1926 General strike was called off, an action which the Communists referred to as the 'greatest crime that has ever been committed . . . against the working class',[40] trade unions were easier to convince. The war of words between the TUC and the Communist party, in the wake of the General Strike, served to nullify the limited influence which Communists had within the Labour party. By 1928, the Communist party's new 'Class Against Class' policy, which viewed the Labour party as the third capitalist party in Britain and committed it to opposition, brought to an end Communist attempts to infiltrate Labour during the 1920s.

The difficulties with the ILP were potentially more damaging since in some areas, like the textile district of Yorkshire, it was the ILP which still shaped the pattern of local Labour activities and organization. Also, until the mid 1920s, it was a growing political party, funded by middle-class sympathizers and led by Clifford Allen, who had raised the intellectual level of debate within the party.

By the mid 1920s this small but burgeoning party was proving difficult to the Labour party. In the early 1920s it had rejected the ideas of dissolution and drawn up a new constitution. Its membership increased and its parliamentary representation was significant. Given this context it was hardly surprising that some of its leading figures,

[39]Quoted from A. Bullock, *The Life and Times of Ernest Bevin, I* (London, Heinemann, 1960), p. 349.
[40]*Workers Bulletin*, 13 May 1926.

such as Jimmy Maxton, were critical of the failure of the first Labour government to introduce socialist measures. By 1925 relations had become so tense that the ILP and the Labour party were meeting regularly to resolve their differences. On one such occasion, in May 1925, Clifford Allen was at pains to stress the educational, intellectual and propaganda role of the ILP:

> It is claimed that it is the special duty of the ILP to develop in detail the Socialist objective of the Movement and supplement its general propaganda with the advocacy of fundamental Socialist principles.[41]

Arthur Henderson, for the Labour party, sought to play down the distinctive role of the ILP, stressed the responsible actions of the Labour party and warned that

> So long as the two bodies presented their individual policies without regard to each other, it was obvious that overlapping and friction would continue, but in the view of the Party Executive circumstances had arisen which rendered it desirable that there should be a frank and full discussion of the whole position.

That 'frank and full discussion', conducted through a sub-committee composed of representatives of both organizations, led nowhere. Such negotiations were to prove futile once Clifford Allen was replaced by John Wheatley and Jimmy Maxton and the Clydesiders gained control in 1926.

Relations worsened when the ILP produced its 'Socialism in Our Time' policy and *The Living Wage* pamphlet in 1926. The primary aim of 'Socialism in Our Time' was to bring about an increase of purchasing power as the way out of the depression. Unemployment would be cured by redistributing wealth and introducing a scheme for family allowances, to be paid out of taxation. Further purchasing power would be injected by imposing statutory wage minimums throughout industry, which would be paid fo· by printing money. Though this was obviously inflationary it was felt that the added purchasing power of workers would absorb industrial capital leading to a rise in production. These sections were to be supported by a variety of Socialist controls – including the nationalization of the Bank of England and the nationalization of industries which did not introduce the minimum wage level.

Such policies were anathema to Philip Snowden and Ramsay MacDonald, MacDonald's antipathy ensured that the ILP programme would receive short shrift. He argued, in the *Socialist Review* of March 1926, that the ILP proposals would be a 'millstone' around the parliamentary party's neck and noted the contradictory approach to capitalism exhibited in the policy – which anticipated the collapse of

[41]Labour Party, NEC, Minutes, 23 May 1925.

capitalism but seemed intent upon offering proposals which would strengthen and perpetuate capitalism. The 1927 Labour party conference debated the 'living wage' and referred it to the executive where MacDonald condemned it to political oblivion.

Many trade unionists also felt hostile to the ILP proposals. It was argued that they would interfere with the free collective bargaining of unions and that family allowances could be used to hold down wages.

It would be misleading to suggest that such internecine conflict did not undermine some support for the local Labour party organization in some areas, such as West Yorkshire. In addition, there was clearly a loss of funds to the party following the Trade Union Act of 1927. But these difficulties were more than offset by the more overt interest of the trade-union movement in the Labour party after the General Strike and the stepping up of individual membership campaigns in the late 1920s. There was great confidence in the party that it would win the next general election. The only doubt, for a time, was who would lead the party to office?

During 1925 Snowden's name was mentioned, along with those of Henderson and Clynes, as possible leaders of the Labour party. Nothing came of this, but it is indicative of the mood of frustration which was developing towards MacDonald. Throughout the mid and late 1920s, there was a feeling abroad in the PLP that MacDonald was drifting away from his colleagues. In a letter to MacDonald in 1927, Snowden reflected upon this mood.

> You must excuse me for writing quite plainly. I am expressing the feeling of all my colleagues who have talked with me on the subject. We are feeling that somehow – it is difficult to explain – we cannot get inside you. You seem to be protected by some inpenetrable barrier. I called it aloofness in my last letter. It was not so in the old days of the NAC.[42]

But, once the general election approached, differences were forgotten as Labour leaders and the rank and file savoured the prospect of victory.

Conclusion

Labour's political growth in the 1920s owes little to the political opportunities provided by the Liberal split in 1916. Though the Asquith v. Lloyd George conflict did enhance Labour's political prospects it has to be remembered that Labour was already winning the progressive vote from the Liberals before the war and had radically improved and altered its organization between 1912 and the late 1920s.

---

[42]Public Record Office, 30/69 item 1753. MacDonald Diaries, 1910–37.

It had emerged as the party of socialist idealism, but it must be remembered that its overriding feature was its close association with the trade-union movement – which was more concerned with loyalty than the implementation of political ideals. For this reason the failure of the first Labour government to introduce a programme of wide-ranging socialist measures did not injure the party, though it did offend many members of the ILP. Equally, the collapse of the General Strike, and the economic and political repercussions which followed it, were less important than the annealing qualities which the dispute provided for Labour and the trade unions.

Throughout the 1920s the image of Labour as a vibrant, expanding new party was not an illusion. By 1929 the party was better organized, more unified and strongly supported than it had ever been in its history. Its political opponents were keenly aware of its power – so much so that they recognized that the only way to stem the tide of Labour in local politics was to form numerous 'Anti-Socialist' alliances. Above all it was a party where loyalty counted for more than principle and ideal – a fact which Ramsay MacDonald would have been wise to remember in the financial and political crisis of 1931.

5 'LUCIFER OF THE LEFT': RAMSAY MACDONALD AND THE COLLAPSE OF THE SECOND LABOUR GOVERNMENT, 1929–31

No British political leader this century has been more reviled than Ramsay MacDonald, Britain's first Labour Prime Minister in 1924 and 1929 to 1931. His decision to offer the resignation of the second Labour government and to accept the King's commission to form a National government during the financial crisis of August 1931 provoked much animus amongst many who knew him and believed in him, sustaining the view that he had planned to ditch the Labour government. It has long been an axiom of the Labour party that MacDonald's actions in 1931 marked him as a traitor to the cause. William Lawther remarked that MacDonald was 'bereft of any public decency'.[1] Harold Laski described him as 'betraying his politics' and 'betraying his origins'.[2] The Labour party, in order to distance itself from its estranged and inconsistent creator, shrouded his name and reputation with invective. A popular catch of the time ran

> *We'll hang Ramsay Mac on a sour apple tree,*
> *We'll hang Snowden and Thomas to keep him company;*
> *For that's the place where traitors ought to be.*[3]

There was also the obituary written by J. S. Clarke and sent to MacDonald

> *Here lies Ramsay Mac*
> *A friend of all humanity,*
> *Too many pats upon the back*
> *Inflated Ramsay's vanity.*
> *The Blarney stone he oft-times kissed,*
> *But departed in his glory:*
> *Having been born a socialist*
> *He died a bloody Tory.*[4]

[1] Quoted by D. Marquand, 'A Traitor's Grave', BBC Radio 4 broadcast, 2 March 1977.
[2] *Harper's*, September 1932.
[3] M. Foot, 'Ramsay MacDonald', review article of D. Marquand, *Ramsay MacDonald, Bulletin of the Society for the Study of Labour History*, 35 (1977), p. 70.
[4] R. C. Challinor, 'Letter from MacDonald to Clarke', *Bulletin of the Society for the Study of Labour History*, 27 (1973), pp. 34–5.

Interpretations

The most damaging accusation of MacDonald, however, comes from L. MacNeill Weir in his book *The Tragedy of Ramsay MacDonald* (1938). Referring to the last days of the second Labour government, he wrote that

> The members of the Labour Cabinet naturally assumed on that Sunday night, 23 August (1931) that Mr Baldwin would be asked to form a government. But it is significant that MacDonald had something quite different in view. Without a word of consultation with his Cabinet colleagues, without even informing them of his intentions to set up a National government with himself as Prime Minister, he proceeded to carry out his long-thought-out plan.

Snowden throws a side-light on MacDonald's attitude at this time:

> When the Labour Cabinet as a whole declined to agree to a reduction of unemployment pay, Mr MacDonald assumed too hurriedly that this involved the resignation of his government. He neither showed nor expressed any grief at this regrettable development. On the contrary, he set about the formation of the National government with an enthusiasm which showed that the adventure was highly agreeable to him.

> It was therefore amazing to them, when the Cabinet assembled next morning. MacDonald came in and announced that a new government had been formed – in short, *that he was in and they were out.*[5]

In a book of almost 600 pages, MacNeill Weir captures the essence of the Labour hostility to MacDonald, presenting the vituperation of a betrayed follower instead of evidence. Nevertheless, such hostility became entrenched within the Labour party and it was accepted, almost as an article of faith, that MacDonald had deliberately and cynically betrayed the Labour movement by his formation of the National government in August 1931.[6]

It is only in recent years that historians have begun to re-examine MacDonald's career with a more dispassionate eye. Almost twenty years ago C. L. Mowat made an appeal for a reappraisal of MacDonald's contribution to the Labour movement on the grounds that the events of 1931 were a collective, not an individual, responsi-

---

[5]L. MacNeill Weir, *The Tragedy of Ramsay MacDonald* (London, Secker & Warburg, 1938), p. 383.
[6]Weir, *MacDonald*, pp. 377–96.

bility,[7] a view which was echoed by Michael Foot in 1977.[8] More recently, the major corrective to earlier views has been presented by David Marquand who, in 1977, published a monumental biography of Ramsay MacDonald, portraying him 'warts and all'.[9] It is easily the most detailed and best evidenced of all that has been written on MacDonald, although it caused controversy by suggesting that there is little to suggest that he schemed to ditch the second Labour government. It drew upon the extensive MacDonald papers and diaries which the family had first consigned to the PRO and then put into Marquand's hands for more than a decade until about 1977. Armed with such partial evidence Marquand argued that the decision to form a National government was a product of MacDonald's concern for national interests.

> All his life, MacDonald had fought against a class view of politics, and for the primacy of political action as against industrial; for him the logical corollary was that the party must be prepared, when necessary, to subordinate the sectional claims of the unions to its own conception of the national interest.[10]

To Marquand, MacDonald's real fault was that he held on to his nineteenth-century principles far too long. His almost religious conviction that the preservation of the gold standard was essential to British economic growth, plus his belief in the primacy of the state over party, ensured that he lacked the 'ability and willingness to jettison cherished assumptions in the face of changing realities'.[11] He was not prepared to take a gamble.

Although Marquand's views and invariably moderate approach have not found favour with many members of the Labour party they have forced some softening of the attitude to MacDonald, Michael Foot has noted that to blame MacDonald alone for the events of 1931 is something of an 'indecency'.[12] Humphry Berkeley, in seeking to explain the reason for MacDonald's decision to form the National government has broadly endorsed Marquand's views: MacDonald felt that the nation had to remain on the gold standard and that unemployment benefits would have to be cut in order to permit the balancing of the budget which would allow this. 'He had', according to Berkeley, 'as he thought, put country before party. He did not realize at the time that the sacrifice was unnecessary'.[13] Indeed, the National

---

[7]C. L. Mowat, 'Ramsay MacDonald and the Labour Party', in A. Briggs and J. Saville (eds), *Essays in Labour History* (London, Macmillan, 1971).
[8]Foot, 'MacDonald', pp. 67–71.
[9]D. Marquand, *Ramsay MacDonald* (London, Jonathan Cape, 1977), p. xiv.
[10]Marquand, *MacDonald*, p. 624.
[11]Marquand, *MacDonald*, p. 795.
[12]Foot, 'MacDonald', p. 70.
[13]H. Berkeley, *The Myth that will not die* (London, Croom Helm, 1978), p. 117.

government went off the gold standard in September 1931 and abandoned some of the previously sacrosanct principles of budget management.

Two recent articles have also called into question the whole notion that the formation of the National government was a product of some grand design on the part of MacDonald, the bankers and the Conservative party. Philip Williamson's article, which uses a wide range of banking archives, government records and private papers, some of which have only just become available, specifically examines the notion that the second Labour government had fallen victim to the 'bankers' ramp' – the imposition of cuts in expenditure which many members of the Labour administration would find difficult to accept.[14] He argues that the whole notion of the 'bankers' ramp' was developed by the Labour movement in order to castigate MacDonald, Snowden and other former Labour ministers and as a means to exculpate those Labour ministers who had not been prepared to join the National government from responsibility for the Labour government's collapse. Despite the attempts of some historians to use this theory to explain the collapse of the Labour government,[15] Williamson maintains that

> The final point to be made about the bankers' ramp accusation is that the bankers did not want the Labour government to collapse during August 1931. The Bank of England directors brought the Conservative and Liberal leaders into the discussions because they feared that a minority government might alone be unable to deal with the crisis, and in order to increase pressure upon ministers to take immediate action – not in order to replace them. [. . .]
> Moreover, in the context of a world-wide decline in financial confidence, the London and New York bankers were hardly likely to have risked causing international financial chaos by indulging in merely political manoeuvres.[16]

If there are doubts about a bankers' plot to get rid of the Labour government there are, according to Stuart Ball, similar doubts about the view that MacDonald conspired with the Conservative party to form the National government.[17] It is true that the press had been speculating on the likelihood of such an arrangement since the summer

[14]P. Williamson, 'A "Bankers' Ramp"? Financiers and the British political crisis of August 1931', *English Historical Review*, XCIX (October 1984).
[15]R. McKibbin, 'The Economic Policy of the Second Labour Government 1929–1931', *Past and Present*, lxviii (August 1975); B. Pimlott, *Labour and the Left in the 1930s* (Cambridge, CUP, 1977), p. 12; J. Fair, 'The Conservative Basis for the Formation of the National Government of 1931', *Journal of British Studies*, xix (1980), p. 150.
[16]Williamson, 'Bankers' Ramp?', pp. 805–6.
[17]S. Ball, 'The Conservative Party and the formation of the National Government: August 1931', *Historical Journal*, 29, I (1986).

of 1930 but Ball convincingly demonstrates that Stanley Baldwin, the Conservative leader, was reluctant to become involved in such an administration, that Neville Chamberlain had declared his hope that 'it won't come to pass',[18] and that it was obvious that such an arrangement was unlikely to be to the benefit of the Conservative party which was already riding high in the political opinion polls.

> The Conservative party sacrificed much in the tactical short term and risked much more in the electoral long term by its actions during the crisis of August 1931. (. . .) In one sense, in view of its uncritical acceptance of the bankers' urgency and therefore of the limitations on its freedom whilst parliament remained adjourned, it could almost be argued that the Conservative party was, more than any other party, the victim of the bankers' 'ramp'.[19]

Recent published research has thus thrown doubt upon Weir's suggestion that MacDonald was carrying out his 'long thought-out plan' when he abandoned the Labour government in favour of the National government.[20]

There are now several shades of opinion towards MacDonald's actions. It is now more readily accepted that he made a significant contribution to the Labour party and that his actions in 1931 were also shaped by other Labour leaders, such as Philip Snowden. It is generally appreciated that there is little hard evidence that MacDonald schemed to overthrow the second Labour government and a greater willingness to accept that he was a victim of circumstances. Nevertheless, his name remains emotive within the Labour party, the odium and the appellation 'traitor' persists. In such circles, MacNeill Weir's views still carry as much, if not more, support than those of David Marquand – especially since the latter did his own form of 'MacDonaldism' by defecting to the Social Democratic party in 1981.

The contrast between the views of Weir and David Marquand are substantial. Weir sees MacDonald as a Liberal opportunist who schemed to ditch the second Labour government and betray the Labour party. On the other hand, Marquand is far more generous, believing that MacDonald was committed to socialism, a principled opportunist, and was driven to form a National government when his Cabinet could not find it possible to support the deflationary policies which were necessary if the country was to remain on the gold standard. Their different interpretations raise four main questions. Was MacDonald a Liberal or a Socialist? Was he a political opportunist? Did he scheme to ditch the Labour government? Does he deserve the appellation 'traitor'?

[18]*Op. cit.*, p. 161.
[19]*Op. cit.*
[20]Weir, *MacDonald*, p. 383.

Liberal or Socialist?

To MacNeill Weir

> MacDonald was always the most accommodating of socialists. His Socialism was of the kind that Sir William Harcourt meant when he said on a famous occasion: 'We are all Socialists now'. His Socialism is that far-off Never-Never Land, born of vague aspirations and described by him in picturesque generalities. It is a Turner landscape of beautiful colour and glorious indefiniteness. He saw it, not with a telescope, but with a kaleidoscope. . . . Anyone can believe in it without sacrifice or even inconvenience.
>
> It is evident now that MacDonald never really accepted the Socialist faith of a classless world, based on unselfish service.[21]

There are many other instances of Weir's doubts about MacDonald's genuine commitment to socialism. But how accurate a picture has he presented of MacDonald? Was his socialism vague and flimsy?

To understand MacDonald one must know something about his early life. He was born in October 1866, the illegitimate son of a farm labourer, at Lossiemouth in Scotland. Despite his working-class background he quickly aspired to the lower middle class. He was a bright child, did well at school and stayed on as a pupil-teacher until he was 19, before going to seek his fortune in Bristol and London. In these cities he pursued a varied career as a teacher, secretary to the National Cyclist Union and, in 1888, secretary to Thomas Lough, a Liberal Radical politican. From then on he was a journalist, writer and, eventually, organizer of the Labour Representation Committee. It was his marriage to Margaret Gladstone, in 1896, which gave him the financial independence to pursue his political career.

As a professional secretary and organizer he was not all that distinct from many of the young men, clerks, civil servants, and other lower-middle-class groups, who flooded to London in the mid 1880s and early 1890s in the hope of finding a niche in society. Rather like Sydney Webb, Bernard Shaw and others who were detached from industry and seeking to find new values to live by, MacDonald was attracted to the socialist ideas which were being widely discussed in the metropolis. He joined the London Fabians and envisaged the gradual modification of existing institutions through the extension of collectivist principles. He believed that socialism could be extended by encouraging municipal authorities to extend their control over most industries and services and by encouraging Parliament to widen the franchise and to introduce legislation to extend public control through nationalization. Indeed, like many other Fabians, MacDonald saw the gradual transference of

[21]Weir, *MacDonald*, p. xi.

industry from private to public control, there to be organized by impartial civil servants driven by the desire to service the community rather than obtain profit.

Fabian socialism was well suited to the strategical course which MacDonald charted, first within the ILP and then as secretary of the LRC. It permitted him virtually to ignore the differences between the ILP and the left wing of the Liberal party. This was vital for MacDonald, like many others in the 1890s, was not certain where his future lay. He only joined the ILP in 1894, after his failure to secure a Liberal nomination and in frustration at the local policies pursued by Liberal associations. In the late 1890s he was not entirely convinced that the ILP provided an alternative to Liberalism and was, with others, struggling to form a Progressive Alliance, drawn together broadly by the belief that the Liberal party was dying and that a new aggressive party had to be forged in order to unite progressive groups and to obtain necessary social legislation. In 1896 he became a member of the Rainbow Group, a body of frustrated Liberals and Radicals dedicated to such changes, and contributed to its journal the *Progressive Review*.[22] Although that particular movement did not get far it revealed that MacDonald was a dedicated gradualist and believed in working through the existing political institutions. Evolution, rather than revolution, was to be the central theme of the MacDonald's ideology. Gradual improvements would bring about socialism not a catastrophic collapse of society. Indeed, he once informed an ILP conference (1909) that

> Socialism is not to come from the misery of the people . . . I know that there is a belief still fairly prevalent amongst one school of socialist theorists that the more capitalism fails, the clearer will the way to Socialism be. I have never shared that faith. . . . Poverty of mind and body blurs the vision and does not clarify it.[23]

MacDonald's gradualism extended to maintaining that there was no incompatability of interests between the classes: 'Socialism is no class movement . . . It is not the rule of the working class, it is the organization of the community.'[24] It was thus necessary to educate the whole community to the need for socialism.

Early in 1905 MacDonald launched a Socialist Library designed to overcome the deplorable lack of a Socialist literature more exhaustive and systematic than pamphlets and newspaper articles.[25] The Library included translations of important continental works on socialism as

[22]Marquand, *MacDonald*, pp. 56–7.
[23]ILP, *Conference Report* (London, ILP, 1909), MacDonald's chairman's address.
[24]R. MacDonald, *Ramsay MacDonald's Political Writings*, ed., B. Barker, (London, Allen Lane, Penguin, 1972), pp. 48–9 and, again, p. 162.
[25]Marquand, *MacDonald*, pp. 88–9.

well as much of MacDonald's own work. The second volume to be produced in the series was MacDonald's *Socialism and Society*. In this eclectic piece, MacDonald rejected the competitive struggle for existence as the chief characteristic of social evolution in favour of an increasing tendency towards cooperation.[26] This was a theme which he was to return to in later writings, and in particular in his *Parliament and Revolution* (1919), *Parliament and Democracy* (1921) and *Socialism: Critical and Constructive* (1921) – which also stressed his belief that socialism would come as the state needed to control the activities of expanding business organization.[27]

There is no doubt that vague and imprecise as MacDonald's ideas may have been they, nevertheless, constituted a body of socialist principles. These principles may not have satisfied some socialists, whose views were more Marxist in orientation, but they represented a body of thought which would have been regarded as socialist by the majority of Labour party/LRC supporters at the beginning of the twentieth century. They accorded with the Fabian gradualist views which were beginning to permeate the Labour party and which became dominant in the 1918 Constitution. Why then does Weir accuse Mac-Donald of being a Liberal rather than a socialist?

The accusation appears to be based partly upon the vagueness of MacDonald's socialist ideas – though they were no more general than the majority of socialists at this time whose ethical commitment was based upon the need to remove obvious inequality in society. The accusation was also partly based upon MacDonald's propensity for compromise. It is true that MacDonald worked closely with the Liberals in the 1890s and maintained associations with Radical Liberals through the Rainbow Group. It is also the case that he was party to the secret pact with Liberalism which bears his name – the Gladstone-MacDonald pact of 1903. Indeed, it was this pact, whereby the LRC was given a free hand in some 30 constituencies in return for MacDonald's agreement to support Liberals in other constituencies, which paved the way for the Labour party's electoral successes in the 1905–6 General Election.[28] These arrangements and compromises, plus the fact that the LRC/Labour party had no socialist clause in its constitution between 1900 and 1918, confirm Weir in his view that MacDonald was truly a Liberal Radical.

Yet Weir's criticism appears unfair for it tends to ignore the amorphous nature of Liberal Radical and Socialist policies which existed in the late 1890s and the early twentieth century. Weir, who was closely associated with MacDonald until 1931, does not appear to have voiced

[26]*Op. cit.*, p. 88; MacDonald, *MacDonald's Political Writings*, extract from *Socialism and Society*.
[27]Marquand, *MacDonald*, pp. 89–93.
[28]P. Adelman, *The Rise of the Labour Party 1880–1945* (London, Longman, 1972), pp. 107–8.

dissent at MacDonald's style at that time and it could be argued that the secret pact did hasten the growth of the Labour party. It might also be added that hard party divisions had not emerged in 1903 in quite the form that existed in 1918. Some Labour MPs were still floating between the Liberal party and the LRC in 1903 and, from the perspective of 1938, MacNeill Weir imposes a solidarity in Labour ranks that did not then exist.

In the 1890s MacDonald, as with many Labour politicians, was not far removed from Liberalism. He had been reared in Liberalism and continued to accept many of its tenets – peace, retrenchment and reform – well after his departure from its political organization. However, by 1900 he was as much a socialist as any other leader in the Labour party. His essential Liberal Radicalism did not impair his commitment to Fabian gradualism – which became the central tenet of Labour party policy after 1918. It is true that the Liberal Radical strand of the Labour party left with MacDonald in 1931 – but that does not mean that he was not a socialist. Just because MacDonald was a master of obfuscation throughout his political life, and wrote about socialism with consistent imprecision, that does not mean that he did not hold strong socialist views. Indeed, until 1931 it was a commonplace suggestion that he was a socialist. It was only the events of 1931 which undermined that assumption – not the experience of the previous three decades.

Opportunist?

There is much evidence to suggest that MacDonald had an eye to the main chance. His rejection of the Liberal party in 1894, the Lib-Lab secret pact of 1903 and his seizure of office in 1924, when he had previously stated that it would be a mistake for a minority Labour government to take power, confirm this view. Yet Weir's charge of opportunism is one which could be levelled at just about any successful politican. In MacDonald's case such a charge is complicated by the fact that he gave up his political dominance of the Labour party in 1914, rejecting its support for the First World War.

Indeed, MacDonald suffered for his opposition to the war. He was mercilessly attacked by Horatio Bottomley, editor of *John Bull*, who called him 'Traitor, Coward, Cur' and demanded 'his trial by Court Martial, his condemnation as an aider and abetter of the King's enemies, and that he be taken to the Tower and shot at dawn'.[29] The culmination of that campaign led to the publication of a facsimile of MacDonald's birth certificate which revealed that his registered name

[29]Marquand, *MacDonald*, p. 189, quoting from *John Bull*, 19 June 1915.

was James MacDonald Ramsay, the illegitimate son of Ann Ramsay.[30] As Weir noted of this stage of MacDonald's life, he was like Milton's Lucifer for

> *He hears*
> *On all sides, from innumerable tongues,*
> *A dismal universal hiss, the sound*
> *Of public scorn.*[31]

In the 1918 General Election, he lost his seat at Leicester, which he had held since 1906, due largely to his anti-war activities.

Marquand has referred to MacDonald as a 'principled opportunist', a description which fits him more accurately than Weir's simple dismissal of his opportunism. As further proof of this qualification, it might be noted that not only did he give up his place within the Labour party in 1914 but he also refused a title in the 1930s, when he ceased to be Prime Minister. He remained, as he said he would, plain 'Jimmy MacDonald, without prefix or suffix'.[32]

The major accusation that he was opportunist, however, surrounds the events of 1931. The general gist of the views put forward by Weir and many Labour party activists is that faced with an increasingly unhelpful Labour party, dominated by the trade unions, MacDonald was pleased to be able to ditch his troublesome colleagues. Snowden, hardly the most impartial commentator, reinforced his view, reflecting that MacDonald neither 'showed nor expressed any grief at this [the formation of the National Government] event'.[33] But did MacDonald scheme to overthrow the Labour government?

Grand Scheme?

It was the events of the 23 and 24 August 1931 which led to the accusation that MacDonald had schemed the downfall of the Labour government and had opportunistically jumped upon the National government bandwagon. Weir argues that

> The impression left on the minds of those who heard that speech [about the formation of the National government] . . . was that the whole thing had been arranged long before and that, while in Cabinet and Committee they had been making panic-stricken

[30]*John Bull*, 4 September 1915.
[31]Weir, *MacDonald*, p. 62.
[32]Marquand, 'A Traitor's Grave'.
[33]P. Snowden, *An Autobiography*, II (London, Ivor Nicholson & Watson, 1934), p. 952.

efforts to balance the Budget, the whole business had been humbug and make-believe.[34]

He asked why MacDonald had been careful to prevent the Labour Cabinet meeting the Liberal and Tory leaders and why he had misled his junior ministers on 24 August 1931? There are also numerous asides about MacDonald's clear intention to 'fix' things. Sydney Webb was one of the first to suggest that there had been a plot by MacDonald to overthrow the Labour government, that it formed 'a single drama, in all its developments seen in advance . . . only by the statesman who was at once its author, producer and principal actor'.[33] Philip Snowden also outlined his views in his *An Autobiography* (1934), supporting the Webb analysis. L. MacNeill Weir also includes numerous newspaper cartoons in his book implying that MacDonald was in negotiations to form a new government with the Conservative and Liberal leaders, including Low's 'Eve-of-the-Session Party at the Borgias', depicting MacDonald wining with Baldwin, Churchill, and other political leaders, in the poisoned atmosphere of intrigue.[36] Yet although there is plenty of evidence of rumour and innuendo, Weir offers no evidence of the 'Grand Scheme'.

Marquand's book, although based very much upon the MacDonald papers – something of a partial source – goes to the other extreme and suggests that MacDonald did not arrive at his decision to form a National government until somewhere between the night of the 23 August 1931 and the late morning of the 24 August. He notes that on 22 August, Malcolm MacDonald, Ramsay's son, records that his father had telephoned at lunchtime and that 'He feels pretty certain that he will resign either tonight or tomorrow'.[37] According to Marquand, MacDonald changed his mind due to the conflation of several factors – the appeal from the King to form a National government, his belief that he would have to support the gold standard, whether in office or in opposition, and his own conviction, nurtured by the King and his Liberal and Tory opponents, that he was the only man who could pull the country through the financial crisis. Combined with several weeks of intense pressure, these considerations led him to the decision to form a National government.

Most of the available evidence supports the view that MacDonald was involved in no 'Grand Scheme'.[38] Indeed, given the economic context in which the National government was formed it is difficult to see how MacDonald could have ever contrived such a scheme.

[34]Weir, *MacDonald*, p. 384.
[35]Sydney Webb (Lord Passfield), 'What Happened in 1931: A Record', *Political Quarterly* (January – March 1932).
[36]Weir, *MacDonald*, p. 313.
[37]Marquand, *MacDonald*, p. 631.
[38]Williamson, 'A Bankers' Ramp'; Ball, 'Conservative Party and National Government'.

The fact is that MacDonald was a prisoner of economic circumstances. Ever since the end of the First World War, successive governments had attempted to return to the gold standard, which had been suspended during the war. In order to raise the pre-war parity of the pound to the dollar successive governments followed the policies laid down by the Cunliffe Committee in 1918 – which advocated a six-year programme of deflation to strengthen the pound. The hope was that once the pound returned to its pre-war parity and the gold standard was restored then all international trading nations would follow suit, moving from protectionism to free trade, increasing international trade and the demand for industrial goods. The end product would be the end of unemployment.

In 1925 Britain returned to the gold standard, raising the value of the pound by 10 per cent in the process according to J. M. Keynes, thus imposing upon all exporting industries the need to reduce their costs by about 10 per cent in order to maintain their former competitiveness. The result was the decline of Britain's exports and balance of trade, as J. M. Keynes had predicted in his pamphlet *The Economic Consequences of Mr Churchill*, although a recent article by K. G. P. Matthews has suggested that the actual level of overvaluation was minimal.[39] By the late 1920s and early 1930s, with rising unemployment and the international depression following the Wall Street crash, the economic situation worsened and, in order to remain on the gold standard, Britain had to borrow from abroad.

It was in this climate of acute economic and financial crises that the second Labour government foundered. It did so largely because MacDonald had to rely upon the financial advice of Philip Snowden, the Chancellor of the Exchequer, who stubbornly adhered to the economic orthodoxy of the day. There were economic choices being suggested to Snowden and the Labour Cabinet. Britain could have gone off the gold standard, devalued the pound and adopted protectionist policies, similar to those subsequently introduced by the National government in 1931 and 1932. The prices of British exports would have been reduced by devaluation and British competitiveness in the home market would have been increased. Alternatively, there was the possibility of expanding out of slump by pump-priming British industry with increased demand through the introduction of a 'living wage' policy or by offering cheap credit to the working class. There was, perhaps, even a third major alternative: the nationalization of industry and the introduction of a broad set of collectivist policies – though they may not have got very far given the second Labour government's minority position. But Snowden had serious objections to all these devices. His political upbringing had been in the

---

[39]K. G. P. Matthews, 'Was Sterling Overvalued in 1925', *Economic History Review*, xxxix, 4 (November 1986).

atmosphere of Liberal Radicalism. The fact is that Snowden's political socialization and his own personal political history made it virtually impossible for him to act in any other way than he did.

Lacking vision, Snowden had no alternative strategy to offer. He thus met rising unemployment with a greater determination than ever to balance the budget by increasing taxation and reducing expenditure. The strategy helped to increase unemployment. Nevertheless, Snowden's policies went largely unchallenged within the Labour party. He was masterful and convincing in Cabinet and had the support of the Treasury, which could operate to deny his Cabinet critics access to financial information. Above all, MacDonald had faith in him. Given this fact, it is hardly surprising that the expansionist ideas of Oswald Mosley, the ILP and other groups made little or no headway within the second Labour government.

With unemployment rising from about one-and-a-quarter million in 1929 to about three million by 1931 the crucial problem for the Labour government was the rising cost of unemployment benefit, which made it impossible for Snowden to come anywhere near balancing the budget in 1931. The Gregory Commission, a Royal Commission set up in December 1930, to examine the whole issue of unemployment and the financing of the Unemployment Insurance Fund, reported in June 1931 and called for reductions of up to 30 per cent in benefits and that 'anomalies' should be eliminated. The Labour government retreated from accepting such a sweeping cut but it was clear that the reduction of unemployment benefit was now central to British politics.

This issue was amplified by the findings of the May Committee. This had been formed in March 1931 as a compromise measure to head off the threatened parliamentary censure of Snowden. It was an all-party committee, headed by Sir George May, which was to advise Snowden on how to reduce national expenditure in such a way as to ensure a balanced budget. It reported at the end of July, estimated that the budget deficit for 1931–32 would be £120 millions and advocated that £67 millions of savings should come from increases in unemployment insurance contributions, changes in benefits and a reduction of the standard benefit by 20 per cent. Whatever rhetoric was used, it was clear that the reduction of unemployment benefit would be the crucial issue in August 1931.

It was Snowden, not MacDonald, who was to be the major influence upon the actions of the second Labour government in the heady atmosphere of financial crisis. Throughout August 1931, he laid down the parameters for discussion and decision making, although the focus of concern began to widen. Declining international confidence in the pound, despite the continuance of high interest rates in London, had led to a flow of money and gold from Britain. The City banking institutions were under strain and there was the very real prospect that Britain could be forced off the gold standard and into protectionism.

Snowden's priority now became the securing of an £80 million loan from New York and Paris to help the City bankers. In order to secure this loan he endorsed the Treasury view that the budget had to be balanced. But at the moment of most severe crisis he also had to deal with the Cabinet, the General Council of the TUC, the Labour party and the opposition parties – all of whom had varying objectives and concerns.

The first meeting of the Cabinet Economy Committee (MacDonald, Snowden, Henderson, Thomas and Graham) had been arranged for the 25 August. But the drain on gold continued and Snowden urged an early meeting. MacDonald arrived back in London on 11 August, declaring of the government, that 'We are of one mind . . . we intend to balance the budget'.[40] This was not so. Though the Cabinet Economy Committee agreed to cuts of £78 million, as part of a package which included increases in taxation, the full Cabinet would only agree to £56 million cuts on 19 August and would not consider a reduction in the rate of unemployment benefit. On the 10 August, MacDonald and Snowden met the Opposition leaders, who felt that the cuts were too little, and the TUC leaders, who felt that they were too great.[41] The full Cabinet considered the matter again but refused to change its decision and MacDonald agreed to offer the package to the Opposition leaders again. But events overtook the government. On 21 August MacDonald was informed that the 'flight on the pound' was worsened and that New York and Paris were not willing to offer a loan unless 'tough' action was taken. A feverish round of discussions in Cabinet and with New York eventually convinced MacDonald that the only course of action was to get the Cabinet to accept the need for a cut of 10 per cent on unemployment benefit. When the Cabinet was forced to express a view on this issue on 24 August eleven ministers, including MacDonald, favoured the cut with nine against.[42] Since the opponents included Arthur Henderson, and some other leading ministers, MacDonald felt that he had no option but to offer the King the resignation of his government. This resignation having been tendered on the morning of 24 August the King, having consulted with the Opposition leaders, asked MacDonald to form a National government. This was duly announced at noon, 24 August 1931.

What is clear is that MacDonald was very much a prisoner of economic events, though it would be an exaggeration to suggest that he was a prisoner of economic orthodoxy for the Cabinet meeting of Thursday 20 August clearly discussed protectionist measures in order

[40]Adelman, *Labour Party*, p. 68.
[41]PRO, 30/69, item 1753, MacDonald Diaries 1910–1937, 20 August 1931; PRO, Cab. 23, report of meeting 20 August 1931.
[42]MacDonald Diaries, 21–24 August 1931; Cab. 23, report of meetings of 23, 24 August 1931.

to avoid serious cuts in expenditure.[43] MacDonald noted of this meeting that fifteen members of his Cabinet favoured a revenue tariff, that eleven wanted a 10 per cent reduction in benefits and that seven favoured a 5 per cent reduction.[44] It is quite clear that decisions about balancing the budget lay between introducing a revenue tariff, which Snowden would reject, and reducing unemployment benefit. There was no choice for MacDonald, since the situation would have been aggravated by the resignation of Snowden.

In addition, research, drawn from recently available Cabinet and Treasury records, has suggested that Snowden undoubtedly misled his Cabinet colleagues, and MacDonald, over the wishes of the New York bankers, and the necessity of attempting to pay £60 million to the Sinking Fund – a fund designed to pay off the National Debt which the National government decided to partly suspend when it came to office.[45] Whatever his economic attitudes, MacDonald was quite clearly not primarily responsible for the economic context of events which led to the collapse of the second Labour government. Nevertheless, it was his decision alone to form a National government under his leadership.

Why did he do it? There was clearly no 'Grand Scheme' as L. MacNeill Weir would have us believe. Marquand's impression that MacDonald was convinced that there was no alternative to continuing with the gold standard, especially given MacDonald's political upbringing and Snowden's rigidity, and that he was the only man capable of saving the country seems more plausible. After all, there is no hard evidence that MacDonald schemed, ample proof that he was under pressure and willing to resign, and that the offer of forming the National government came from the King and the Opposition. Perhaps, the problem was that MacDonald remained too wedded to the values of Victorian Liberalism. Most certainly, when he left the second Labour government in 1931 he led most of the Liberal Radical section out of the Labour party. Undoubtedly, MacDonald felt that his actions were justified on the highest of principles – the need to put state before party. Clearly there is no evidence of a 'Grand Scheme', but does that mean there was no betrayal?

Betrayal?

Although there was initial equivocation amongst MacDonald's closest friends about the action he had taken, the majority of Labour supporters felt a deep sense of outrage at what they considered to be betrayal.

---

[43]Cab. 23, report of meeting 20 August 1931.
[44]MacDonald Diaries 1910–1937, 20 August 1931.
[45]B. C. Malament, 'Philip Snowden and the Cabinet Deliberations of August 1931,' *Bulletin of the Society for the Study of Labour History*, 41, (1980), pp. 32–3.

Marquand, quite rightly, suggests that the MacDonald correspondence revealed a degree of generosity amongst his former colleagues –
Willie Leach, a Bradford MP, wrote that 'I trust you will allow me to
continue to count myself your friend – very troubled and very
anxious'.[46] Ben Riley, Labour MP for Dewsbury, hoped that MacDonald would be 'successful in his efforts' and that 'the severance for [sic]
the Party may be of short duration.[47] But these views did not find
favour with the average Labour MP, party activist or local constituency party. Just about every Labour party organization in the
country disowned MacDonald and his new-found friends. Fred
Jowett, a Labour MP of a Bradford seat, was terse: 'The government
need not have resigned'.[48] In addition he added that the Labour
government had not attempted to offer socialist policies and that it
should have had the determination to do so.

Nonetheless, initial reactions were tinged with regret rather than
outright hostility. Attitudes did not harden until MacDonald's
National government decided to come off the gold standard, in September 1931, and to suspend the full payment of the Sinking Fund. If
either action had been taken in mid-August there would have been no
reason for the resignation of the Labour government. MacDonald's
decision to call a general election in October 1931, which led to the
return of 556 National government candidates – most of them Conservatives – compounded the treachery for most Labour supporters.
Trade unionists were soon to be found referring to MacDonald as a
political blackleg – a man who was not prepared to remain loyal to his
party.

There were many who felt personally betrayed by MacDonald, and
perhaps he did deserve the obloquy which was heaped upon him.
Nevertheless, it should be remembered that the actions he took in 1931
were partly conditioned by the actions of the rest of the Labour
Cabinet. Barbara Betts, the later Barbara Castle, recognized this
when she reported on the Labour party annual conference in October
1931: 'It was almost as if it feared to probe too deeply lest it should be
disillusioned as to the integrity of Uncle Arthur [Henderson]'.[49]
Skidelsky made much the same point in criticizing the entire leadership
of the Labour party,[50] and the point has been made more recently by
Michael Foot: 'there was always something squalid about the affair
when Henderson and Co. and other leaders joined the chorus as eagerly

[46]Marquand, MacDonald, p. 649.
[47]Marquand, *MacDonald*, p. 649.
[48]*Bradford Pioneer*, 28 August 1931.
[49]*Bradford Pioneer*, 9 October 1931.
[50]R. Skidelsky, *Politicians and the Slump: The Labour Government of 1929–1931*
(London, Macmillan, 1967).

as most of them did. The scapegoat theory was an indecency as well as a falsehood . . . .'.[51]

Conclusion

The events of 1931 tend to hide the achievements of MacDonald. One must remember that for more than 30 years he was the key figure in the Labour party. As secretary, MP and parliamentary leader he was clearly the architect of his new progressive organization and his highly eclectic and imprecise brand of socialism left the Labour party sufficiently vague enough to allow many ex-Liberals as well as socialists to join it. He left his mark on the Labour party, which has normally adopted his type of leadership.[52] Had it not been for the events of 1931 it is fair to suggest that he would have been considered one of Labour's great heroes.

If one examines the accusations levelled against MacDonald as a result of the collapse of the second Labour government it is clear that most are at best half-truths. He was a socialist, very much of the ilk of many ethical socialists and Fabians of the 1890s, and had certainly made his departure from the Liberal party, though he remained influenced by Victorian Liberalism – as did many of Labour's leaders. He was an opportunist – though, perhaps, of the 'principled' type. He did not scheme to ditch the Labour government but he did eventually betray his own principles and many of those who had placed faith in him. In the end he probably was, as Marquand suggests, a victim of his nineteenth-century principles, and stuck to them when they were no longer relevant. Nevertheless, he must not be allowed to take the blame alone. In many ways Philip Snowden was just as guilty as MacDonald for the events of 1931. The other Labour leaders also played their part.

There is no evidence that MacDonald planned to replace the Labour government with a National government. Nevertheless, the myth lingers on, perpetuated by the memory of what came after – Labour's electoral disaster in the general election of October 1931. In the final analysis, MacDonald had not remained true to the party and the movement which had supported him. It is for this reason that the Labour party have assigned him to a 'traitor's grave'. Nevertheless, one must also remember Mowat's reflection that 'If the Labour Party condemns MacDonald it condemns itself for having chosen and retained him as leader.'[53]

---

[51]Foot, 'MacDonald', p. 70.
[52]Mowat, 'MacDonald', p. 151.
[53]Mowat, 'MacDonald', p. 151.

6 THE REVIVAL AND TRIUMPH OF LABOUR, 1931 – 45

MacDonald's defection and the disastrous October 1931 General Election were a trauma for the Labour party. The confidence gained in the 1920s was suddenly swept away as Labour, apparently, revealed its inability to administer the economy or to bend to the needs of the nation. Yet within 14 years, in July 1945, the Labour party swept back to power with 393 MPs, giving it a substantial majority in Parliament for the first time in its history. Why did this occur? What factors permitted the Labour party to re-emerge as the vital force in British politics?

Interpretations

Unlike previous chapters, there are no obvious centripetal forces gathering historians into clear schools of thought. Nevertheless, there are many minor debates which have divided historians. Three questions have been predominant in their minds. First, why did the Labour party lose so badly in 1931 and what impact did this have upon the party? Secondly, how important was the rise of fascism and the Spanish Civil War in preparing the Labour party for an active role in the 'People's War'? Thirdly, how relevant was the experience of war to the Labour victory of 1945?

The catastrophic election defeat of 1931, when the Labour party was reduced from 289 MPs to a mere 52, has often been seen as the inseparable consequence of MacDonald's betrayal. Up to two million voters, many of them members of the working class, are seen as having ebbed away from Labour and responded to the nationalistic demands of MacDonald and Snowden. Ralph Miliband reflects upon the difficulties faced by the Labour party in meeting the challenges of ex-Labour Ministers who had ranged alongside the Tories:

> Labour's voice had been muffled throughout the crisis and it remained hesitant and defensive during the campaign. The Labour Ministers had been too deeply implicated in the policies of MacDonald and Snowden for their efforts at dissociation from them to carry conviction.[1]

[1] R. Miliband, *Parliamentary Socialism* (London, Merlin, 1972 edition), p. 191.

The contemporary analysis of the Labour party supports such a view. The NEC blamed the hostile election broadcasts of Snowden, which included his description of Labour policy as 'Bolshevism Run Mad', for the loss of support and to the fact that people regarded the Labour party as one which had 'run away' from the crisis.[2]

Nevertheless, John Stevenson and Chris Cook have argued that the link between MacDonald's departure and the election defeat of 1931 is a false connection.[3] They believe that the Labour government was frustrating many of its supporters, that political support was ebbing away and that this was partly reflected in the party's poor parliamentary by-election results. In addition, the Labour party was in a precarious position. Its 1929 General Election victory was a shallow success. Although it was the largest parliamentary party it had obtained fewer votes than the Conservatives and it appeared that the collapse of the Liberal party in 1929 might ultimately benefit the Conservatives. They thus maintain that the Labour party was bound to lose the 1931 General Election, whatever circumstances it was fought in. However, they do admit that the 1931 General Election did contribute something to the Labour party's decline: 'The simple reason why Labour had lost four out of five seats it was defending was that its opponents were united.'[4] Indeed, there were 449 straight fights against Labour candidates in 1931 compared with only 99 in 1929. In addition, they maintain that the middle class, not the working class, deserted Labour and supported the National government in the crisis. Thus, the gist of their argument is that Labour would have done badly without MacDonald's 'betrayal' – though it did contribute something to Labour's political failures.

But how did the Labour party react to its defeat? Did it, as some have suggested, move leftwards at its 1932 Party conference and prepare the ground for the socialist policies which were ultimately introduced after 1945?[5] Alternatively, did the defeat simply strengthen the hand of the trade-union movement within the party? There also seems to be some dispute about how quickly the party organization recovered from its setback. Was the confidence in the party largely destroyed at the local level or did enthusiasm for the cause lead to a quick revival in its fortunes?   .

The threat of fascism and the outbreak of the Spanish Civil War, in 1936, has been the second significant area of debate concerning the Labour party in the 1930s. The most perplexing problem facing members of the Labour party was how to reconcile their advocacy of

[2] J. Stevenson and C. Cook, *The Slump* (London, Jonathan Cape, 1977), chapter vi.
[3] *Op. cit.*, pp. 94–5.
[4] *Op. cit.*, p. 107.
[5] P. Adelman, *The Rise of the Labour Party 1880–1945* (London, Longman, 1972), p. 74; J. Hinton, *Labour and Socialism: A History of the British Labour Movement 1867–1974* (Brighton, Wheatsheaf, 1983), p. 148.

peace with the urgent need to deal with the threat of European fascism. This concern was adumbrated in the early 1930s by the rise of Oswald Mosley's British Union of Fascists. Historians have varied in their interpretations of how the Labour party approached these problems and the effectiveness of its responses.

Michael Newman argues that the Labour party adopted the view that fascism only emerged where parliamentary democracy was not well established. Since such a system seemed well founded in Britain it chose to ignore British fascism, unlike the Communist party, which was prepared to fight it on the streets at Olympia in 1934 and Cable Street in 1936. Broadening out his topic, he concludes that

> In this sense, Labour's respect for the constitution and its willingness to collaborate with an increasingly strong State against 'extremism' of the Left as well as the Right did not save Britain from fascism: it merely helped capital at the expense of the working class.[6]

This type of accusation against Labour has been extended to the whole sphere of foreign affairs, ranging over the period from the Abyssinian invasion, to the Spanish Civil War and Munich. Its leading exponent has been Ralph Miliband. Assiduously, he has gathered together evidence of the dilatory attitude of the Labour party towards meeting these various challenges. He notes Sir Charles P. Trevelyan's speech at the 1936 Labour party conference, accusing the NEC of 'being beggared of policy at this moment' in saving the Spanish Republican Government.[7] He concludes in chilling style:

> The Conservative derelictions in that period have been sufficiently documented for the verdict passed on the guilty men not to have been reversed by history. But the Labour leaders of those years have been fortunate that Conservative guilt was as great as it was. For it helped to obscure their own share of the guilt and their own contribution to the politics of appeasement through the immunity from effective challenge they provided to the actual culprits.[8]

Less frenetically, K. W. Watkins has attempted to explain why the Labour party was slow to respond to the challenge of fascism in Spain, a foreign event which bitterly divided the British people.[9] Kenneth Harris, on *Attlee*, Ben Pimlott on *Hugh Dalton* and Philip Williams on *Hugh Gaitskell* provide a more balanced and less critical approach to

[6]M. Newman, 'Democracy versus Dictatorship', *History Workshop*, 5 (Spring, 1978), p. 85.
[7]Miliband, *Parliamentary Socialism*, p. 240.
[8]*Op. cit.*, p. 271; C. Fleay and M. L. Saunders, 'The Labour Spain Committee: the Labour Party Policy and the Spanish Civil War', *Historical Journal*, xxviii (1985).
[9]K. W. Watkins, *Britain Divided* (London, Nelson, 1963).

Labour's response to foreign affairs.[10] Indeed Pimlott notes how determined Dalton was that the Labour party should face up to the threat of Hitler and Mussolini. As a result of visiting Germany, where he saw at first hand the persecution of the Jews, he pressured the Labour party to face up to the European fascist nations and to abandon the pacifist policy which it had more or less accepted in 1933. The culmination of his triumph in getting the Labour party to accept armed deterrence occurred at the party's Bournemouth conference of October 1937, following a year when he had acted as chairman of the party. He spelt out the Party's new position to the delegates, who gave their overwhelming support:

> In this most grim situation, not of the Labour party's making, our country must be powerfully armed. Otherwise we run risks immediate and immeasurable. Otherwise, a British Labour government, coming into power tomorrow, would be in danger of humiliation, intimidation and acts of foreign intervention in our national affairs, which is not tolerable for Englishmen to contemplate.[11]

In other words, the Labour party faced up to the problem of the European fascist states with commendable speed and considerable fortitude.

Thus historians are divided between those who feel that the Labour party's response to fascism was inept and those who maintain that, given the cumbersome nature of the party machine, it responded as quickly, and effectively, as it could to the issues of fascism, appeasement and war. But such a debate may have to be tempered by the view that the Labour party has no option but to take a spectator role, developing policies for the future at a time when it was incapable of affecting the present.

The third area of concern is the impact of the Second World War upon the Labour party. Opinions vary about the extent to which the war contributed to Labour's political success in the 1945 General Election. One view sees the war as creating the conditions for the Labour victory: 'For it was the experience of war which caused the emergence in Britain of a new popular radicalism, more widespread than at any time in the previous hundred years. It was of that popular radicalism that the Labour party was, in 1945, the electoral beneficiary.'[12] Another argues that whilst the war was important in shaping the Labour victory that success could have been achieved at a general election in 1940 had the war not intervened.[13] This argument tends to

[10]K. Harris, *Attlee* (London, Weidenfeld & Nicolson, 1982); P. M. Williams, *Hugh Gaitskell* (Oxford, OUP, 1982).
[11]B. Pimlott, *Hugh Dalton* (London, Jonathan Cape, 1985), pp. 247–8.
[12]Miliband, *Parliamentary Socialism*, p. 272.
[13]Adelman, *Labour Party*, p. 82.

suggest that the mid and late 1930s saw the highpoint of the working-class attachment to Labour and such an association was bound to push the party forward beyond the interim level of success it had achieved in 1929 – to be so cruelly set back by the events of 1931.

In so far as there are common arguments concerning the three issues under discussion they tend to focus on the state of party organization and leadership in the 1930s. On the one hand, there is a widespread belief that Labour recovered well at all levels in the 1930s, so much so that the war simply galvanized its claim to office in 1945. On the other hand, the view prevails that Labour fared badly in the 1930s, was effete and ineffectual and that it was the radicalism produced by the war which saved it from political oblivion at the hands of Churchill in 1945.

The 1931 General Election and Labour Organization in the 1930s

The 1931 General Election set the PLP back a generation to the end of the First World War when it had 61 MPs. In fact with 52 MPs, it had only 10 more MPs than it had had following the December 1910 General Election. The obvious question is to what extent was this political disaster due largely to the unusual circumstances of the 1931 General Election? The subsidiary is, how quickly did the party recover?

Table 6.1 The Labour vote: 1922–31 general elections

General Election	National %	West Yorkshire %
1922	29.7	30.4
1923	30.7	37.5
1924	33.3	· 41.6
1929	37.1	46.0
1931	30.8	32.5

Stevenson and Cook obviously feel that the Labour party would have been defeated in 1931, even without MacDonald's departure and opposition. They thus throw doubt upon the Labour party's view that defeat was entirely due to the crisis of 1931. But what evidence is there that Labour was ailing before the autumn of 1931?

Certainly, evidence for such a view exists for the Labour stronghold of West Yorkshire, the textile district of the West Riding of Yorkshire covering the districts of Bradford, Leeds, Halifax, Huddersfield and Wakefield. One very telling fact about West Yorkshire is that whilst it remained a Labour heartland the Labour party experienced a much more substantial drop in its vote than occurred nationally. Does this indicate greater dissillusion with Labour in West Yorkshire than in the country as a whole?

There was obviously much evidence of rising frustrations within Labour ranks both nationally and within West Yorkshire before 1931. The ILP was critical of the Labour government's policy towards unemployment benefit and there was considerable frustration at the government's economic policy. Yet the criticism was directed at MacDonald and Snowden and such critics would be expected to remain loyal to the Labour party after the defection of its leaders. Indeed, the collapse of the second Labour government appears to have been a healing factor within Labour ranks. This was reflected in Willie Leach's comment that 'It was MacDonald who had left the Labour movement, not the Labour movement which had left MacDonald.'[14]

West Yorkshire Labour parties passed numerous resolutions against MacDonald's action and were determined in their opposition to him. But what was the attitude of the working-class and middle-class voters who had supported Labour in 1929? Unfortunately there is little direct evidence by which to measure the fluctuations in these sources of support.

The evidence of trends emerging from parliamentary by-elections is rather thin. There were in fact only two by-elections in West Yorkshire between the 1929 and 1931 general elections. One was held in Leeds South East in August 1929, following the appointment of H. H. Slesser as Lord Justice of Appeal. That by-election was only forced by the fact that the Communists put forward a candidate – and Labour won an overwhelming majority in a low poll. The other, at Shipley in 1930, is far more interesting for it was one of only three parliamentary seats which Labour lost during the period of the second Labour government.

William Mackinder had been returned with a majority of almost 5,000 in 1929. At the by-election following his death the Labour party lost the seat by almost 2,700 votes. This was a considerable shock and the *Bradford Pioneer* reflected that

> Shipley is a first-class electoral disaster, and following as it does the depressing municipal results, something like a portent. What does a 27 per cent fall in the Labour poll in a Northern industrial constituency mean?[15]

It went on to argue that the wool lock-out of 1930 might well have led to a loss of support for Labour but that this alone could not have accounted for a loss of 5,500 votes. Rather, it was suggested that the lack of militancy of the Labour government, rather than the militant activities of the wool textile workers, offers an explanation.

[14] *Bradford Pioneer*, 11 September 1931.
[15] *Op. cit.*, 17 October 1930.

The Government may be an honest and gradual Government, but it is certainly not a militant one. It avoids sharp issues, it does not put the question, it is above all not at war with Authority.

The last reference is presumably directed at the Establishment.

Yet a closer inspection of the events undermines the speculative comments of the *Bradford Pioneer*. In 1930 the Labour party had performed well in maintaining its much improved municipal position in West Yorkshire: its 90 representatives of 1924 had been increased to 157 in 1929 and was maintained at 156 in 1930.[16] There was little suggestion from municipal results that Labour was losing support.

Table 6.2 Shipley: 1929 General Election result and 1930 by-election result

General Election, May 1929	Votes	% of Poll
W. Mackinder (Lab)	18,654	42.3
Sir R. Clough (Con)	13,693	31.1
J. W. Hirst (Lib)	11,712	26.6
Turnout 85% of 51,838 voters		
By-Election, 6 November 1930		
J. H. Lockwood (Con)	15,238	36.0
W. A. Robinson (Lab)	13,573	32.1
A. Davy (Lib)	12,785	30.2
W. Gallacher (Comm)	701	1.7
Turnout 80.0% of 52,856 voters		

The reference to the wool textile lock-out is also unclear. The fact is that textile workers had been faced with numerous attempts to reduce their wage during the 1920s. The dispute in 1930 had been caused by further attempts by the employers to reduce wages. The unions had agreed to a reduction of 5 per cent but this was rejected and, in June 1930, after a 10 week lock-out, the workers were forced to accept the employers' terms. It was the textile employers who were the aggressors, but at the end of May 1930, the *Bradford Pioneer* accurately reflected public opinion, noting that 'Half the general public think that the textile workers are heroic martyrs and the other half think they are terrible Bolshies'.[17] Labour votes were undoubtedly lost.

Also it may well be that some of Labour's middle-class and working-class supporters – faced with the economic failings of the Labour government – began to doubt the party they had voted for in 1929. Certainly there was a switch of votes from Labour to National candidates, as is indicated in Table 6.1. In fact 430,227 out of 935,276 voters

[16]J. Reynolds and K. Laybourn, *Labour Heartland* (Bradford, Bradford University Press, 1987), p. 100.

[17]*Bradford Pioneer*, 23 May 1930.

in West Yorkshire had voted for Labour in the 1929 General Election. Labour's vote had fallen by 110,000 and allowing for the fact that there were another 50,000 voters registered – 46 per cent of whom would probably have noted Labour in 1929 – the real loss of support was probably nearer 133,000. Almost 30 per cent of the Labour voters appear to have deserted the party in West Yorkshire between 1929 and 1931. There is no clear guide to who deserted. Undoubtedly, as Stevenson and Cook suggest, the middle-class support for Labour slipped away quickly, collapsing completely in the 1931 General Election. Yet, contrary to their view of national developments, working-class support does not appear to have held up well in West Yorkshire.

The fact is that the MacDonald government could not have secured some of their parliamentary success in West Yorkshire without such working-class support. Stevenson and Cook have noted that MacDonald's victory at Seaham was indicative of the extensive working-class support there was for 'MacDonald and his associates'.[18] There were certainly constituencies in West Yorkshire which could not have been won by National candidates without similar support. This was most obvious in Bradford South, where Labour lost a majority of 12,500 in the 1931 General Election. In eight other constituencies a Labour majority of between 7,000 and 10,000 was overturned.

Quite clearly there was some loss of political momentum within the Labour ranks before 1931, but it is difficult to gauge how much this contributed to the Labour defeat in October 1931. What is evident, however, is that a significant proportion of the working classes had drifted away from Labour. But how did this affect the party?

J. H. Hudson, a one-time friend of Snowden and ex-MP for Huddersfield, reflected, in December 1931, that 'It is no use denying the facts. The treachery of Snowden and MacDonald had a profound effect upon many of our people'.[19] The *Leeds Citizen* was more blunt about Snowden:

> He did smash the Labour government because some of its members dared to contemplate a revenue tariff as better than an attack upon the unemployed. He remains in this government, which carried out both.[20]

There was clear resentment that the old Labour leaders had deserted the party and that some Labour supporters, both working-class and middle-class, had responded to their appeal to support the National government in this moment of crisis. But the Labour party was resilient.

The fact is that the Labour party recovered quickly from its political

[18]Stevenson and Cook, *The Slump*, p. 110.
[19]*Huddersfield Citizen*, December 1931.
[20]*Leeds Citizen*, 12 February 1932.

defeat. At the national level, it recovered from 52 to 154 seats between the 1931 and 1935 General Elections, and the Labour vote in 1935, at 8,325,491, was only about 64,000 less than it had been in 1929. Indeed, the national percentage of the poll rose, from 37.1 per cent in 1935. The fact that the number of Labour representatives did not recover to the 1929 level is entirely due to the fact that Labour candidates normally faced only one other candidate, a National candidate, in their contests.

There had been some municipal losses for Labour in the 1931 municipal elections but these had been recovered by 1933.[21] In areas like West Yorkshire, this was clearly the case. The 156 municipal representatives of 1930 were reduced to 137 in 1931 but had recovered to 162 by 1933. By 1936 the number had reached a pre-war peak of 194.[22]

There were many reasons for the revival of Labour fortunes. For one thing, the election defeats of 1931 had exaggerated the real losses to the Labour party. For another, the departure of the ILP had, ironically, led to improvements in party organization in some areas.

Faced with a Labour party which was intent upon demanding that all its MPs should vote according to the wishes of the PLP, the ILP decided to reject the insistence on observing Standing Orders. Gradually, but perceptibly, the ILP drifted out of the Labour party, amidst rancour and debate. One newspaper suggested that if 'the ILP is dissatisfied with the Labour Party it will not improve it by committing suicide in a passion of indignation'.[23] Unfortunately, this is precisely what it did at Jowett Hall, Bradford at the end of July 1932 when it voted, by 112 to 86, in favour of disaffiliation. Fenner Brockway, who strongly supported disaffiliation, has since referred to it as 'a stupid and disastrous error, and appointed chairman at Easter, I was largely responsible'.[24] He added that

> It was stupid because we departed just when the party was turning Left in reaction to the MacDonald failure and betrayal. It was disastrous because, outside the Labour Movement, the ILP dwindled to relative insignificance and because the Labour Party lost the inspiration of the socialism, evangelism and dynamism which the ILP at its best contributed. My support of disaffiliation was the greatest political mistake of my life.

Nevertheless, whatever the Labour party lost in inspiration it gained back in organizational improvements in the old ILP stronghold. For instance, the departure of the ILP left the Bradford Labour party free

[21]Stevenson and Cook, *The Slump*, pp. 116–17.
[22]Reynolds and Laybourn, *Labour Heartland*, p. 110.
[23]*Leeds Citizen*, 29 January and 1 April 1932.
[24]F. Brockway, *Towards Tomorrow* (London, Hart-Davis, MacGibbon, 1977), p. 107.

to establish a more effective ward system. The ILP had always prevented the creation of a separate Labour party ward system ever since the introduction of the 1918 Constitution: 'Now all is changed. . . . There are no territorial rights to settle.'[25] Soon after the disaffiliation of the ILP, new ward branches were formed throughout the city.[26]

Structure and intention were central to the recovery of Labour's political position. Despite its parlous financial state, the national Labour party had set about the urgent task of rebuilding its confidence and organization. In early 1932 it began its new 'A Million New Members and Power' campaign. Within a year its individual membership had risen by about 100,000. In January 1933 it set up a central By-Election Insurance Fund to help needy constituencies to put forward candidates. But perhaps more important than improvements in organization was the decision that it would develop its 'socialist' policies.

At first these policies lacked precision – though the arrangement of a number of area conferences helped to provide the broad outlines of a programme. The Policy Sub-Committee of the party, influenced by Hugh Dalton and Herbert Morrison, attended to the issues of unemployment, banking, housing and transport. These policies were underpinned by the oft-stated general commitment to the introduction of a planned national economy and the desire for the 'socialization of industry'. The whole package of policies was presented in a series of leaflets and pamphlets, such as *For Socialism and Peace* and *Labour's Immediate Programme* (1937). Although Brockway detects that the Labour party was moving 'Leftwards' at this stage, it is interesting to note that the party's commitment to public control of industry was softened by the slow and gradual approach to its introduction.

This commitment and activity was quickly transmitted to the local level. The sheer volume of organizational and propaganda work was enormous. There were vast outpourings of activity in even the weakest of constituency parties. The Bradford Labour party held a 'Victory for Socialism' conference in 1934, Labour League of Youth organizations began to expand, and by-election victories – such as Arthur Greenwood's at Wakefield in April 1932, provided the impetus for further propaganda work.[27]

Very quickly, the Labour party became identified with the social issues of the day and, as James Cronin has suggested,[28] reached its zenith as the party of the working class in Britain. It was involved in attempts to fight the Household Means Test, introduced by the National government. Its representatives occupied positions on the

[25] *Bradford Pioneer*, 2 September 1932.
[26] *Op. cit.*, 30 September 1932.
[27] *Leeds Citizen*, 29 April 1932.
[28] J. E. Cronin, *Labour and Society in Britain, 1918–1979* (London, Batsford, 1984).

Public Assistance committees, in the hope of nudging relief provisions up, and its councillors were responsible for many public schemes – most notably the tremendous slum-clearance and house-building schemes which occurred in Leeds during the mid 1930s.[29] This association with the working class was also strengthened by the closer link of the Labour party with the trade-union movement.

Trade unions controlled the Labour party through their domination of the NEC after 1918. Nevertheless, they were not overbearing in their impositions and the trade-union movement tended to nudge Labour in its direction through the National Joint Council, a body which brought the General Council of the TUC and the NEC of the Labour party together for discussions. It was only after the failure of the General Strike that the National Joint Council, which was later renamed the National Council of Labour, began to assume more importance as Ernest Bevin and the TUC became more enamoured of political action. More trade-union sponsored Labour candidates were put forward at general elections and, after MacDonald and most of Labour's Liberal Radicals departed in 1931, the trade union movement effectively became the dominant force in Labour politics. This strengthened the link of the party with the working class, tended – as we shall see later – to isolate middle-class left-wing intellectuals and produced a counter-response in the form of the Constituency Labour party movement.

The fact is that by the mid 1930s, the Labour party was truly, as it had never been before, the party of the working class. Why then was its recovery in the 1935 General Election rather less than might have been supposed?

Most Labour politicians did not expect the return of a Labour government though many felt that the party would win between 200 and 250 seats. In fact its parliamentary representation rose from 52 in 1931 to 154. What explains this relative failure? Stevenson and Cook have certainly offered a battery of possible and plausible explanations. They have suggested that Labour could not attract the middle ground and that most of the former Liberal voters went to the Tories.[30] C. P. Trevelyan was clear on the point: 'the Liberals as an organization are gone. Roughly one-third voted Labour, two-thirds Tory. If it had been the other way round, we should have had 50 to 100 more seats'.[31] Labour also fought the election on Socialism which, according to Trevelyan, was a mistake since 'The middle class are not ready for it or the black-coated workers. Therefore in Sunderland, Darlington, Leeds, Newcastle, the middle class have won. In the mining areas and

[29] Leeds Citizen, 10 April, 11, 17 November, 2 December 1932; 3 March 1933, 26 October 1934; 13 March, 8 May, 18 September 1936; Bradford Pioneer, 31 August 1934, 7 June 1935; City of Leeds Labour party, Minutes, 19 July 1933.
[30] Stevenson and Cook, The Slump, p. 257.
[31] Op. cit., p. 257.

proletarian London they did not'.[32]

Yet there were other reasons as well. If the Labour party had failed to capture the middle ground that may have been because it was so closely identified with the trade unions and the working classes. But there is also the possibility that, faced with a National government, the party appeared to have little prospect of forming a government – even more so when it had only just acquired a new leader in Clem Attlee, for George Lansbury had not resigned until 8 October 1935.

The 1935 General Election was a sad disappointment for the Labour party. Nevertheless, it augured well for the future. Labour was demonstrably the only alternative to the Conservatives, who continued to dominate the National government. For those expecting significant social reform, Labour was the only possible party to support. It was also regaining much of the ground it had lost in the industrial areas in 1931. In West Yorkshire the party increased its parliamentary representation from one to 10 and its percentage of the vote from 32.5 per cent to 43 per cent. One cannot be certain how well the party would have done if there had been a general election in 1940, but there is at least some basis for the views of Henry Pelling and others that it might well have won the election – especially given the performance of the National government in foreign affairs.

Fascism at Home and Abroad

There seems little reason for the Labour party to have dealt with British fascism in any other way than it did – that is, to ignore it as far as it could. Recent work on Mosley and British fascism has concurred about the basic unimportance of Mosley and the British Union of Fascists.[33] After the Olympia meeting of 1934, which saw the clash between the communists and the fascists, there was little interest in the movement. Beaverbrook and Rothermere, the press barons, withdrew their support and those who had joined the movement to be on the bandwagon had thought better of their actions. As S. Rawnsley suggests, it was the small hard-core who sustained their support.[34]

There were in fact few centres of fascist support outside London, Manchester, Birmingham and Leeds. The Labour party's 1934 circular on fascism revealed this thinness of support. Even in Leeds, occasionally suggested as one of the most powerful and well-organized of fascist centres, it found only 100 to 200 fascists. Indeed when Mosley addressed a meeting of 1,500 people at Leeds Town Hall in May 1934 it

---

[32]*Op. cit.*, p. 257.

[33]G. C. Webber, *The Ideology of the British Right* (London, Croom Helm, 1987); R. Thurlow, *Fascism in Britain: a history, 1918–1985* (London, Hackwell, 1987).

[34]S. Rawnsley, 'The Membership of the British Union of Fascists', in K. Lunn and R. Thurlow, eds., *British Fascism* (London, Croom Helm, 1979), pp. 150–65.

was estimated that about 400 fascists were present, 'most of whom had come to Leeds by bus'.[35]

The Labour party was quite right to play down the fascist challenge. What they could not do is ignore the threat of European fascism.

Throughout the inter-war years Labour politicians had been concerned about the preservation of peace. They posed numerous questions. Could European peace be guaranteed by disarmament? How would Germany be prevented from entering another major international conflict? Could French fears of, and hostility towards, Germany be removed? To these and similar questions they offered three policies for peace in Europe: disarmament, collective security operating through the League of Nations and the restoration in Germany of her territories stripped away by the Treaty of Versailles. It was widely believed that these policies would provide the basis of peaceful coexistence between nations. Yet mutual distrust between France and Germany persisted, Hitler rose to power in Germany, the Spanish Civil War presented the stark challenge of fascism, and the Italian intervention in Abyssinia revealed the contempt which the Italians had for the League of Nations. Some Labour politicians continued to cling to their previous peace strategies but by the late 1930s the majority had come to accept that war was inevitable – a view confirmed by the events in Czechoslovakia, Austria and Poland which preceded the outbreak of the European war. This change of attitude created problems for the large and cumbersome structure of the Labour party, where the commitment to peace was a deep-rooted and sensitive issue. In a slow, confused, process of adjustment the Labour party attuned itself to the fight against fascism, and eventually the need to abandon its emphasis upon political independence.

It was Ernest Bevin and the trade-union movement which forced the Labour party to change direction. In 1933, at the Hastings Conference, the party had shown its commitment to two potentially contradictory policies. It supported a resolution that it would oppose war by 'organizing working-class action, including a general strike' and yet accepted a resolution committing it to a general reduction of armaments within the security of the League of Nations' willingness to take action against aggressor states. The difficulty was that Labour could have found itself supporting military action against a fascist state at the same time as it threatened a general strike against war.

In fact the Labour party was divided on how to maintain peace. Arthur Henderson, Ernest Bevin, Dr Dalton, Clement Attlee, and their supporters, favoured disarmament based upon collective security. The young Hugh Gaitskell, who had become aware of the dangers of fascism in his visit to Austria in the summer of 1933 and who was being greatly influenced by Hugh Dalton, later summed up the attitude of

[35]Labour party archives, LP/FAS/34/20.1.

this group by arguing that a general strike against all wars was 'an invitation to the fascist aggressors'.[36] A second, rather small, group, led by George Lansbury, the party leader, advocated pacifism. A third, composed of ex-members of the ILP, favoured an international general strike to prevent conflict and the need for working-class institutions to offer a revolutionary socialist programme. A fourth, led by Sir Stafford Cripps and the Socialist League, a body founded in 1932 when a large minority group in the ILP refused to follow the ILP leadership and majority in the decision to break away from Labour, favoured a 'united front' with the Communists against the fascism.[37] Cripps explained that the fascist threat was serious and that the Communist hostility towards the Labour party had now changed. They had 'disavowed any intention, for the present, of acting in opposition to the Labour movement in the country, and certainly their action in many constituencies during the last election gives earnest of their disavowal'.[38]

These factions come into conflict at the 1935 Labour party conference. This took place at Brighton in the climate of Italian aggression against Abyssinia and Ernest Bevin, with the overwhelming support of the trade-union movement, swept away the protests of Lansbury and Cripps's Socialist League to win conference support for collective security through the League of Nations sanctions, including, if necessary, military sanctions against Italian aggression in Abyssinia. Bevin, with the support of the major trade unions, put paid to any pacifist policies which George Lansbury still harboured for the party. Bevin dealt brutally with Lansbury and his pacifist reservations, thus forcing Lansbury to quit as leader of the Labour party. Rather dramatically, Dr Dalton recorded that Bevin 'hammered [Lansbury] to death'.[39]

This conference also provoked two major, and related, controversies: the Socialist League mounted a major challenge against the conference policy and constituency parties began to protest that the block-vote of trade unions was limiting their influence within the party. The two movements were linked by Sir Stafford Cripps, who operated in both. Defeated at the 1935 Labour party conference, the Socialist League and Cripps attempted to forge an alliance with *Tribune* (formed to encourage the 'united front' against fascism), the Communists and the Constituency Labour party association through a new 'united front' campaign.

The international events of 1935 and 1936 tended to confirm the view of both extremes of the Labour party. Bevin and Dalton felt that

[36]Williams, *Gaitskell*, p. 69.
[37]B. Pimlott, *Labour and the Left in the 1930s* (Cambridge, CUP, 1977), pp. 77–99.
[38]*Socialist*, March 1936, quoted in Pimlott, *Labour and the Left in the 1930s*, p. 93.
[39]Quoted Pimlott, *Labour and the Left in the 1930s*, p. 73.

the invasion of Spain by Franco's fascist forces justified rearmament whilst Cripps and the Socialist League supported the united front campaign since the National government was considered to be untrustworthy. As a result the Edinburgh conference of 1936 passed resolutions leaving the Labour party supporting collective security but opposing rearmament. However, the Spanish Civil War did make a difference. The conference condemned the Non-Intervention policy adopted by the major powers, for it was being flouted by Italians, Germans and Russians, and recommended that the Spanish Republican government should be allowed to buy arms.[40]

After the conference, the Socialist League continued to oppose rearmament, opposed sanctions against Italy threatened as a result of the Italian invasion of Abyssinia, and advocated a policy for the Labour movement of preparing for the 'mass resistance to war', by which it meant a general strike. In January 1937 it patched together a new 'united front' campaign in association with the ILP, the Communists, the Left Book Club and *Tribune,* around a programme of defence for the Spanish Republic, opposition to rearmament by the National government, support for the struggles of the unemployed and the affiliation of the Communist party and the ILP to the Labour party. The campaign was in defiance of the Labour party ban on joint work with the Communists and the Socialist League was condemned by the party, its members being forced to choose between disbanding the organization or expulsion. The Socialist League was thus dissolved in May 1937.

The failure of the 'united front' campaign persuaded the anti-fascist movement to reconsider its strategy. The direction of the campaign moved towards a broader 'popular front' to be drawn up between the left in Britain, France and the Soviet Union. When this campaign faltered the idea of the 'popular front' was extended to include an alliance between the Labour party, the Liberals and some dissident Conservative opponents of the National government, such as Winston Churchill, who were expressing their opposition to appeasement with Hitler and Mussolini.

In this climate, Cripps decided to mount a 'popular front' campaign in 1937 and 1938, which might enable Labour to enter a coalition government with anti-fascist and anti-appeasement Conservatives and Liberals if a split could be engineered within the Conservative party. Indeed, such a split appeared possible in February 1938 when Sir Anthony Eden resigned from the National government because of Neville Chamberlain's attempt to recruit Italy as an ally against Germany.[41] At that time, as George Orwell reflected, the campaign appeared to be exerting some impact upon British politics for 'In

[40]Harris, *Attlee,* p. 128.
[41]D. Carlton, *Anthony Eden* (London, Unwin paperback ed., 1986), pp. 128–30.

England the Popular Front is only an idea, but it has already produced the nauseous spectacle of bishops, Communists, cocoa-magnates, publishers, duchesses and Labour MPs marching arm in arm to the tune of of "Rule Britannia".[42]

The 'popular front' idea was, however, rejected by the Labour party, which wished to maintain its political independence, mindful of the general election which was due in 1940. As a result Aneurin Bevan and Cripps, with several others, were expelled from the party. Their rank and file supporters were also rooted out of the party in a flurry of activity throughout 1939.[43]

The fact is that after 1936 the tide turned to the right in British Labour politics. In that year Bevin became Chairman of the General Council of the TUC and Dalton became the Chairman of the NEC of the Labour party. In 1937 Dalton and Attlee got the PLP to support the armed forces estimates and the Bournemouth Conference supported rearmament. There was now a new firmness in British Labour party policy.

Miliband is unfair, to say the least, in his criticism of the Labour party at this time. Although it was fragmented in its approach to foreign affairs, and slow to respond to events in Europe, it did strongly oppose Fascism and appeasement even before the 1937 Bournemouth Labour party conference. The right wing within the party has shown more realism about events in Europe than the left wing. Nevertheless, there remains the issue of the 'popular front' and the 'united front' against fascism – both of which were anathema to a Labour party which was hostile to a Communist party whose declared intent was to use Labour, and a Coalition with fascist forces which might create the same problems which the minority Labour government had faced between 1929 and 1931.

The Second World War

The Labour party firmly supported the British government's declaration of war on Germany on 3 September 1939, and agreed to an 'Electoral Truce', though it initially refused to join the Chamberlain government in the prosecution of the war. It did not enter the Coalition government until May 1940, when Winston Churchill had replaced Chamberlain as Prime Minister.

Labour did well out of the allocation of offices in the new government and, ultimately, did well at the end of the war. But was Labour's success in the 1945 General Election primarily a result of the

[42]Pimlott, *Labour and the Left in the 1930s*, p. 143.
[43]Huddersfield Labour party, Minutes, 21 February 1939; Halifax Labour party, Minutes, 25 May 1939; *Leeds Citizen*, 3 February 1939.

wartime experience?

There was certainly much evidence that Labour was recovering well before 1939 and that, whatever the views of Miliband, its policies were commanding more respect as it was seen to be more forceful in its attitudes to fascism than the National government. There were difficulties, but the fortunes of the party were clearly reviving. However, its recovery may not have been sufficient to have put it in power had there been a general election in 1940 – since a good proportion of ex-Liberal support still attached itself to the Conservative party. Indeed Paul Addison feels that Labour had looked all set to lose another general election: the war years represented a great revolution in the party's fortunes.[44]

Indeed, many writers have argued that the wartime experience encouraged the growth of a new popular radicalism which strongly favoured the views and policies of the Labour party. Richard Titmuss's book *Problems of Social Policy* (1951), an official history of the Second World War, suggested that the circumstances of war created an unprecedented sense of social solidarity among the British people, which made them responsive to the great increase of egalitarian policies and collectivist state intervention.[45] The bombing and evacuation had exposed social problems which had hitherto remained hidden from public view and generated a sense of commitment by central government to the strategic necessity of having a contented and healthy civilian population. In contrast, recent writers on the Second World War have been far more cautious and more ambivalent. Paul Addison argues that the war helped to establish a new political consensus and that the leftward shift in popular attitudes began as early as 1940, with the appointment of 16 Labour ministers in Churchill's wartime government, the emphasis that was placed upon establishing a fairer society, and the organization of wartime evacuations. However, the crucial factor in this change appears to have been the military catastrophe at Dunkirk, which appears to have forced the government, faced with the need to restore calm and instill unity into the war effort, to cater for the welfare provision of all. In the wake of Dunkirk, William Beveridge and many other Whitehall mandarins began to organize the war effort, and, according to Addison, 'The home front organized for war was becoming a model, and an inspiration, for the reorganization of the peace'.[46] Nevertheless, he believes that the atmosphere of optimistic solidarity was by no means as universal as Titmuss had supposed. Yet Labour benefited from those social changes for the new consensus represented a 'dilution of

[44] P. Addison, *The Road to 1945: British Politics and the Second World War* (London, Jonathan Cape, 1975), p. 15.

[45] R. M. Titmuss, *Problems of Social Policy* (London, HMSO, Longman, Green, 1951), p. 508.

[46] Addison, *The Road to 1945*, p. 118.

Conservative rather than Labour politics'.[47] Indeed, it appears that the mood of the nation was changing rapidly between 1940 and 1942 and that the Labour party benefited from its barrage of activity and propaganda.

Addison's views have been broadly supported by a wide range of historians, including Angus Calder, Henry Pelling, Arthur Marwick, Ralph Miliband and H. L. Smith.[48] Whatever their views on the nature of the impact of war, they are clear that the Labour party was the great beneficiary of the growth of wartime radicalism. Even Correlli Barnett and Max Beloff, who have recently criticized the whole episode whereby wartime radicalism imposed upon Britain a commitment to a post-war welfare state, admit to the impetus this gave to the political popularity of the Labour party.[49] Their reservation, as Barnett suggests, is that the British economy was forced to accept a social burden, the welfare state, which she could not afford: 'Britain's postwar decline began in wartime British dreams, illusions and realities. The British people had brought it on themselves even before the bunting was hung across the streets in rejoicing and hope on VE-day.'[50]

There seems to be no doubt that Labour was the party which benefited most from the wartime radicalism and the new political consensus which emerged. The only significant difference of opinion seems to be over the timing of this changed political mood. Addison suggests that there was a leftward swing in political opinion in 1940 whilst Henry Pelling tends to suggest that this was occurring from about 1942. Certainly, by 1942 there was evidence of rising political support for Labour in the Gallup polls and, in December 1942, Mass-Observation estimated that about two people out of five had changed their political outlook since the beginning of the war.[51] The new wartime radicalism may not have been a 'formed socialist ideology',[52] but it was one from which the Labour party was well equipped to benefit.

The fact is that the Labour party was well prepared to deal with the war, contrary to its experiences in 1914. From the beginning of the war it had been looking to the future. It had produced *Labour War Aims* in October 1939 and *Labour, the War and Peace* and *Labour's Home*

[47]*Op. cit.*, p. 271.
[48]A. Calder, *The People's War* (London, Jonathan Cape, 1965); H. Pelling, *Britain and the Second World War* (London, Fontana, 1970); A. Marwick, *Britain in the Century of Total War* (London, Bodley Head, 1965); Miliband, *Parliamentary Socialism*; H. L. Smith, ed., *War and Social Change: British Society and the Second World War* (Manchester, Manchester University Press, 1986).
[49]C. Barnett, *The Audit of War: The Illusion and Reality of Britain as a Great Nation* (London, Macmillan, 1986); M. Beloff, *Wars and Welfare* (London, Edward Arnold, 1982).
[50]Barnett, *Audit of War*, p. 8.
[51]Addison, *The Road to 1945*, p. 126.
[52]Miliband, *Parliamentary Socialism*, p. 274.

Policy in 1940. In these statements, the Labour party and Attlee outlined the way in which a strengthened League of Nations could be used to maintain the peace once the 'rule of law' had brought about peace. But of more immediate importance was Labour's belief that 'for the Labour Party a Socialist Britain is not some far-out Utopia, but an ideal that can be realized within our time'.[53]

These policies and expectations were given a boost by the fact that Clem Attlee was effectively Deputy Prime Minister throughout the period of the Churchill Coalition government. It fell to Attlee, and Bevin, to provide what became known as 'War Socialism'. Health and housing provision emerged, the Household Means Test was abolished, day nurseries were provided, cheap school meals were made available for all school children and the war economy was regulated. Ernest Bevin, the Minister of Labour, took powers to control the movement of Labour through the Essential Works Order (March 1941). Under this legislation, workers could be prevented from leaving jobs. Bevin was given the powers of direct Labour and trade-union recognition and collective bargaining were encouraged.

In many respects these were simply piecemeal responses to the wartime situation, a fact which was revealed in the debate over the Beveridge Report of 1942, *Social Insurance and Allied Services*.[54] Nominally it was the product of the Social Insurance Committee set up by the Ministry of Health in May 1941, but in fact it was almost entirely the work of William Beveridge. In it he gave systematic shape to ideas about social security. Social insurance was to be reorganized to provide a national minimum income and his proposals depended upon three assumptions: a national health service, family allowances, and full employment guaranteed by the government. It was a controversial and comprehensive scheme which, unlike the other legislation, threatened to reorganize the whole structure of society.

Churchill was suspicious about where such demands might lead and was already on record as having noted that 'Reconstruction was in the air' and that there was 'a dangerous optimism . . . growing about post-war conditions'.[55] The Beveridge Report confirmed him in his suspicions. Indeed his government refused to implement this policy straight away and thus provoked the only major anti-Government revolt by the PLP during the war.

Attlee had given interviews to the effect that social security was effectively socialism: 'Socialism does not admit an alternative, Social

[53]G. D. H. Cole, *A History of the Labour Party since 1914* (London, Allen & Unwin, 1948), p. 380.
[54]*Social Insurance and Allied Services*, report by Sir William Beveridge (London, HMSO, 1942); J. Harris, 'Some Aspects of Social Policy in Britain during the Second World War', in W. J. Mommsen, ed., *The Emergence of the Welfare State in Britain and Germany* (London, Croom Helm, 1981).
[55]Pelling, *Britain and the Second World War*, p. 170.

Security to us can only mean Socialism'.[56] To him and his supporters it was essential that the Beveridge Report should be quickly accepted as an essential commitment by the government. But it was quite clear that Churchill intended to delay its publication, and Attlee even felt that it might be saved until the end of the war to form part of the Tory programme. He was also hostile to the Churchill memorandum sent round government circles in which it was suggested that the economics of life might be such as to force a choice 'between social insurance and other urgent claims on limited resources'. Attlee sent a counter-memorandum to the government urging that 'decisions must be taken and implemented in the field of post-war reconstruction *before* the end of the war'.[57] Churchill relented, the government accepted most of the report but gave the impression that it was committed to nothing. A Labour resolution that the government should support the Beveridge Report and implement it was defeated by 335 votes to 119, but 97 Labour MPs had voted against the government, 30 or so abstained and only 23 voted for the government – 22 of those being government ministers.

It is clear that the Beveridge Report became a sensitive issue, especially after the midsummer Gallup polls in 1943 when Labour registered a lead of 11 per cent over the Conservatives.[58] In the end the government was forced to set up a Reconstruction Committee towards the end of 1943, a committee which inherited and developed a scheme which became the 1944 Education Act.[59] In 1944 the Reconstruction Committee put forward a scheme, which gained White Paper status, for guaranteeing 'Full Employment' through government action on Keynesian lines if large-scale unemployment occurred. Ernest Bevin moved its adoption by Parliament in June 1944 and found himself opposed by Aneurin Bevan who felt that it was simply a device for propping up capitalism and that socialism alone was the cure for unemployment.[60] Hugh Dalton was barely less critical, constantly referring to the vanity of Beveridge and the 'Beveridge muddle' in his diary.[61] Whilst accepting the bulk of the Beveridge Report, acknowledging that it was a 'fine stimulating document' he warned a group of delegates from the Bishop Auckland Labour party that

> . . . I knew Beveridge better than most people having served both under and over him; that he is not 'one of us' and has no first-hand knowledge of industrial conditions; that there are a

[56]Harris, *Attlee*, p. 220.
[57]*Op. cit.*, p. 220.
[58]*Op. cit.*, p. 223.
[59]*Op. cit.*, pp. 227–30.
[60]*Op. cit.*, p. 231.
[61]H. Dalton, *The Second World War Diary of Hugh Dalton 1940–45*, ed., B. Pimlott (London, Jonathan Cape, 1986), pp. 455, 538, 564.

number of things in his Report to which we could not subscribe, e.g. the penalizing of miners and railway workers because their jobs are inherently more risky than a carpenter's, and the proposal to take twenty years to reach the appropriate rate of old-age pension.[62]

If contemporary politicians expressed doubts about the Beveridge Report, and the 'welfare state' which it anticipated, their concerns are as nothing compared with the reactions of recent right-wing writers such as Max Beloff and Correlli Barnett.[63] Just as Mrs Thatcher's early traumas in office focused upon the war years and the restrictions of the 1940s, so have they criticized the social policies forced upon Britain by the Beveridge Report and wartime radicalism. To Barnett it was the 'Beveridge Report that provided the battlefield on which the decisive struggle to win a national commitment to New Jerusalem was waged and won'.[64] And it was Beveridge who was the main architect of the Report and the commitment to the post-war welfare state:

> As appropriate for a prophet and a brilliant Oxford intellect, Beveridge thought a lot of himself, so that righteousness went hand in hand with authoritarian arrogance and skill at manipulating the press to make him the Field Marshal Montgomery of social welfare.[65]

According to Barnett, the War Cabinet was misguided by its advisers, most notably Beveridge, into building a comprehensive welfare state system, the 'New Jerusalem', which Britain's industrial economy has been unable to support. For good or ill, it was the Labour party which seemed most suited to creating the 'New Jerusalem'.

By 1945 the Labour party was demonstrably the party most likely to introduce the social reforms which were essential if Britain was to avoid the mistakes of the inter-war years. In addition, it had revealed its ability to operate in government. Herbert Morrison said later that 'During the Coalition the Labour members had learnt a great deal from the Conservatives in how to govern'.[66] Other Labour leaders concurred. The party was thus well positioned to win a general election – though it doubted its ability to win when faced with a victorious Churchill.

Yet Labour won the general election of July 1945, called within two months of the end of the European war, by a substantial majority: 393 seats to the Conservatives 213. The Liberals won only 12 seats. Though

[62]*Op. cit.*, p. 564.
[63]Barnett, *Audit of War*; Beloff, *Wars and Welfare*.
[64]Barnett, *Audit of War*, p. 26.
[65]*Op. cit.*, p. 26.
[66]Herbert Morrison to King George VI, November 1945, quoted in Miliband, *Parliamentary Socialism*, p. 272.

Labour candidates did not win an overall majority of the votes, the 48.3 per cent of the vote it gained was more than enough, under the British electoral system, to ensure that the Labour party was capable of forming its first majority Government with an overall majority of 146.

The Labour victory would appear to have been the product of a number of factors. The long-term revival of Labour since 1931, when its failures had been exaggerated, conflated with the wartime collectivism to favour the return of a majority Labour government – an event which seemed increasingly likely from about 1942 onward when the Gallup polls began to show a substantial Labour lead. In this climate the Conservative manifesto, *Mr Churchill's Declaration of Policy to the Electors,* which simply emphasized political continuity and the full programme of post-war reconstruction agreed by the Coalition, proved no answer to the Labour programme, *Let Us Face the Future,* which stressed the need to avoid the failures of the 1930s and to introduce domestic legislation which would include nationalization of industries, full employment and improved social services. Labour's campaign proved to be more attractive and appropriate than the Conservative one which reflected the arguments of Professor Friedrich von Hayek of the London School of Economics, whose book *The Road to Serfdom,* published in 1944, argued that economic planning necessitated the apparatus of tyranny. In addition, the Labour party had demonstrated its ability to govern and was now faced with no effective challenger on the Left of British politics: the Liberals, with only 307 candidates in 1945, had no chance of forming a government.

Conclusion

The Labour party took fourteen years to shake off the election defeat of 1931 and to return a Labour government with a landslide victory. Nevertheless, the portents were there for all to see. The Labour party might have been destroyed as a parliamentary force in 1931 but its local organization remained vibrant and vital. The 1935 General Election may have proved disappointing, but it was now evident that the party had recaptured its working-class vote and that it was no longer faced with a challenge from the Liberal party for the progressive vote. It may have been slow to react to the challenge of European fascism but there were good reasons for that and when it did react it was firmly opposed to appeasement – thus avoiding a close association with the 'Guilty Men'. The wartime experience had demonstrated that the party could govern and that it was more likely than the Conservatives to introduce the social legislation which a more radical electorate was prepared to entertain. The Gallup polls also provided continuing evidence of Labour's popularity with the electorate. Despite the fears of Labour leaders in 1945, any objective assessment of the political situation must have come to the conclusion that Labour would be returned to office – although the precise scale of its victory was open to doubt.

The Second World War quite clearly provided the final push to Labour's success. Paul Addison has noted that the wartime conditions did alter the context of debate: 'Had they [the Labour Party] gone to the country in 1939 with the programme of 1945, they would have been issuing a strongly radical challenge. But in 1945, they had only to consolidate and extend the consensus achieved under the Coalition, and build upon the new foundations of popular opinion'.[67] But it should also be realized that the platform for that success was laid down in the 1930s. The electoral victory of 1945 was the culmination of years of sedulous hard work. But it also provided a serious challenge to the Labour party, which was now faced with demonstrating that it was capable of implementing its socialist programme – a programme to meet the social optimism which had help sweep it to power in 1945.

[67] Addison, *The Road to 1945*, p. 261.

7 LABOUR IN OFFICE, 1945–51

The Attlee governments have been the real locus of debate for Labour historians in recent years, producing a spate of publications. In 1979 Philip Williams's book on Hugh Gaitskell appeared, to be followed four years later by his edition of the diaries of Hugh Gaitskell.[1] Kenneth Harris's monumental work on Attlee was published in 1982[2] and two years later both Kenneth Morgan and Henry Pelling produced their own versions of the history of the Attlee years.[3] More recently Ben Pimlott has been prolific, producing his splendid biography of Hugh Dalton as well as editing the *Political Diary of Hugh Dalton*.[4] In 1987 John Campbell reassessed Nye Bevan's career, in a less romantic fashion than did Michael Foot, his previous biographer.[5] This flood of weighty publications, the result of the increasing availability of family archives and the new deposits of records in the British Library, have been of more than usual interest because of the disastrous electoral performance of the Labour party in the general elections of 1983 and 1987. They have added flavour to the recent political debate about the future of the Labour party: should it look back, as Tony Benn suggests, to the years of planning and democratic socialism of the Attlee governments, or should it look forward beyond the primitive and fragmented efforts of those years.[6]

Politicians, of all political parties, have tended to treat the Attlee years with respect, viewing them variously as evidence of the success of planned socialism, of the shift to the Left, of the working out of Liberal policies forged in the 1930s and the Second World War or even as a period of Conservative social reform – 'Butskellism'. Yet if the Attlee years have been the apotheosis of Labour's planned socialist economy for many politicians this is not a view held by many historians. They

[1]P. M. Williams, *Hugh Gaitskell* (Oxford, OUP, 1982); H. Gaitskell, *The Diary of Hugh Gaitskell*, ed., P. M. Williams (London, Jonathan Cape, 1983).
[2]K. Harris, *Attlee* (London, Weidenfeld & Nicolson, 1982).
[3]H. Pelling, *The Labour Governments 1945–1951* (London, Macmillan, 1984); K. O. Morgan, *Labour in Power 1945–1951* (Oxford, Clarendon Press, 1984).
[4]B. Pimlott, *Hugh Dalton* (London, Jonathan Cape, 1985); H. Dalton, *Political Diary of Hugh Dalton, 1918–40, 1945–1960*, ed. B. Pimlott (London, Jonathan Cape, 1987); H. Dalton, *The Second World War Diary of Hugh Dalton 1940–45* (London, Jonathan Cape, 1986).
[5]J. Campbell, *Nye Bevan and the Mirage of British Socialism* (London, Weidenfeld & Nicolson, 1987); M. Foot, *Aneurin Bevan, 1897–1945* (London, MacGibbon & Kee, 1962), *Aneurin Bevan 1945–1960* (London, Davis Poynter, 1973).
[6]*The Guardian*, 29 September 1980, quoted in Morgan, *Labour in Power*, p. 1.

have been less sympathetic, willing to challenge the mythology which has been built around the events of 1945 to 1951, though not without the type of partiality shown by practising politicians.

Interpretations

Recent historians have asked three major questions about the Labour government of 1945. First, to what extent was the early legislation of that government a product of the social blueprint laid down during the Second World War? Secondly, and more vital, were the Labour leaders committed to introducing socialism and taking Britain into new directions? Thirdly, how far could Britain have operated independently from the USA, given the extent of her economic dependence upon American money?

Marwick, Addison, Miliband and Hinton have all implied that Labour's socialist programme owed much to wartime radicalism and planning and comparatively little to a genuine demand by Labour politicians to introduce socialism. The Labour leaders were seen to be Addison's 'social patriots' carrying out the wartime measures demanded by a radicalized electorate or, in Miliband's less generous estimation, mere managers of the demand for state capitalism which had emanated from the war.[7] These views, whatever their motives, are at variance with those expressed by Pelling and Morgan.[8] Pelling, now less resolute than he once was, sees the war as having only a limited impact upon the Attlee governments. Morgan has come to a similar conclusion, noting that several of the wartime proposals fell short of what Labour might reasonably have demanded, and had been demanding since the mid 1930s. He also stresses the tenuous link between the wartime health blueprints and the measures introduced by Nye Bevan in 1949. J. Hess, in a detailed study of the social policy of the Attlee governments, tends to support Morgan's line of argument, whilst admitting that the Beveridge Report did dictate that they would introduce the type of welfare capitalism which he envisaged.[9] He maintains that any post-war administration would have had to introduce the type of measures which the Attlee governments introduced. José Harris also notes much the same point.[10]

More right-wing historians, such as Barnett, Beloff and Blake, also

[7]Morgan, *Labour in Power*, chapter 1; P. Addison, *The Road to 1945: British Politics and the Second World War* (London, Jonathan Cape, 1975).

[8]Pelling, *Labour Governments 1945–51*, pp. 97–8.

[9]J. Hess, 'The Social Policy of the Attlee Government', in W. J. Mommsen, ed., *The Emergence of the Welfare State in Britain and Germany* (London, Croom Helm, 1981).

[10]J. Harris, *William Beveridge: A Biography* (Oxford, Clarendon Press, 1977).

have few doubts that the Beveridge Report shaped the politics of the Attlee governments.[11] They accept that any post-war government would have had to introduce the welfare policies put forward by Beveridge and agreed by the wartime Coalition government. Any other course of action would have been unthinkable given that the wartime consensus favoured the creation of a welfare state, even though it was manipulated by the 'vain and egotistical as well as very clever' Beveridge who, with the help of Keynes in the Treasury, lobbied ceaselessly among the media to achieve a revolution in social policy.[12] Their work forms part of the 'New Right' philosophy which has emerged since the mid 1970s which seeks to re-establish the *laissez-faire* policies which existed before the Second World War and were destroyed by the Beveridge welfare state.[13] They have no doubt that the Attlee governments and the 'Butskellism' of the 1950s were controlled and conditioned by the Beveridge Report.

Whatever the origins of Labour's economic and social reforms, the real battle is joined over the question: how genuine were the attempts of Labour leaders to introduce socialism? Marxist historians have tended to suggest that the Labour government appeared vague and uncommitted to anything more than the nationalization of industries and services to which there was little public hostility. There was, apparently, no intention by Attlee, Morrison and Labour's other leaders, to use public ownership as an effective weapon to control the economy. According to Miliband,

> In regard to nationalization, there is no ambiguity at all. From the beginning, the nationalization proposals of the Government were designed to achieve the sole purpose of improving the efficiency of the capitalist economy, not as marking the beginning of its wholesale transformation, and this was an aim to which Tories, whatever they might say in the House of Commons were easily reconciled.[14]

Hinton makes a similar point.[15] But these views are hardly surprising, coming as they do from historians who perceive the parliamentary system to be an inefficient and ineffective method of achieving socialism. They contrast sharply with those of Morgan who has

[11]C. Barnett, *The Audit of War: The Illusion and Reality of Britain as a Great Nation* (London, Macmillan, 1986); M. Beloff, *Wars and Welfare* (London, Edward Arnold, 1984); R. Blake, *The Decline of Power 1915–1964* (London, Granada, 1985).

[12]Blake, *Decline of Power*, p. 284.

[13]J. Clarke, A Cochrane and C. Smart, *Ideologies of Welfare* (London, Hutchinson, 1987).

[14]R. Miliband, *Parliamentary Socialism* (London, Merlin, 1972), p. 288.

[15]J. Hinton, *Labour and Socialism: A History of the British Labour Movement* (Brighton, Wheatsheaf, 1983), pp. 171–2.

emphasized the achievements of the Attlee governments, even if they evaded rather than resolved the 'beguiling vision of socialism in our time'.[16] To Morgan, the Labour administration

> was without doubt the most effective of all Labour governments, perhaps amongst the most effective of any British government since the passage of the 1832 Reform Act and the first partial advance of the dynamic of democratization in our political processes. . . . It brought the British Labour movement to the zenith of its achievement as a political instrument for humanitarian reform.[17]

The point is that both Pelling and Morgan feel that the Labour government fell short of the ideal but that this was due to the difficult circumstances in which they operated rather than from a lack of will. This was not a faltering and opportunistic administration but one which had a clear vision of the socialist society it was aiming to create. However, the reality of government intervention was always likely to be less attractive than the utopian vision of socialism which drove it forward. Even though the nationalization programme lost its impetus and direction the Attlee governments had taken a vital step towards displacing the old order of government attitudes.[18]

These two rival interpretations differ on numerous points of detail. Marxist writers, on the whole, tend to see the Labour policies on national insurance, health, housing and food subsidies as leaving a good deal to be desired.[19] They also decry Labour's efforts at nationalization, emphasizing that it was the Labour Left which had to force the reluctant Labour government to nationalize iron and steel in the face of strong employer opposition, and that the Government only did so after several years of prevarication. They also rant against Labour's foreign policy which saw Ernest Bevin become a leading architect of the North Atlantic Treaty Organization, and Britain become a military appendage to the United States in its dealings with the USSR. The views of Morgan and Pelling are far more generous. It is to the overall success of the work of the Attlee governments, rather than their specific problems and failures, which they urge their readers to look. The nationalization policy had its successes as well as its failures; social welfare was greatly improved and the achievement of Indian independence a significant development in the emergence of the new Commonwealth.

For both schools of thought, the events are the same though the interpretations differ. The difficulty is that in developing their main

[16]Morgan, *Labour in Power*, p. 503.
[17]*Op. cit.*
[18]*Op. cit.*, pp. 502–3.
[19]Hinton, *Labour and Socialism*, pp. 173–4.

ideological approaches, from the Marxism of Miliband to the almost nostalgic respect paid by Morgan, their interpretations cannot easily account for obvious aberrations. Hinton, for instance, tends to play down Labour's successes, such as its nationalization of the iron and steel industry. To him, it is clear that it was only the Labour Left, which he admits was weak, that forced the government to face up to this task.[20] He does not explain how a weak Labour Left could have prevented Morrison, with the support of the vast majority of the Parliamentary Labour Party and a generally acquiescent Labour party, from abandoning the nationalization of iron and steel. Morgan's praise for the Labour government also seems at odds with some of the evidence he presents, especially when he refers to the attempt to control private industry as being half-hearted, indirect, and in many ways unsuccessful.[21] Although he constantly refers to the innovative side of Labour's policy and the overall pattern of success within the wider social and economic context, his accounts of the individual events reveal that the Attlee administration was cautious rather than ambitious. But perhaps the difficulty is that the Labour governments of 1945 to 1951 were perplexing and contradictory – providing evidence to support both their critics and their admirers from the plethora of autobiographies, biographies and diaries that have been produced by, or on, their leading figures.

As a side issue to the second debate, Miliband and Hinton criticize the almost slavish loyalty of the Attlee governments to the USA – in their attitude to the USSR, their involvement in the Korean War and other issues. This contrasts sharply with the evidence presented by Morgan and Pelling, who stress that despite the crippling financial difficulties which the governments faced, which threw them on the financial mercy of the USA, they exercised a remarkable degree of independence on such matters as the atomic bomb and Palestine. The fact is that there were other factors at work in British foreign policy, not just a desire to work with a capitalist USA against a socialist and communist Eastern Europe.

Labour's Victory and Expectations

The young Hugh Gaitskell began his diary on 6 August 1945 by writing that 'It had been an extraordinary 10 days'.[22] Indeed it had been so, for the Labour party had won a landslide victory on 25 July, with 393 MPs (from about 48 per cent of the poll) to the Conservatives' 213 MPs (from 39.6 per cent of the poll). It enjoyed a majority of 146 over the

[20]*Op. cit.*, pp. 173–4.
[21]Morgan, *Labour in Power*, chapter 1.
[22]Gaitskell, *Diary*, p. 4.

other political parties and Attlee had no hesitation in accepting the King's commission to form a government. A Cabinet was formed and expectations were high that Labour would be able to introduce the programme of social welfare and nationalization which it had envisaged over the previous decade and in its electoral programme *Let Us Face the Future*. But if the socialist dawn had arrived in political terms it is clear that some of Labour's leading figures were doubtful of the new government's ability to deliver its socialist programme.

Within days of the Labour victory Hugh Dalton, the new Chancellor of the Exchequer, had called an informal meeting with some of the young but aspiring men of the party, including Harold Wilson, Hugh Gaitskell, Richard Crossman, George Brown and John Freeman. Its purpose was to discuss the 'future policy and problems' of the Labour government. One of those present expressed the view that 'too many people had voted Labour in the hope that it meant more pay and less work'.[23] Another spoke of the major problems of food, homes and fuel which would be 'extraordinary difficult to handle at any rate in the first two years. It was, therefore, necessary that there should be first-class publicity to make it clear that these difficulties were inevitable and inherited by the Labour government'.[24] Such fears were well founded, for the new Labour government faced horrendous economic difficulties.

During the war British industry had been converted to war production at the cost of exports, facilitated by loans from the United States and the sale of British overseas assets. The result was that Britain's invisible earnings declined and that her visible exports were down to about one-third of their pre-war level. The Labour government's first priority was thus to secure financial support, which could only come from the United States, in order to buy food and raw materials whilst she was building up her export industries. The sudden end of the United States 'lend-lease' aid in August 1945 exposed the weakness of the British economy and forced the government to send J. M. Keynes to the USA in order to secure a new loan. But the final conditions of that loan were harsh, for Britain was expected to remove exchange controls and to make sterling freely convertible within a year of taking up the loan. In fact when Britain attempted to honour this agreement, in July 1947, the economy was still too weak to withstand such a change of policy, and the government was soon forced to re-introduce exchange controls. The continued fragility of the economy was further revealed by the balance of payments crisis in 1949, which occurred despite the fact that Britain's exports had increased by about 60 per cent since 1945. And matters were not helped by a variety of setbacks over which the government had little control – most notably the severe

[23]*Op. cit.*, p. 15.
[24]*Op. cit.*, p. 14.

winter of 1946–47, which led to coal shortages, the closure of factories and a temporary increase of unemployment to two millions.

Labour historians, whether critics or admirers of the Attlee governments, attest to the seriousness of the economic situation which faced Britain at this time, and even the critics admit that there 'seemed little alternative to soliciting a new loan on whatever terms the Americans may see fit to offer'.[25] This is a view which has been strongly endorsed by Alec Cairncross who feels that the weakness of the post-war British economy meant that there was no alternative to obtaining the American Loan.[26] Indeed, it appears that Keynes had already anticipated that there would be an 'overriding need to look to the United States for the finance necessary to cover Britain's post-war deficits', even before the war had ended.[27] The later reliance upon the Marshall Aid programme tightened that link with the United States. Inevitably, there were political consequences.

Attlee and Bevin have frequently been criticized for their almost slavish acceptance of the alliance with the United States and against the Soviet Union. This was certainly evident in the fact that Bevin helped forge NATO, which came into existence in April 1949. But it had also been apparent before in the way in which Bevin constantly referred to the 'special relationship' between Britain and the USA. It was also evinced in the support which Britain showed towards the neo-Fascist government of the Shah of Iran in the face of the Soviet threat to Britain's sources of oil in the Middle East. It might also be remembered that Attlee was one of the most anti-Soviet ministers in the wartime coalition. Britain's pro-American and anti-Soviet policy in foreign affairs accorded well with the sympathies of some of the leading members of the Labour Cabinet, though such policies owed much to the immense economic problems she faced in the post-war world.

The Welfare State – a Legacy of the War?

Despite the horrific and frightening economic problems it faced, the new Labour government was able to extend greatly the responsibilities of the state during its early years in office. Although associated with nationalization, its greatest claim to fame is that it created the welfare state. The Labour manifesto of 1950 proclaimed that 'Labour had honoured the pledge it made in 1945 to make social security the birthright of every citizen. Today destitution has been banished. The

---

[25]Hinton, *Labour and Socialism*, p. 169.
[26]A. Cairncross, *Years of Recovery: British Economic Recovery: British Economic Policy 1945–51* (London, Methuen, 1985).
[27]*Op. cit.*, p. 90.

best medical care is available to everybody in the land'.[28] Allowing for the natural exuberance of a party manifesto, the claims were largely true. Indeed the creation of the welfare state led to the apotheosis of the Attlee governments.

There is little doubt that Labour's social welfare programme would not have been possible without the American loan which provided the financial flexibility essential to the expansion of social provision. If this is accepted, the main issue for many historians is the originality of the programme: was it a product of the war, the result of Labour party policies or an extension of the Liberal policies of Beveridge and Keynes?

Social-welfare measures have never been the prerogative of any one party, but it is clear that the Labour party had laid claim to some of the detailed welfare planning before the Second World War. It had built up its social welfare policies during the mid 1930s and, in 1937, issued *Labour's Immediate Programme,* written by Dalton, which advanced schemes for social welfare and the creation of full employment. In essence it was the programme which was presented to the electorate in the party's *Let Us Face the Future,* published in 1945. Both documents made vague references to the need for a National Health Service, national insurance and a house-building programme. Although specific detailed programmes were thin it was widely assumed that the Labour party would by the one likely to introduce comprehensive welfare measures.

In a sense the question is artificial for the Labour party was part of the Coalition government and played its full part in the development of the blueprints of social welfare. It was Arthur Greenwood, Labour MP for Wakefield, who, as Minister concerned with reconstruction, was responsible for setting up the Inter-Departmental Committee on Social Insurance and Allied Services, out of which sprang the Beveridge Report. There were also many common features between the pre-war Labour policies and the Beveridge recommendations on social insurance, national health and full employment, though the Beveridge Report was far more detailed.

In as far as they shared a common objective, Labour's welfare proposals and the wartime blueprints complemented each other. In some areas the Beveridge Report did provide the basis of Labour's social welfare provisions but in other areas it, and other war-time reports, were far removed from what the Labour government introduced. In fact the Labour government's welfare programme was a rich mosaic of wartime collectivism, Labour policies and practical necessity.

In a wide sense, the Beveridge Report had provided the context in which the Labour party was able to press the reluctant Churchill to

---

[28]The Labour Party, *Labour Believes in Britain* (London, Labour Party, 1949).

accept some form of commitment to post-war reconstruction and social welfare. The wartime conditions also ensured that the 1944 Education Act, the Butler measure which recognized the need for secondary education for all in secondary modern, central and grammar schools, would be accepted. It was this Act which Ellen Wilkinson, as Minister of Education, began to apply in 1945.

Yet the strongest evidence of the influence of the Beveridge Report is the National Insurance Act of 1946. James Griffiths, the Minister responsible for National Insurance, was intent upon implementing the Beveridge Report and introduced a scheme along similar lines in 1946, committed to the principle of providing a 'National Minimum Standard'.[29] Sick benefit was raised to 26 shillings per week, unemployment benefit was set at the same level and the time period was extended, and family allowances, maternity and widow's benefits were also introduced. There were minor differences from the Beveridge Report, and there was an element of means testing, but to all intents and purposes the Labour government proved to be a faithful advocate of Beveridge's scheme – of which it had been part instigator.

Nevertheless, there was no straight line of argument flowing from the Beveridge Report and the work of the Reconstruction Committee to the post-war Labour government's welfare state and Hinton is wrong to suggest that 'the 1946 legislation on National Insurance and on the National Health Service gave concrete form to the reconstruction promises of the wartime coalition'.[30] This was generally true of the National Insurance Act; it was most certainly not the case for the National Health Service, which was largely the product of Aneurin Bevan's initiatives, as has become clear with the recent availability of Cabinet and government records.

The Beveridge Report deliberated on the need for a comprehensive health and rehabilitation service and emphasized the need for a universal contributory scheme of health provision which would make medical and dental treatment immediately available whether in private or public health hospitals. There was an assumption, however, that the contemporary provision of private and public health provision might be better organized.[31] The Labour party's *A National Service for Health* (1943) more or less accepted these ideas, though it envisaged the creation of a 'national, full-time, salaried and pensionable service' for general practioners.[32] Henry Willink, Churchill's Minister of Health, offered a scheme which contemplated some state control over doctors. But none of these reports or schemes ever envisaged the nationalization of the hospitals which Bevan's National Health Service

[29]Morgan, *Labour in Power*, pp. 170–3.
[30]Hinton, *Labour and Socialism*, pp. 169–70.
[31]*Social Insurance and Allied Services*, report by William Beveridge (London, HMSO, 1942), pp. 158–9.
[32]Pelling, *Labour Governments 1945–1951*, p. 103.

Bill intended, nor the extent to which Bevan's scheme contemplated GPs being drawn into the NHS on a quasi-salaried basis. The fact is that the National Health Service Bill put forward by Bevan in 1946 went much further than the wartime blueprints had suggested and it is just not good enough for Hinton to suggest that 'the scheme did not go significantly beyond what had been accepted in principle by all during the war'.[33] This is simply not the case. Bevan's scheme was innovative and, in contrast to the Beveridge scheme, non-contributory. The National Insurance Act might have provided a contributory sickness benefit scheme but it did not pay for the National Health Service, only for loss of earnings. The NHS was paid out of taxation and Bevan was rightly peeved when he wrote that

> Its revenues are provided by the Exchequer in the same way as other forms of public expenditure. I am afraid this is not yet fully understood. Many people still think they pay for the National Health Service by way of their contribution to the National Insurance Scheme. The confusion arose because the new service sounded so much like the old National Health Insurance, and it was launched on the same day as the National Insurance Scheme.[34]

The passing of the National Health Service Bill in 1946 and its introduction in 1948 were, of course, accompanied by a tremendous outburst of opposition from the British Medical Association, which held plebiscites of its members to reveal their opposition to what they saw as the loss of professional independence. But in the end Bevan appeased the bulk of the profession. The creation of the National Health Service was, by any terms, a success. Bevan could rightly stress, with a certain amount of pride, that the 'National Health Service and the Welfare state have come to be used as interchangeable terms . . .'.[35]

Housing policy also owed rather less to wartime measures than it did to pre-war Labour policies and post-war practicalities. The inter-war Labour governments had laid down the commitment to local authority mass housing programmes and slum clearance, through the Wheatley Act of 1924 and the Greenwood Act of 1930. Bevan followed directly in this line by ensuring that four out of every five houses were built by local authorities. But even this commitment to planning and local authority involvement could not ensure that there was a speedy return to the late 1930s situation when house building reached up to 350,000 per year. Though, given the financial difficulties they faced, the Labour governments did remarkably well to increase house building

[33]Hinton, *Labour and Socialism*, p. 170.
[34]A. Bevan, *In Place of Fear* (London, Heinemann, 1952), p. 80.
[35]*Op. cit.*, p. 81.

from 3,000 in 1945 to around 200,000 per annum between 1948 and 1951.[36]

It is far too simple to suggest that Labour's welfare state was simply a legacy of the war. The fact is that it drew upon some aspects of the Beveridge scheme and the work of the Reconstruction Committee, but it also drew upon some of the distinctive qualities of Labour policy and was largely entrusted to Aneurin Bevan whose policies owed distinctly less to liberal thinkers than to the ideas of some of his colleagues.[37]

Nationalization and Labour's Commitment to Socialism

The most serious doubts about the Labour government's commitment to socialism arose from its plan for the 'socialization of industry'. Although it moved quickly to nationalize both services and industry it has been argued that it had little compunction to go further than those measures which were deemed to be absolutely essential in order to redeem its political pledges and to improve the efficiency of the economy. The different attitude of Attlee towards the whole process of public control and the modest and vacillating conviction of Herbert Morrison did little to reassure the left wing of the party that public ownership would ever be used as a weapon of regulation and control for the whole economy. The slowdown of the public ownership programme from 1948 and the hesitancy displayed by the government in nationalizing iron and steel seems to have confirmed the worst fears of Bevan and the Labour Left that the government lacked a firm-rooted commitment to socialist planning and control. And, it is true to say that its whole programme for industry was haphazard and piecemeal. Cairncross goes so far as to suggest that the whole process of nationalization 'may even have weakened the government's grip on the economy' since it was directed at industries, with the exception of iron and steel, which 'created almost exclusively for the home market' and excluded those multi-national businesses, like ICI and Unilever, who were forced to adapt to the competitive situations in the international markets.[38]

The Labour government lacked a clearly thought out strategy for public ownership. Before and during the war, the party had drawn up and constantly revised its list of industries and services due for nationalization but had invariably failed to draw up detailed plans or schemes. Emmanuel Shinwell, as Minister of Fuel and Power in 1945,

[36]Pelling, *Labour Governments 1945–51*, p. 110.
[37]Campbell, *Nye Bevan*; J. Campbell, 'Demythologising Nye Bevan', *History Today*, Vol. 37 (1987), pp. 13–18.
[38]Cairncross, *Years of Recovery*, p. 495.

was given to reflect that

> I had believed, as other members had, that in the Party archives a
> blueprint was ready. Now, as Minister of Fuel and Power, I
> found that nothing practical and tangible existed. There were
> some pamphlets, some memoranda produced for private circula-
> tion, and nothing else. I had to start with a clear desk.[39]

This was an exaggeration, even though it did reveal the intellectual
void at the centre of Labour's proposals for nationalization. The path
of change had not been thought out and it was Shinwell who was partly
responsible for the lacuna in Labour thought for he had been Minister
of Mines in 1924 and between 1929 and 1931, and Chairman of the
party's Reconstruction Committee towards the end of the Second
World War.

Herbert Morrison's nationalization list in *Let Us Face the Future,*
and his belief that the newly-nationalized industries should be managed by independent corporate central bodies, were effectively the
only plans on offer. There was evidently no commitment to link the
nationalized industries and services into some overall grand strategy
for an assault on the bastions of capitalism – despite the numerous
committees and sub-committees which Morrison set up through the
office of Privy Council, which he used to co-ordinate domestic policy
and expenditure during the Attlee years.

From the start the imperfections of the plan for public ownership
were overridden by the government's desire to fulfil its pledge as
quickly as possible. The Bank of England, civil aviation, cable and
wireless were nationalized in 1946; railways, transport and electricity
in 1947; gas in 1948 and the early measures for iron and steel were
introduced in 1948 and 1949. The bulk of the activity occurred between
1945 and 1947, and it was only by trial and error that the organizational
structure, finances, compensation, pricing policy and relations with
the workers were worked out.

Much of this programme caused little political or economic disturb-
ance. Even coal nationalization went through without major dissent.
But this was hardly the consensual society which Keith Middlemass
would have us believe in, where government, trade unions and
employers worked within an acceptable framework to ensure balance
in domestic policy.[40] Matters were far more adversarial. The fact is
that the nationalization of coal, under the independent National Coal
Board, did not prevent conflict between a monolithic and centralized
coal industry and a frustrated workforce – as was demonstrated in the
summer of 1947 when Grimethorpe and other South Yorkshire pits

---

[39]Morgan, *Labour in Power*, p. 79, quoted from E. Shinwell, *Conflict without Malice*
(1955), pp. 172 ff.
[40]K. Middlemass, *Politics in Industrial Society* (London, Deutsch, 1979), pp. 11–23.

took strike action.

Indeed there were other problems which made the task of the Labour government far from easy. The shortage of coal in the bad winter of 1946–47 led to some criticism of the NCB, and there were some on the Left who objected to the generous compensation terms offered to the coalowners for the nationalization of their property.

Nevertheless, although the government may have lacked the zeal which the Left hoped for, it was committed to implement its piecemeal programme and was quite prepared to meet the challenge of the employers and the Conservative party. It had the stomach for the fight. Indeed it needed it for, from the early legislative programme, there had been fierce opposition to the 1947 Transport Act and the 1948 Gas Act.

The Transport Act nationalized railways and road haulage. The nationalization of railways provoked little debate but the nationalization of road haulage proved most controverted. The Conservative party fought strongly against the measure, defending the 'C' Licence holders whose activities covered distances of less than forty miles. In the end the government relented, though the rest of the road haulage sector was taken into public ownership.[41]

There were similar problems in achieving the public ownership of gas. The Conservative opposition produced over 800 amendments to the Gas Bill, much to the annoyance of Gaitskell, and the Standing Committee of the House of Commons remained in session for two nights in a row. But at the end of the sitting, which was an odd affair given that much of the gas supply was already in municipal ownership and that the wartime Heyworth Committee had provided the blueprint, Gaitskell won the day. He wrote in his diary:

> The whole thing created a minor sensation in the Party with the satisfactory result that our Members on the Committee who had been getting very disgruntled ended up much mollified by the limelight, being regarded as heroes and receiving a letter from the Prime Minister, and above all defeating the Opposition.[42]

Up to a point then, the Labour government had revealed its resolve, if not its coherence, in approaching matters of public ownership. Quite clearly, each bill was treated as a separate measure and the whole strategy of public ownership was closely confined to the industries and services involved. Hinton and Miliband are thus vindicated in the views they hold, as is Morgan, who has emphasized the fragmented and piecemeal nature of the whole operation.

There is similar agreement over the more contentious issue of the nationalization of iron and steel. Most historians agree that the party

---

[41] Morgan, *Labour in Power*, pp. 107–8.
[42] Gaitskell, *Diary*, p. 66.

was reluctant to introduce the measure. It had only been Ian Mikardo's intervention in the 1944 Labour party conference that had driven the issue forward, much against Morrison's wishes. The fact is that Morrison had always been opposed to the proposal, and support for his attitude had increased when Britain faced financial and economic problems in 1947. By that time the majority of the Cabinet favoured either its deferment or its abandonment, though some favoured an interim measure which would fall short of complete nationalization along the lines of the Iron and Steel Control Board which had run the industry between 1946 and 1948.[43]   A pusillanimous Labour Cabinet thus faced hostile steel manufacturers, a determined Opposition and an obdurate House of Lords. But, in the end, the industry was formally nationalized in 1950. It is at this juncture that the various writers part company. Hinton is emphatic: 'It had always been apparent that there would be more capitalist resistance to public ownership of steel than any other nationalization measure prepared by the government. Keeping steel nationalization in the programme was, therefore, a real victory for the left'.[44] But this explanation seems unlikely. It is true that *Tribune* and the Keep Left movement were active at this time but, as both Miliband and Hinton acknowledge, they carried little weight in a party of government where there was little dissent from the prevalent and dominating spirit of the Parliamentary Labour party and the trade unions. The more plausible explanation is offered by Morgan who suggests that a variety of factors – the need to appease Bevan in Cabinet, the general commitment to steel nationalization in the face of opponents who saw in its failure the end of moves towards public ownership and the general indecisiveness of the government – which were rather more important than the marginal efforts of a pathetically weak left wing. In a halting and stumbling manner, steel nationalization was given legislative life in the face of redoubtable difficulties. The pressure of the Left was just another of those incalculable factors pushing the measure forward.

Yet there is no doubt that the momentum of change was slowing down. Though committed to a new programme of nationalization, the second post-war Labour government of 1950–51 did not achieve a great deal in this direction and some of its emergent young leaders, including Gaitskell, who became the new Chancellor of the Exchequer in October 1950, were reluctant to go much further along the road to 'socializing industry'. Indeed, by this time Gaitskell had already indicated his preference for redistributing income and removing poverty.

There is also little evidence that the Labour government of 1950–51 prepared to exert greater control over private industry. Its plans for the formation of Development Councils, to link employers and unions

[43]Morgan, *Labour in Power*, p. 115.
[44] Hinton, *Labour and Socialism*, p. 174.

together, foundered and the government's share of the economy, never more than about 20 per cent, was simply not sufficient to cajole private industry into a more positive response to government planning.[45]

The government generally lacked a clear planned strategy for the whole economy. Miliband, Hinton and Morgan all agree about the failings of Labour's schemes for public ownership: they were piecemeal, failed to use nationalization as a weapon of change and rarely provoked debate. What they differ about is the overall result. To Hinton and Miliband the end product was a badly thought-out mixed economy where capitalism was, if anything, strengthened. To them, there seems to be little evidence of a strong socialist commitment. On the other hand, Morgan feels that the warts of nationalization do not negate the general shift that it had brought about in the economy: 'A vital step forward had been taken in the displacement of the old order, even if its successor was far from clear in 1951. Without nationalization above all, the morale and impetus of the 1945 Labour government could not have been sustained. For most members of the party and the movement, that was its ultimate justification'.[46]

Indeed, it would appear that nationalization was the driving force behind the post-war Labour governments. If they lost their way and had no clear comprehension of how to use what was, to the Labour party, this symbol of socialism that did not make their efforts less worthwhile. They did at least attempt to take the country in a socialist direction in domestic affairs. It is not quite so clear that they attempted to do this in foreign, overseas and defence matters.

Foreign Affairs, the Commonwealth and Defence

In the immediate post-war years it was widely expected that a Labour government would be committed to the policies of disarmament and international reconciliation which it had advocated for most of the inter-war years. It was further expected that it would preside over the end of colonial rule and the creation of the new Commonwealth. By the late 1940s there was no longer an illusion that Labour would implement the pacific policies of the past, though there was a sense of satisfaction at the fact that Britain was disengaging from Empire and had, under difficult circumstances, created the independent new Commonwealth states of India and Pakistan. These contradictory responses have helped to produce a variety of interpretations of Labour's overseas policy – some of which call into doubt the commitment of the government to socialist policies.

[45]*Op. cit.*, pp. 175–6; Morgan, *Labour in Power*, p. 129.
[46]Morgan, *Labour in Power*, p. 141.

Miliband is hostile to the whole framework of Labour's overseas policies. He has argued, first that Labour's foreign policy was not distinctive from that of the Conservatives: 'Winston Churchill was not vainly boasting when he said, as he often did, that the government had consistently followed his own recommendations and proposals'.[47] On Colonial policy he added that 'The government's response to the anti-colonial challenge it faced was a mixture of minimal constitutional reform on the one hand, and of repression on the other, including, as part of the defence of the "free world" against Communism, the waging of a fierce colonial war in Malaya'.[48] However, neither observation is well balanced, and historical amnesia seems to have occurred when it comes to the Labour government's successes in these areas of policy.

There is no doubt that the Labour government disappointed the 'Keep Left' movement and *Tribune* over its foreign policies – and most notably in its attitude towards the Soviet Union. At the end of the war there had been clear hopes of strengthening the ties with the Soviet Union, but, in April 1949, the Washington Conference had fully confirmed the anti-Soviet attitude of the Labour government in its decision to form NATO. But much had changed during the intervening four years.

Labour's switch to the right, and to the alliance with the United States against the Soviet Union, had been conditioned by many factors. The most obvious was the appointment of Ernest Bevin as Foreign Secretary, though the government's need of the American Loan and its wariness of the pacific policies of the inter-war years were contributory factors. Bevin brought with him a reputation of being something of an anti-Communist largely due to his battles with Bert Papworth and the Communist-led London busmen within his own union, the Transport and General Workers.[49] During the Second World War he held few illusions about the difficulties which would be faced in dealing with the Soviet Union in the post-war world.[50] He was confirmed in his own fears when he found the Russians reluctant to agree to the reunification of Germany, imposing the blockade on Berlin and criticizing Britain's policies in the Middle East.[51]

Bevin was also mindful of the need to avoid a repeat of the inter-war years, when the United States adopted an isolationalist policy. The end of Lend–Lease raised memories of this event and motivated him to

[47]Miliband, *Parliamentary Socialism*, p. 303.

[48]*Op. cit.*, p. 304.

[49]A. Bullock, *The Life and Times of Ernest Bevin, Vol. I: Trade Union Leader, 1881–1940* (London, Heinemann, 1960).

[50]A. Bullock, *The Life and Times of Ernest Bevin, Vol. II, Minister of Labour, 1940–1945* (London, Heinemann, 1967).

[51]A Bullock, *Ernest Bevin: Foreign Secretary* (London, Heinemann, 1983), pp. 478–9, 549–85.

strengthen the link with the USA in the context of Britain's need to negotiate an American loan and what he perceived to be the rising threat of the Soviet Union to Britain's interests in the Middle East and Western Europe.

Alan Bullock's monumental work on Bevin as Foreign Secretary, based upon the recent availability of the Bevin papers in the Public Record Office, has demonstrated the extent to which Bevin was still convinced that Britain was a major world power and that she was threatened by the Soviet Union.[52] At the end of the war, it appears that Bevin was prepared to attempt to work with the Soviet Union to produce an acceptable peace settlement. But his involvement with the Russians convinced him of the need to conclude a series of bilateral defence treaties with France and the Benelux countries as well as maintaining a military presence in 'West' Germany, in order to protect the West. He also publicly announced the idea of a 'Western Union' in the House of Commons on 22 January 1948. His two main themes were that the Soviets were aiming to get Communist control in Eastern Europe and that Western Europe would have to consider ways of defending its independence. He argued that the 'free nations of Western Europe must now draw together. . . . I believe the time is now ripe for consolidation. . . .'[53]

Bevin carefully avoided mentioning any sort of relationship with the United States and did not define what was meant by the 'Western Union'. But, after that speech, Bevin sedulously sought to get a commitment to the defence of Western Europe from the USA. At first, the USA refused to give such an undertaking. But events moved quickly in 1948. On 5 March 1948 there was a Communist coup in Czechoslovakia,[54] the Russians were pressuring the President of Finland to visit Moscow and also imposed a blockade on West Berlin in the summer of 1948.[55] The Berlin blockade, which consisted of the Russians cutting off the road and rail links between Berlin and the West and the ending of the supply of electricity to the Western sector of the city from the Soviet sector and the Eastern zone, necessitated the Berlin airlift which involved American cooperation with the British in order to maintain 'West' Berlin.

By the autumn of 1948, amidst genuine fears that the Western European nations would be overrun by the Russians in the event of war, there were clear signs that a Western Alliance was likely to be formed. The United States finally agreed to commit itself to the support of the Western European nations at the Washington Conference on 4 April 1949, after protracted and intense discussions. As Bevin signed the NATO agreement he commented:

[52]*Op. cit.*, pp. 116–17.
[53]*Op. cit.*, pp. 519–21.
[54]*Op. cit.*, pp. 525–8.
[55]*Op. cit.*, pp. 571–80.

> I am doing so on behalf of a free and ancient parliamentary
> nation and I am satisfied that the step we are taking has the
> almost unanimous approval of the British people . . .
>   Our people do not want and do not glorify war, but they will
> not shrink from it if aggression is threatened.[56]

Nevertheless, it must not be assumed that Britain was slavish in her
support for the United States. There were, in fact, many points of
disagreement on international matters. The United States did not, for
instance, favour other nations sharing in the development of the
atomic bomb and so Attlee committed Britain to developing an
independent atomic capability.[57] There were also many other points of
departure, none more obvious than the events in Palestine.

Ever since the Balfour Declaration of 1917 Britain had been committed to a 'national home for the Jewish people',[58] though this intent
had always been tempered by the desire to protect the interests of the
non-Jewish communities. It soon became apparent that these joint
objectives were not possible. The flood of Jewish immigrants into
Palestine during the 1930s was too much for the Arab community and
too little for the Jews. Whilst various inter-war governments
attempted to regulate the flow of immigration it appeared that the
Labour party favoured Jewish immigration more than it feared Arab
reaction. Poale Zion, the Jewish Labour party, was affiliated to the
Labour party and Jewish Labour MPs, such as Manny Shinwell and
Lewis Silkin, campaigned strongly to win Labour support for the
creation of an independent Jewish state. Thus it is no surprise that the
Labour party conference of 1944 strongly associated itself with the
continued Jewish immigration into Palestine and the gradual withdrawal of the Arab community. But neither Ernest Bevin or the Labour
government pursued such a line when in power.

From the start they adopted a more even-handed approach, which
certainly did not please President Truman who demanded the
immediate admission of 100,000 Jews into Palestine in 1945.[59] The
Palestine Committee of the Cabinet, dominated by Morrison, limited
Jewish immigration to 1,500 per month, although it was agreed that an
Anglo-American Commission would be set up to examine the issues
involved. Even though it confirmed the need to admit 100,000 Jews
Attlee refused to accept the recommendation without an agreement to
reduce the size of the military forces being mustered by both the Jews
and the Arabs. From the start, British and American interests were at

---

[56]*Op. cit.*, p. 672.
[57]Morgan, *Labour in Power*, pp. 280–4, 427–9; Pelling, *Labour Governments 1945–1951*, p. 127.
[58]Pelling, *Labour Governments 1945–1951*, p. 127; Bullock, *Bevin: Foreign Secretary*, pp. 45–8, *passim*.
[59]Pelling, *Labour Governments 1945–1951*, p. 128; Morgan, *Labour in Power*, pp. 280–4, 427–9.

odds, a situation which was not helped by Ernest Bevin's cutting comment that 'they [the Americans] did not want too many Jews in New York'.[60]

Bevin's acrimonious outburst did not endear him to the Americans and, eventually, the continued illegal immigration of the Jews, the naval blockade and the episode of the ship *Exodus*, violence against British troops, the United Nations Committee and its advocacy of the partition into Jewish and Arab states, and the civil war, forced Bevin to allow the creation of the state of Israel in January 1949 and led to the ignominious withdrawal of British troops. Bevin's even-handed approach to the Palestine question seriously underestimated the extent of American support for the Jews and the commitment of the Jewish people to their homeland. In the end, he fell foul of what has been referred to as 'the endless imbroglio of Palestine'.[61]

Yet it cannot be denied that the Labour government's foreign policy was remarkably right-wing and lacked a clear socialist perspective. The fear of Communism and the need to identify with the USA for financial reasons saw Britain support the United States in its actions over the Korean War. But even if the foreign policy record of the Labour government looks tawdry to some, it is at least explicable in terms of the need for the American Loan and the fear of Soviet expansionism. What is more surprising is how readily it was accepted by the party and the PLP. What left-wing opposition there was quickly evaporated as the Soviet Union registered its threat to British oil supplies in the Middle East, blockaded West Berlin and engineered the Communist coup in Czechoslovakia. Granted his own assumptions Miliband is probably right to criticize the failure of the Labour government to adopt a socialist foreign policy, though he studiously avoids offering a realistic alternative. But he is almost certainly too harsh in rejecting, out of hand, the Labour government's policy towards the colonies.

The monumental achievement of the Attlee government in relationship to India was rather more than the 'minimal constitutional change', or signs of repression, which Miliband refers to in his general attack upon Labour's colonial policy.[62] British Labour politicians had been committed to Indian independence before the Second World War and Attlee's government had indicated its intention to offer some measure of independence to India. Attlee had sent a delegation of Cabinet Ministers – Stafford Cripps, Pethick-Lawrence and A. V. Alexander – to India in February 1946 to conduct intricate

---

[60]Pelling, *Labour Governments 1945–1951*, p. 128.
[61]Morgan, *Labour in Power*, p. 2.
[62]Miliband, *Parliamentary Socialism*, p. 304.
[63]Morgan, *Labour in Power*, pp. 219–20; Bullock, *Bevin: Foreign Secretary*, p. 234.

negotiations with the Congress and the Muslim leaders.[63] They found no consensus and were forced to produce a complex three-tier system of government which ruled out the idea of creating the state of Pakistan. As a result an interim government was formed, under Pandit Nehru, in September 1946. But the rising level of violence between the Hindus and the Muslims threatened its continued existence and provoked the Viceroy, Lord Mountbatten, to bring forward the withdrawal of British troops to 15 August 1947 – the day on which the Indian Congress agreed that India and Pakistan would formally become independent states, and full members of the Commonwealth. The occasion was also marred by widespread bloodshed throughout India. It is possible that the end of the British Raj could have been handled more effectively, though doubtful given the contending forces at play. What is not justified is the view that the Labour government was repressive. It was certainly much less so than previous administrations and the term seems highly inappropriate in the light of the withdrawal, or 'scuttle', from India. What was there to be repressive about when the subcontinent was being given back to the native population?

The Labour government was clearly deflected from part of the political course which it aimed to pave in 1945. Its foreign policy, conditioned by a variety of events, was never to be the socialist policy which many of its supporters had hoped for, though there was some credit to be drawn from its actions in India and Palestine. But this aberrant foreign policy was partly conditioned by Britain's post-war economic problems, many of which would have been unsurmountable without the American Loan. Even with that Loan, and further financial help, there were serious economic constraints upon the Labour government's ability to fulfil its objectives.

The Financial Crises

The dominating force behind the actions of the Labour government was the exigent need for financial stability without which there could have been no significant progress towards socialism. Yet, as Cairncross has suggested, it is evident that, despite rising industrial output and thriving exports, the British economy was desperately constrained by the enormous debts incurred directly in war.[64] It was this factor which dominated Britain's economy during the years between the 1940s and the early 1960s. Labour ministers were aware of the situation as soon as they entered office and were soon to be found pushing for the foreign borrowing which would ensure financial stability. In the first

---

[63]Morgan, *Labour in Power*, pp. 219–20; Bullock, *Bevin: Foreign Secretary*, p. 234.
[64]Pimlott, *Hugh Dalton*; S. Howson, 'The origins of cheaper money, 1945–47', *Economic History Review*, XI, 3 (August 1987); Cairncross, *Years of Recovery*, pp. 428–41.

instance, that stability was provided by the American Loan. Later, the Marshall Aid programme provided the Labour government with the financial flexibility to implement its extensive programme of domestic and social legislation between 1945 and 1947. But it was primarily the terms of the American Loan which slowed down the pace of legislative change after 1947. The decision to make the pound sterling convertible with the dollar on 15 July 1947, a condition of the Loan, paved the way for a change in direction in the economic and social programme of the Labour government and brought about the Morrison 'Consolidation' policy which Miliband has seen as evidence of Labour's retreat from socialism.

As Chancellor of the Exchequer, Hugh Dalton had pursued economic policies which, though they were not Keynesian, sought to offer expansion rather than the deflationary policies of the inter-war years. The American Loan had provided him with the resources to pay for nationalization, the recovery in house building and the whole panoply of social reform. There is little doubt that the Labour government's legislative programme would have been severely restricted without American financial support. But in 1947 matters began to go wrong. The fuel crisis and coal shortage, conditioned by the bad winter of 1946–47 destroyed the conviction that socialist planning could cope with any situation and there was a temporary rise of unemployment to about two millions. Indeed one critic, from inside the party, felt that the government's economic strategy was 'haphazard and profoundly unsocialist'.[65] Imposed upon this evident failure of planning was the sharp rise in American prices in 1947 which undermined the value of the American Loan and contributed to the balance of payments crisis of the summer and the constant dollar drain from the British gold and currency reserves. By the summer of 1947 more than half of the arranged loan of $3,750 millions, which was supposed to last until 1951, was gone and it appeared that the rest would disappear by 1948. In such circumstances, the decision to make the pound convertible was a foolish step, though an inevitable one if the government was to honour its pledge. The result was a financial disaster and the run on the pound was so heavy that the government was forced to impose a temporary suspension of convertibility on 20 August 1947. That became permanent in December.

This financial mistake changed the whole course of the Labour government's approach to the economy. Within a few months, Dalton was replaced as Chancellor of the Exchequer by Sir Stafford Cripps. With him went the freedom which domestic policy had enjoyed, although there were already signs of the new austerity measures before the Cripps era began. The new era brought with it a major export drive

---

[65]Thomas Balogh quoted in Morgan, *Labour in Power*, pp. 334–5. This view is challenged in Pimlott, *Hugh Dalton*, pp. 450–75.

coupled with austerity at home, associated with the reduction of food imports, the strict rationing of food and the extension of the wages freeze.

The economy was greatly strengthened by these actions and the devaluation of the pound in 1949 ran very much against the economic trends. In fact it was a temporary decline of the US economy, leading to a worsening of the British balance of payments situation, that led to the devaluation of the pound from \$4.03 to \$2.40 in September 1949.

The financial crises of 1947 and 1949 had their origins in the serious balance of trade situation which Britain faced after the war and did not accurately reflect the enormous improvements brought about by the Labour government. Between 1945 and 1949 the value of exports had risen from about 50 per cent below the pre-war level to almost 55 per cent above, paying for about 85 per cent of the imports compared with only a third in 1945. Industrial production was, by 1949, 30 per cent above that of 1938.[66] By 1949 great strides had been made to revive the British economy and the devaluation of that year produced a Cabinet which, according to Gaitskell, was doubtful of the need for, or the necessary extent of, any devaluation.[67]

Whatever the legitimacy of the financial adjustments produced by the foreign trade situation the impact was clear – the rate of social reform and public ownership would be slowed down. The issue of steel nationalization was fought in an atmosphere of financial difficulty and other measures of public ownership were discussed in less exalted tones after 1947.

Morrison's call for 'consolidation' simply imposed itself upon the natural cautiousness of a government which was always reluctant to go beyond the pledges made in *Let Us Face the Future*, and was now faced with a difficult financial situation. His speech to the Labour party conference at Scarborough in 1948 indicated that there was strong support within the government that it should not vigorously pursue further nationalization, but to allow 'Ministers adequate time to consolidate, to develop, to make efficient the industries which have been socialized in the present Parliament'.[68] This was clearly a policy conditioned by economic events and designed to prepare Labour for the next general election. By 1949, when the Labour party produced its new policy statement *Labour Believes in Britain*, there was little substance to its nationalization programme beyond some general commitment to the public ownership of industrial life assurance and sugar, and some perfunctory threats to nationalize those industries which were 'failing the nation'. Consequently, apart from the protracted debate on steel nationalization relatively little was achieved.

[66]Gaitskell; *Diary*, p. 125.
[67]*Op. cit.*, pp. 125–54.
[68]Miliband, *Parliamentary Socialism*, p. 298.

'Consolidation' was not confined to public ownership alone, for the health welfare measures of the Labour government were about to be implemented fully in 1948 and there were immediate fears about the cost of these policies. In addition, it would be unfair to suggest that the move towards 'consolidation' was in some way evidence of the expiry of socialist intent – the fact is that the new welfare schemes moved the Labour government into new areas of provision and cost which no previous government had ever faced. Confronted by the financial difficulties of 1947, and Cripp's demand for self-sufficiency and austerity, it was obvious that there would be arguments concerning expenditure on welfare measures. To suggest that Morrison's caution was somehow less socialist than Bevan's demand for social expansion is to devalue the real and substantial contribution made by Labour's welfare measures to the life of the ordinary citizen. It also ignores the financial and strategic context within which the Labour government operated.

This is not to deny the fact that there were major disagreements between the key figures in the Labour government concerning the extent of their commitment to socialism. Indeed, it would be difficult not to be aware of these conflicts, especially in connection with the National Health Service.

Morrison and Gaitskell v. Bevan

Herbert Morrison was appointed Lord President of the Council in 1945. The formal duties of that post were hardly demanding for he was responsible for the work of the Privy Council Office and presented the business to the King and the Council when it met, which was infrequently. But the post brought with it the position of deputy premier and the leadership of the House of Commons. Between 1945 and 1947 the Privy Council Office gained additional responsibilities – most notably that of co-ordinating the principal measures of nationalization and planning Labour's legislative programme over five years. In effect Morrison was to act as a sort of overlord on the home front.[69] He was the fulcrum around which Labour policy revolved and was seen, especially by his critics, as the personification of the domestic policy of the Labour government. But the Labour Left also saw Morrison as the stumbling block to the rapid transition to socialism which it sought, though it was his battles against Aneurin Bevan, Minister of Health, which produced most animus. Just at the moment that Morrison was pronouncing the need for 'consolidation' Bevan was presiding over the formation of the National Health Service, which was to prove an

[69]B. Donoghue and G. W. Jones, *Herbert Morrison* (London, Weidenfeld & Nicolson, 1973), pp. 348–51.

increasing financial burden to the Labour administration faced with the need to administer the Cripps programme of austerity. The widely different policies being advocated by Morrison and Bevan were to make the provision of the National Health Service one of the most contentious issues faced by the Labour government – ultimately leading to the highly emotional resignation of Bevan from the government in 1951.

The National Health Service came into existence in July 1948, at a time when Sir Stafford Cripps was attempting to control public expenditure in the wake of the Dalton years of expansion. When the decision to form the NHS had been taken in 1946 it was estimated that it would cost £126 millions. During its first year, 1948–49, expenditure exceeded £278 millions, rising to £356 millions between 1950 and 1951.[70] These unexpectedly high figures dismayed Attlee, Cripps and Morrison who, by 1949, were strenuously seeking to force the Minister of Health to reduce expenditure.

As Cabinet and government records now reveal, the conflict first emerged in the autumn of 1949, at a time when the Labour Cabinet had decided to devalue the pound. Cabinet and committee discussions were quite clearly leading towards an attack upon the finances of the Health Service and Bevan pre-empted serious debate by announcing, at a Labour rally in Staffordshire on 25 September, that

> I have made up my mind that the National Health Service is not going to be touched, and there is no disposition by the government to touch it. The government had made up their mind to solve the problem without ruining the social services, and the health service is sacrosanct.[71]

On 6 October, holding his first press conference for three years, he said that the government had 'set their face against a Health Tax, if what was meant was a payment made by a patient at the moment he needed treatment.'[72]

Bevan's statements clearly reflected the debate which had been going on within government circles for some time, a debate which continued well beyond the Cabinet meeting on 20 October 1949, when Morrison raised the possibility of charges on teeth and spectacles, and which Morgan suggests saw the end of the preliminary attempts to reduce health costs.[73] The debate in fact raged within government circles into the spring of 1950.

The whole episode stemmed from the attempt by Cripps to reduce

[70]Cab, 124, file 1187, memorandum of Miss J. H. Lidderdale to Herbert Morrison, Lord President of the Council, 4 October 1949.

[71]*The Times*, 26 September 1949; cutting in Cab 124, file 1187, memorandum of Lidderdale to Morrison.

[72]*The Telegraph*, 7 October 1949, cutting in Cab 124, file 1187.

[73]Morgan, *Labour in Power*, pp. 400–1.

and control public expenditure. He and Morrison were already
discussing such matters by September 1949; hence Bevan's attempt to
pre-empt decisions. The matter was raised in Cabinet on 20 October
and Cripps sent a letter to Bevan, on 28 November, suggesting a
variety of ways of reducing NHS costs, including the removal of merit
awards for doctors and the introduction of prescription charges.[74]
Morrison, and his advisers E. M. Nicholson and Miss Jane Lidderdale,
continued to press for further cuts and orchestrated the increasing
isolation of Bevan from the rest of the Cabinet, forcing Cabinet to
demand that he should present a paper to it explaining how he
intended to reduce costs in the NHS.[75] It was Nicholson who, in his
memoranda, paved the way for the final showdown. He informed
Morrison of his fears and remedies:

> It ought, however, to be emphasized that however much the
> Minister of Health can say on the virtue and merits of vast
> expenditure on the sick he is leading the government straight for
> another 1931 crisis in the very near future, and unless the
> government can show that it knows how to adopt a pace of
> development of the Health Service which the National economy
> can bear something will have to go before long.
>
> Probably the best approach would be for the Cabinet to set a
> ceiling figure on the National Health Service as on the Defence
> Services . . . £300 millions. This would still give the Health
> Service well over double the figure (£126 millions) on the basis of
> which the government decided to go forward with the Service in
> 1946.[76]

The emotive threat of a repeat of 1931 carried much weight with a
minister who had lived through those events.

Bevan's response to these pressures was to emphasize that Labour's
supporters would not understand any withdrawal from a completely
free health service. He also urged delay due to the impending general
election. Replying to Cripps on 9 December 1949, he wrote that 'I
think that a proposal to charge two or three shillings for some 40 per
cent of 'prescriptions' would give rise to a lot of surprise, resentment,
and, in many cases, hardship'.[77] He was determined to protect the
NHS and concluded his letter with an emotive flourish:

> I think we must see the problem clearly and make up our minds;
> either we must stand to the health service as a whole, sticking to
> all principles on which we founded it, or else we should clearly

[74]Letter from Cripps to Bevan, 28 November 1949, Cab 124, file 1187.
[75]Cab 124, file 1187. Also quoted on letter of E. M. Nicholson to Lord President
(Morrison), 18 January 1950.
[76]Cab 124, file 1188, letter dated 11 March 1950.
[77]Cab 124, file 1187, letter Bevan to Cripps, 9 December 1949.

admit that – much as we still believe that it was, and is, the right
service to aim at – our economic position renders it impossible to
have it for some years to come; in the latter event, we leave it to
the statute books for the future but in the meantime substitute a
revised, interim and austerity service being worked out on
different principles and after an intensive review of the whole
field. I personally should reject the latter, as you know. But I
should infinitely prefer to tackle it that way, if financially it
proved essential, than to go on with a process of whittling away
which brings small savings coupled with large discredit in many
people's eyes.

In fact he was being less than fair in his assessment for he was drawing
too sharp a contrast between the universal and free provision of health
care and the rejection of that principle which some relatively minor
changes would bring. The principle of free provision would have been
destroyed, though what remained would have been immeasurably
better than what had existed before the war. In any case, Bevan had no
intention of drawing up any schemes of cuts, even when specifically
asked to do so. The timing of the 1950 General Election put paid to the
immediate debate and Bevan indicated to Attlee his reluctance to take
action:

You have, no doubt, noted that at the last meeting of the Lord
President's Committee, it was decided in my absence (unfortunately I had a slight cold and could not attend) that I should at
once proceed with discussions with chemists and doctors about
the arrangements for charging a shilling [5p] for prescriptions,
despite the fact that because of exemptions the savings will now
be no more than £5 millions.

I have submitted a paper to the Cabinet but it was not possible
to discuss it on Tuesday. As you no doubt know, I am now
leaving London on a long speaking tour for the Party and then
must visit my own constituency.

I am, therefore, instructing my office not to proceed with the
discussion until after the Election. This will not prejudice a final
decision on the question of making a charge, but I am sure that
you will appreciate that to start discussions with the British
Medical Association, including Charles Hill, who is a Conservative candidate . . ., would be the height of folly, for our proposals
would be certain to become known and would lend themselves to
grotesque misrepresentation by the Opposition.[78]

Bevan had his way and the issue of health charges subsided for the
time being, as the Labour government fought the 'demure' general
election of February 1950.[79] Bevan was kept away from the limelight

[78]Cab 124, file 1187, letter of Bevan to Attlee, 2 February 1950.
[79]Morgan, *Labour in Power*, p. 403.

and the Labour party played down its commitment to nationalization, thus giving support to the views of those who believed that the Labour party/government had retreated from socialism after 1947. Nevertheless, the Labour party was returned to power with a much reduced parliamentary majority; it had 315 seats to the 298 held by the Conservatives and the nine held by the Liberal party. With its narrow majority the new Labour government seemed reluctant to become involved in controversial and expensive policies, especially when the Korean War threatened to bring about huge increases in the defence budget. In an atmosphere of political hesitancy and economic retrenchment, the rapidly rising costs of the NHS were bound to throw Bevan into conflict with his Cabinet colleagues.

Yet the new assault on the NHS finances was conducted with rather more stealth than previously. Although Bevan and Cripps had clashed over the proposed NHS charges in March and April 1950, what at first appeared to be a victory by Bevan proved a triumph for Morrison and Cripps. Bevan, having reversed his initial views, had 'forced the Chancellor then to drop the charges in favour of a ceiling on Health expenditure' – though this was the fall-back position which Nicholson had previously suggested to Morrison.[80] This was followed by Bevan's removal from the Ministry of Health to the Ministry of Labour in mid-January 1951, and the removal of his former post from the Cabinet. Bevan was no longer in a position to fight off the attacks upon the NHS. Marginalized, his only recourse was to resign from the Cabinet in one of the best-recorded episodes of the Attlee years.

Gaitskell, who had become Chancellor of the Exchequer in the place of Cripps in October 1950, had announced his intention to levy charges on dentures and optical services under the NHS to the Cabinet Committee on Health in March and April 1951, following intensive discussions with the New Health Minister and various committees of government. The precise proposal was that half the cost of dentures, a £1 charge per pair of spectacles (other than for children) and a shilling prescription charge should be raised from patients. Bevan made it clear that 'he had always been opposed to the introduction of charges for dentures and spectacles'.[81]

In the next few days, Bevan threatened resignation, and informed Dalton that he was 'opposed to rootless men like Gaitskell . . . who are dismantling the welfare state'.[82] After some vacillation, he resigned on 22 April 1951 to be followed into exile by Harold Wilson, President of the Board of Trade and John Freeman, a junior minister of Supply. Bevan left, ranting about the threat which Gaitskell, the second Snowden, posed to his Health service. The formal comment of the

[80]*Op. cit.*, p. 444.
[81]Cab 128/1, Cab 25, 9 April 1951.
[82]Morgan, *Labour in Power*, p. 450; Dalton's Diary, 9 April 1951.

Cabinet was more sober: 'It had not been found possible to find a form of words which would satisfy the Minister of Labour, and he had now resigned from the government'.[83] The Cabinet had clearly found in favour of Gaitskell, who had also threatened resignation if the charges were not announced.

In a narrow sense, the conflict over health charges was a conflict between those, like Morrison and Gaitskell, who acknowledged the financial difficulties faced by Britain and others, like Bevan, who believed that the NHS was sacrosanct. In its wider framework, it has been seen as a conflict between the right-wing forces in the Labour government, withdrawing from socialism, and the left-wing forces who saw the expansion of a free and universal NHS as an essential testimony of the Labour government's commitment to socialism. However, the contrast is overdrawn and far too stark for the savings of £20 millions accomplished by the charges was minimal compared with the great improvements made by health provision between 1948 and 1951.[84]

The End of the Attlee Years

By 1950 the Labour government was clearly in difficulty. It had achieved its main legislative thrust in the immediate post-war years, the electorate was less supportive of it in the 1950 General Election and many of its leading spirits were gone – having resigned, died or left through ill-health. The government's initiative was further stifled by the financial difficulties it faced, most notably the rapidly rising costs which the Korean War added to the defence bill. In addition, the trade-union movement was no longer prepared to force its members to accept wage restraint as the consensus between the trade unions and the government began to erode. Ever since 1945 the trade unions had accepted the need to sublimate their sectional interests to the needs of the reforming Labour government. Wage restraint had been accepted by the TUC and its member unions generally discouraged strike action. But this arrangement was beginning to break down in the autumn of 1950, and was indicated by the defeat of the General Council of the TUC in its attempt to extend wage restraint. It became all too evident in the outbreak of industrial disorder in 1950. In June, a strike by Smithfield meat lorry drivers led to the massive use of troops in order to ensure that food supplies were adequate to meet rations. The actual number of strikes in 1950 remained small, and fewer than 1,400,000 working days were lost – the lowest since 1940. But many of them occurred towards the end of the year and demonstrated hostility

[83]Cab 128/1, Cab 30 (51), 23 April 1951.
[84]Gaitskell, *Diary*, p. 246.

against the two-year wage freeze and trade-union anguish at the conti-nuance of Order 1305, passed in July 1940 to settle disputes by joint negotiating machinery.

Labour ministers clearly feared that these strikes were motivated by the desire of the Communist party to promote industrial disorder. Its fears were based upon the fact that, in March 1950, the Communist party held a National Industrial conference at which Harry Pollitt declared that 'the great issues would be settled not in the area of this reactionary Parliament, but by workers' mass struggles in the factories and streets'.[85] The government believed this to be evidence of the deliberate intent of the Communists to cause industrial unrest and it was arranged that a committee would be set up to examine their activities and that Special Branch would be responsible for their surveillance.[86] For a time, it was suspected that the Communists were seeking to disrupt electricity and fuel supplies and a ten-day strike by the workers at the North Thames Gas Board led the government to arrest ten of the leaders, under Order 1305 and other legislation. They were sentenced to imprisonment for one month, though the sentence was later reduced to a fine.[87]

The fear of Communist disruption was undoubtedly exaggerated; the collapse of the wages freeze was not. Recently available Cabinet and government records indicate that Cabinet ministers were being informed that the wages freeze was breaking down, despite a rise of earnings of 18 per cent between April 1947 and August 1950. Indeed, it was suggested that a salvage job could be mounted if a new wages policy, based upon a scientific assessment of skill, bonuses, and an annual economic survey to indicate the 'amount of national surplus available for distribution' could be arranged.[88] Though this scheme did not get very far its formulation at least recognized that the existing wages policy could not last. By early 1951, when Aneurin Bevan was Minister of Labour, the last vestiges of the policy were laid to rest when a national railway strike was avoided by the government urging British Rail to give them a 7.5 per cent increase, rather than the 5 per cent it had offered. It was at this moment that Bevan began the process of dismembering Order 1305 which was proving to be an industrial and political embarrassment to the Labour government.

It was only a matter of time before Attlee, plagued with a variety of domestic and foreign problems, decided to call a general election for October 1951. Though the Labour party remained the most popular political party, with 48.8 per cent of the vote compared with the Conservatives 48 per cent, it captured only 295 seats compared to the

[85]Cab 124, file 1194, draft of broadcast by the Minister of Labour, October 1950.
[86]Cab 124, file 1196, memorandum from Frank Soskice, Attorney General to Lord President.
[87]Morgan, *Labour in Power*, p. 437.
[88]Cab 124, file 1196, memorandum 28 August 1950.

321 gained by the Conservatives. The post-war Labour era drew to a close, though the Labour party could still claim to be the most popular political party amongst the voters.

Conclusion

Recent writers have been right to attack the political myths which have surrounded the Attlee governments of 1945 to 1951. In no way can it be correct to see these administrations as calmly, and with deliberate intent, introducing the planned socialist state devised by democratic socialists and agreed to by the nation as a whole, as some contemporary writers and recent politicians would have us believe. There was much less planning that the myth allows for and far too much hesitancy, produced by the acute financial difficulties within which these administrations worked. The Attlee governments were also profoundly controversial – although the Left was always marginalized in its opposition on such matters as foreign policy.

Historians have been no less partial than politicians in examining the Attlee years in ways which suit their own political perspectives. Marxists have, on the whole, denigrated the achievements of the Labour government due to the fact that their ideology rejects the view that democratic parliamentary socialism could ever be other than inefficient and prone to compromise: most certainly they accept that socialism in Britain cannot be brought about by parliamentary means. They find, in the failures of the Attlee governments, sustenance for their views and note, with disdain, the way in which Labour chancellors of the exchequer have invariably been attracted to the succubus of Treasury orthodoxy when it comes to a conflict between financial prudence and the implementation of socialist measures. Those who are more right-wing are inclined to accept that the Attlee governments had their faults but did achieve a significant shift in the attitude and role of government in society.[89] Morgan, very much in the moderate Labour mould, acknowledges the great achievements of the Attlee years, even allowing for the severe financial constraints which existed. On the whole, Morgan's dispassionate assessment of the Attlee governments appears to be far more objective than the polemical outbursts produced by Miliband and Hinton.

It is true that the Beveridge Report did provide a wartime social blueprint upon which to build the Welfare State but it would be misleading to suggest, as Hinton does of the NHS, that the 'scheme did not significantly go beyond what had been accepted in principle by all the parties during the war'.[90] The fact is that Bevan did add his own

[89]Blake, *Decline of Power*, p. 317; Barnett, *Audit of War*; Beloff, *Wars and Welfare*.
[90]Hinton, *Labour and Socialism*, p. 170.

distinctive ideas to the final programme and the Labour party had been developing a variety of welfare policies before the war. Equally, there is no doubt that Attlee and his colleagues did envisage the creation of a socialist state. But as democratic socialists they did not seek to transform the nation overnight and, from the start, stressed that they had no intention of taking all industries into public ownership. The fact that only about one fifth of the economy fell into government hands, and that the administration failed to manipulate the rest of the capitalist economy in the direction which it intended, is not to deny that the government was socialist so much as to criticize the pace of development which could be achieved under parliamentary democracy. And it is widely agreed that the Labour programme of 1945 to 1947 was one of the most ambitious and successful to be introduced by any post-war administration, let alone Labour administration. It fulfilled the bulk of its political pledges and ultimately nationalized steel, despite enormous difficulties: a weak and ineffective Left was hardly as important in this task as the PLP and an acquiescent Labour party out in the country, and a Cabinet anxious to maintain some semblance of unity. Nationalization was achieved because the thrust of party support was behind the Labour leaders not because of a pusillanimous Labour government giving way to the temperamental outbursts of an effete Left wing.

Nevertheless, even if the Attlee governments implemented more than wartime collectivism in the attempt to introduce democratic parliamentary socialism, they are open to the charge that they kowtowed to United States capitalism in opposing socialist and Communist Europe. It is quite clear that Bevin developed a foreign policy which favoured the US alliance and attempted to isolate the USSR, though this seemed to be more associated with the concern for wider British interests abroad and was remarkably opposed to US interests in Palestine and in the production of the atomic bomb. The government also achieved a remarkable success in withdrawing from Empire and bringing about Indian independence. This indicated that it was intent upon bringing to an end the imperial game. The Attlee administrations were remarkably free from US domination in foreign policy given the extent to which they relied upon the US for a loan and Marshall Aid to counteract Britain's vulnerability to balance of payments crises.

Indeed, the successes of the Labour governments should not be overlooked. They offered the most effective evidence of what could be achieved by a democratic socialist administration. They brought about change in direction for the British nation and moved government towards a more humanitarian concern for its people, committing it to the maintenance of full employment – a sharp contrast to the events which followed the First World War. These achievements were considerable and formed the basis of the policies of successive governments, at least until 1979.

As unemployment has risen to well above three millions, there has been rising nostalgia for the planned policies of the Attlee era by the progressive parties in Britain. Labour politicians have looked at it fondly as a period of party unity when Labour enjoyed widespread popular support. The problem since 1951 has been that the party has experienced a dramatic decline of that support. There seems to be the illusion that if Labour could return to the style and policies of the Attlee years it would be more successful. Unfortunately, for such optimism, the times have changed. As the Labour party has discovered over more than three decades it loses moral legitimacy when it loses the popular vote. The problem of the Labour party since 1951 has been to develop the type of policies which would help it retain popular support at the same time as it extends socialist solutions to the nation. This is a formula which has evaded the party, due largely to the fact that the trade-union movement and traditional Labour supporters have been reluctant to adapt to the changing structure and demands of British society.

8 THE CRISIS IN THE LABOUR PARTY, 1951–79

The summer of 1987 saw the Labour party conduct one of its most impressive general election campaigns. Few would deny that the party won the campaign, but it still lost the election by a substantial margin. There has been a plethora of explanations for this paradox, many of which have invoked the dominating question of Labour history since 1951 – why has the Labour party's popularity declined since the immediate post-war years? The theories have been numerous and varied – though there has been a measure of agreement within Labour ranks that the party failed to recapture the vote of the skilled members of the working class. According to Ken Livingstone:

> This loss of support amongst skilled workers is nothing new. It was a process which began during the 1966 Wilson administration, when that government's incomes policy hit hardest at skilled workers. The pattern was repeated during the 1974 Labour government, as skilled workers' wages were again held back. This has left skilled workers deeply suspicious that it is they who are forced – by higher taxes and rates – to bear the burden of the relief of poverty and the rebuilding of our investment industry.[1]

There was substantial support for this view from the academic world and particularly from Professor Ivor Crewe who analysed the results of a Gallup survey commissioned by the BBC to that effect.[2] His main conclusion was that the Labour party had recaptured the traditional working class through offering full employment and the welfare state as its prime policies but had 'failed spectacularly' to win over the skilled manual workers and the new working class, who may often live in the South, be owner-occupiers and possibly non-union. According to Crewe's survey, Labour won 49 per cent of the vote of skilled workers in 1974, 45 per cent in 1979 and a mere 34 per cent in 1987. In contrast, the Conservatives won 26 per cent in 1974, 45 per cent in 1979 and 43 per cent in 1987. Other surveys have a slight variance but generally tell the same tale, and broadly endorse Crewe's view that

> The party had come to represent a declining segment of the working class – the traditional working class of the council

[1] *The Guardian*, 26 June 1987.
[2] *Op. cit.*, 15 June 1987.

estates, the public sector, industrial Scotland and the North, and the old industrial unions – while failing to attract the affluent and expanding working class of the new estates and new service economy of the South. It was party of neither one class nor one nation; it was a regional class party.[3]

Yet is this loss of the skilled working-class vote, particularly in the South, the prime reason for Labour's electoral decline in recent years? Does this argument offer a plausible explanation of the decline of Labour's political fortunes since 1951, or are other factors at work? What has gone wrong for Labour? To pose Eric Hobsbawm's question, has the forward march of Labour halted?

Interpretations

The decline of the Labour party has been one of the most hotly debated issues of recent years. In broad terms, six main types of explanation have been offered, and they cover the full range of political thought from the Far Left to the New Right.

Historians of the Far Left have tended to suggest that the reason for Labour's failures lies in the fact that socialism cannot be achieved by parliamentary means. Tony Cliff – the effective founder and leader of the International Socialists, now the Socialist Workers' party – doubts the parliamentary pathway and believes in the power of the trade-union movement and the working class to bring about the fundamental changes which he seeks. Beyond this he is prepared to accept that the Labour party's failures in recent years stem from the fact that.

> Wilson put the boot in hard to the workers who voted for him, and in 1970 the Labour vote went down to 43 per cent. Between 1974 and 1979, we had the worst Labour government ever. Unemployment doubled. Hundreds of hospitals were closed. This was a horrible period. And the Labour vote went down again to 37 per cent.[4]

This view has been refined by a second explanation offered by Ralph Miliband. His main argument is that Labour's decline stems from the fact that socialism has not been on the Labour agenda since the 1950s. Miliband is adamant that socialism was a lost issue by the mid 1950s.

> The point has been made: a socialist programme could only have enhanced the Labour party's chances if it had been put forward, and fought for, in Parliament and outside, from 1951 onwards,

[3]*Op. cit.*, 15 June 1987.
[4]*Op. cit.*, 20 July 1987.

and if all the resources and energies of the party and the trade unions had been used to make it known and understood.[5]

Because this was not done he feels that there is little to suggest that a socialist 'programme would have attracted greater support had it been presented in 1955'.[6] To Miliband, the issue is clear – socialism could only have been fought for in the immediate wake of the Attlee years when the electorate was still sensitive, and sympathetic, towards it. These policies were not developed and the Labour party drifted towards Labourism and worse. The whole history of the party since the early 1950s is thus seen as a retreat from the socialism which inspired its founding fathers.

Yet many on the left would disagree with Miliband's pessimistic assessment. They see in socialism, and the development of Clause Four, the real prospect for Labour victory. Hinton accepts that the Labour party quickly drifted away from offering socialist policies in the 1950s but sees this as the cause of a decline which can be reversed. Without a clear socialist philosophy there is nothing to distinguish the Labour party from the actions of the Conservative governments of the 1950s and 1960s who did not dismantle the welfare state and who broadly accepted the Keynesian economic approach which the Attlee governments had adopted.[7] With a clear socialist policy there is a prospect of Labour's revival.

Whatever the varying ideas offered by Miliband and Hinton they do agree that it has been, and may be, possible for the Labour party to achieve socialism through parliamentary means. It is the lack of application to such a policy which is seen by them as the cause of Labour's political decline. But such views are not sufficient for a third group of writers who have attempted to explain Labour's failures in terms of the rigidities of 'Clause-Four Socialism', which sees socialism simply in terms of the nationalization of industry and services.

Tony Crosland, in his book *The Future of Socialism* (1956) made a forceful attempt to reinterpret the meaning of socialism in the light of the changes which had taken place since 1945 – suggesting that Labour had to go beyond Clause Four. It was his view, and those of other Gaitskellites, which became evident in 1959 when Mark Abrams, Richard Rose and Rita Hinden offered their post-mortem on Labour's 1959 General Election defeat entitled *Must Labour Lose?*[8] They maintained that the answer was probably yes for three main reasons. In the first case, they noted the contraction of heavy industry which meant a reduction in the size of the traditional working class and the

---

[5]R. Miliband, *Parliamentary Socialism* (London, Merlin, 1972 edition), p. 331.
[6]Miliband, *Parliamentary Socialism*, p. 331.
[7]J. Hinton, *Labour and Socialism: A history of the British Labour Movement 1867–1974* (Brighton, Harvester Group, 1983), p. 183.
[8]M. Abrams, R. Rose and R. Hinden, *Must Labour Lose?* (London, Penguin, 1960).

comparative expansion of the middle classes and the middling income group. Secondly, they suggested that the social changes in society meant that middle-class values were expanding and that in some way this increased consumerism at the expense of socialism. Thirdly, in consequence, Clause Four was losing its political appeal.

Subsequent events, including the election of four Labour governments, have proved this assessment to be unduly pessimistic. Nevertheless, the view of Abrams and his colleagues did give rise to the 'affluent worker' debate which underpinned the philosophy of the Gaitskellites and the revisionists. The argument of these thinkers and politicians alike was that Labour should diversify its policies since its working-class base was being eroded by the social trends of the 'affluent' society. But this diversification was no longer to be based upon old-fashioned appeals to class consciousness and socialism. Instead it was to be rooted in pragmatism and the rather vague and amorphous commitment to establishing a more equal society.[9]

Support for this view stemmed from the fact that Labour was losing its political popularity. Its overall electoral support in general elections had fallen from 14 million voters in 1951 to 11.5 million in 1979. It fell to a mere 11 million in 1987. By 1979 only about half of all trade unionists were voting for Labour and the individual membership of the party, largely based upon the working class, had declined quickly. Indeed the official individual membership figures had fallen from about one million in 1952 to 630,000 in 1982, though it has been suggested that the real figure was much lower at about 250,000, with only 55,000 activists, by the late 1970s.[10]

A fourth type of explanation is far more optimistic for Labour's future electoral success. It is best presented in the *New Fabian Essays*, produced in the 1950s, and the more recent *Fabian Essays in Socialist Thought* (1984). The general thrust of these works is to suggest that Labour has failed because it did not develop socialist policies beyond Clause Four. Richard Crossman, writing in the first of these collections, felt the need to take socialism forward, in a democratic way, beyond the restrictive framework of the existing welfare state.[11] The more recent *Fabian Essays in Socialist Thought*, edited by Ben Pimlott, offers an eclectic recipe for the revival of socialism.[12] But what gives it unity and purpose is the prevailing belief that Labour will

[9]J. E. Cronin, *Labour and Society in Britain 1918–1979* (London, Batsford Academic and Education, 1984), chapter 9.

[10]P. Whiteley, 'The Decline of Labour. Local Party Membership and Electoral Base, 1945–79', in D. Kavanagh, ed., *The Politics of the Labour Party* (London, George Allen & Unwin, 1982).

[11]R. H. S. Crossman, 'Towards a Philosophy of Socialism', in R. H. S. Crossman, ed., *New Fabian Essays* (London, 1952), pp. 1–32.

[12]B. Pimlott, ed., *Fabian Essays in Socialist Thought* (London, Heinemann Educational, 1984).

best survive and develop if it holds to the views of the Left and develops policies which extend beyond the mere application of Clause Four. There is little in it to suggest that reducing the existing socialist programme of Labour will bring about the party's revival and much to recommend the development of socialist ideas. Indeed, it is salutary to reflect, as does Ben Pimlott in his illuminating opening essay, that monetarism was marginal to Conservative policies in 1979 but soon came to occupy the centre stage of politics when the level of debate was raised. In the best Fabian tradition, the various essayists contradict each other in charting their separate courses. Yet certain strands do emerge. Most obviously there is the conviction that socialists should rid themselves of market economics. Additionally, there is the general acceptance of the need to revive the spirit of brotherhood, fellowship and equality combined with the concern to temper the notion of the socialist state being bureaucratic.

James Cronin has taken this type of view further and suggested that there needs to be a positive attempt to develop the policies of the Labour party to meet the demands of the skilled working class, the lower white-collar workers and women, in order to secure or win back their vote. His argument is that the party has failed to attend to their needs for more than 30 years and stuck firmly, despite the Gaitskellite attempts to challenge it, to Clause Four and the demand for public ownership. In essence, he argues that the Labour party has ossified and defaulted upon the development of policies towards home ownership, taxation and equal pay which are of interest to some sections of society who have demonstrated their willingness to support Labour.

> By the 1950s Labour ceased to offer a compelling reformist vision or even a clear alternative to the Tories. Its middle-class supporters soon began to swing back and forth between Labour and the Conservatives depending on the fickle perceptions of the moment, and its working-class base to alternate between abstention and reluctant support. This was not due, however, to the disintegrating effect of social change upon class structure. Rather, from 1950 until the mid 1970s, Britain exhibited a pattern of structural change whose undiluted political effect could well have been to maintain, or possibly increase, Labour support. For example, the maintenance of full employment and the moderate pace of growth cushioned the impact of industrial shifts upon the economy, the occupational structure and working-class communities. This allowed trade-unions – the main correlate of Labour Party voting – to adapt to the changing composition of the working class and to maintain and even slightly increase their membership.[13]

[13]Cronin, *Labour and Society in Britain*, p. 13.

Interestingly, in analysing the evolution of working-class communities Cronin stresses that they are multi-layered and susceptible to many forces and that there have been many shifting connections between the workers, the trade unions and the Labour party. It was never possible to assume a virtual identity between class membership, participation in class-based organizations and support for class politics.[14] Nevertheless, the Labour party did well out of class politics and Cronin reminds us that consumerism is just one of the many forces which reshape, rather than change, the structure and ambitions of the working class: it doesn't make them less inclined to vote Labour if that party continues to provide the lead. The fragmentation of the working class alone cannot, to Cronin, account for Labour's electoral decline.

Cronin's views are strongly supported by others. Susan Perrigo has stressed the limited response of the Labour party towards equality of pay and opportunity for women.[15] Paul Whiteley has argued that the 'dealignment' of the working class from the Labour party is explained by its reluctance to represent adequately the objectives of its supporters.[16] Ivor Crewe has also suggested as much.[17]

From the outset, Cronin rejects the Gaitskellite revisionist ideas as being far too simple. The problem was not that change was occurring and that Labour needed to drop some of its old shibboleths, such as Clause Four, but that Labour had failed to develop and extend its policies to incorporate all those sections of society which were prepared to vote for it and had not correctly assessed the changes in class which had taken place. In Cronin's view, the Labour party stuck firmly to its roots in the past, the leadership was cautious and defensive, and throughout the 1950s and the 1960s the Labour party was unable to develop new plans and offer new policies.[18] It is thus the conservatism of the trade unions which has restricted the Labour party from moving beyond the conception of socialism as being the effective implementation of Clause Four.

Although trade unionism has had its passionate defenders it is clear that the excesses of trade unionism have formed another, the fifth, explanation of Labour's recent political decline. Ivor Crewe has stressed that the 'dealignment' of the working class and support for the Labour party was not due to the narrowing of any ideological gap, nor was it due to the rising affluence of the working class, but rather it came as a consequence of the unpopularity of trade unions between the mid

---

[14]*Op. cit.,* pp. 13–15.
[15]S. Perrigo, 'Socialist – Feminism and the Labour Party: Some Experiences from Leeds', *Feminist Review*, 23 (June 1986), p. 102.
[16]P. Whiteley, *The Labour Party in Crisis* (London, Methuen, 1983).
[17]I. Crewe, B. Sarlvik and J. Alt, 'Partisan Dealignment in Britain, 1964–1975', *British Journal of Political Science* 7 (1977), pp. 146–7.
[18]Cronin, *Labour and Society in Britain*, pp. 173–83.

1960s and 1970s.[19] There was a general feeling that they were exerting 'too much power' and that, contrary to reality, the Labour party was drifting to the left. To many, according to Crewe, it seemed that Labour was not the party which they had grown up with. The miners' strikes of 1972 and 1974 were pivotal in this changing pattern of attitudes, as would have been the 'winter of discontent' of 1978–79 had Crewe's analysis extended that far. A. J. Taylor, M. Holmes, and many others, concur.[20]

It is fair to suggest that the inability of the Labour governments to control the trade unions had contributed to the loss of electoral support for Labour. Yet, of course, it would be impossible to envisage the continued existence of the Labour party as a mass party without trade-union support. The crux of the matter is that the party has to balance the fact that trade unions are vital to its existence against the equally important fact that Labour governments have to represent the electorate rather than the unions. The trade unions have normally been prepared to subordinate their economic and industrial demands to the need to return the Labour party to office and have generally accepted the need for impartiality to be shown by Labour governments. But their acceptance of the separateness of Labour governments depended upon a *quid pro quo* – the Labour governments would not seek to restrict their freedom to negotiate and would allow them to conduct industrial bargaining in the way they wished. Taylor suggests that Barbara Castle's White Paper, *In Place of Strife* (1969), threatened that relationship and that the 'Social Contract' of the mid and late 1970s loosened the trade union – party link between 1974 and 1979. More than this, many workers, who had once deferred to both trade union and Labour leadership, now consciously recoiled from their old ties as a result of what they saw as the industrial anarchy of the late 1970s. Wilson and Callaghan might have put the boot into the workers at this time but many felt that the unions had kicked out against the patriotic necessity to save Britain from economic ruin.

The obvious economic failures of Britain since the 1960s, the ineffectiveness of Labour governments, and the apparent shortcomings of the welfare state have produced a sixth type of explanation for Labour's decline – the belief that the rising disenchantment with the ways in which the Beveridge-inspired welfare state has developed has reduced Labour's political support. Whilst it is true that some socialists and feminists have been critical in this way, it is the New Right which has been the most vociferous opponent of Beveridge and the welfare

[19]Crewe, Sarlvik and Alt, 'Partisan Dealignment'.
[20]A. J. Taylor, *The Trade Unions and the Labour Party* (London, Croom Helm, 1987); M. Holmes, *The Labour Government 1974–79: Political Aims and Economic Reality* (New York, St Martin's Press, 1985).

state. It would appear that their views have gained much political support since the early 1970s and that, in Thatcher's Britain, they have succeeded in breaking the post-war political consensus, based upon the welfare state, which has done much to sustain the Labour party.

The post-war welfare state was constructed on the assumption that the state was able to manage the British economy and specifically to maintain the condition of 'full employment'. The recession of the 1970s and 1980s had the effects of reviving mass unemployment and of undermining the belief in Keynesian techniques in economic management by the state. Partly as a result of that recession, governments since the early 1970s have been preoccupied with state expenditure and the 'problem' of how to reduce it. What is also clear is that the failures and weaknesses of the welfare state have left it open to the criticism that it is an unhappy compromise, to which few owed political allegiance, rather than the all-embracing brave new world to which all must attest.[21]

The basis of the thinking of the New Right is the work of the Austrian economist Friedrich von Hayek, most particularly his book *The Road to Serfdom* (1944).[22] In this book, dedicated to 'Socialists of all parties', Hayek sets out the dangers which the growth of socialism posed to individual freedom. Identifying socialism as the political twin of fascism, Hayek argued that socialism was a pathway to totalitarianism, for it offered economic and social security which held hidden dangers: 'when security is understood in too absolute a sense, the general striving for it, far from increasing the chances of freedom, becomes the gravest threat to it.'[23] These views were revived and revised by Rhodes Boyson in his collection of essays *Down with the Poor* (1971) and given some support by the actions of the Heath government of 1970–74, which aimed to restrict the powers of trade unions and encourage private enterprise by freeing it from state restrictions.[24] Boyson referred to the end of paternalism and clearly stated that 'Not only is the present welfare state inefficient and destructive of personal liberty, individual responsibility and moral growth, but it saps the collective moral fibre of our people as a nation'.[25] Since the mid 1970s, Margaret Thatcher and Keith Joseph have promoted the Conservative party's 'conversion' to monetarism, free-market principles and a *laissez-faire* view of society. The philosophy of the New Right, which was of marginal importance in the 1960s, has been at the centre-stage of British politics for the last decade. One central theme, evident during the Thatcher

[21]J. Clarke, A. Cochrane and C. Smart, *Ideologies of Welfare: From Dreams to Dissillusion* (London, Hutchinson, 1987), chapters 10 to 13.
[22]Clarke, Cochrane and Smart, *Ideologies of Welfare*, pp. 118–23.
[23]*Op. cit.*, p. 119.
[24]*Op. cit.*, p. 130–4.
[25]*Op. cit.*, p. 133.

administrations has been the freeing of enterprise and initiative from the interference of the state. This has meant that state expenditure on welfare has had to be cut. As Keith Joseph once wrote, 'Cuts mean cuts'.[26]

For more than a decade then, the views of the New Right have been gathering support. The promotion of this new philosophy of 'independence' is supposed to bring with it a whole array of benefits. It re-invigorates the economy; it encourages competition; it fosters moral strength and character; it removes the need for the welfare state; it revitalizes the family and regenerates self-discipline. This new philosophy appears to have strengthened and stabilized support for the Conservative party. For the Labour party, so clearly identified as the party of the welfare state, it appears to have produced the opposite result, especially in the climate of the 1970s when Labour governments were facing serious difficulties in financing the burden of welfare measures. Taken with other factors, then, it is possible that the growth of the New Right philosophy and the problems of the welfare state have cost the Labour party votes. Indeed, Peter Jenkins, in his recent book, *Mrs Thatcher's Revolution: The Ending of the Socialist Era* (1987), has suggested that the bankruptcy of the Croslandite dream of social welfare sustained by growth, and of growth driven by managerial efficiency, finally tipped the scales in favour of Thatcher's New Right philosophy and against the Labour party.[27] From the mid 1970s onwards, when the Croslandite dream began to fade, Mrs Thatcher focused upon her concern for the war years, and on the restrictions of the 1940s. Hence her contemporary attempt to set the people free.

Some historians of the Right have been quick to endorse Thatcher's philosophy through their examination of the Second World War. In chapters 6 and 7, it was stressed that Barnett, Blake and Beloff had all reflected upon the burden which the Beveridge-inspired welfare state had imposed upon Britain.[28] Barnett made it quite clear that the vain, opinionated and arrogant Beveridge, and the civil servants, forced upon Britain a system of welfare provision which even wartime surveys suggested she would be unable to sustain.[29] The 'New Jerusalem' could not be afforded and its acceptance by the wartime government helped to cause Britain's protracted decline as an industrial country after the Second World War.[30] According to Barnett, the 'illusion of

[26]K. Joseph, *Monetarism is not enough* (London, Centre for Policy Studies, 1977), quoted in Clarke, Cochrane and Smart, *Ideologies of Welfare*, p. 133.
[27]P. Jenkins, *Mrs Thatcher's Revolution: The Ending of the Socialist Era* (London, Jonathan Cape, 1987).
[28]C. Barnett, *The Audit of War: The Illusion & Reality of Britain as a Great Nation* (London, Macmillan, 1986); M. Beloff, *Wars and Welfare* (London, Edward Arnold, 1984); R. Blake, *The Decline of Power 1915–1964* (London, Granada, 1985).
[29]Barnett, *Audit of War*, pp. 26–9, 276–304.
[30]*Op. cit.*, pp. 1–8.

limitless possibility', which arose in the war, was due to two basic
fallacies – that Britain had won the war because she had organized her
economy successfully, and that she was industrially and technologi-
cally developed. Both were misleading assumptions and 'the burdens
of the New Jerusalem were not being wished on a first-class modern
industrial system well able to bear the weight but on one which even in
the crisis of total war had manifested the classic symptoms of what was
later to be dubbed the "British disease".'[31] Thus, in Barnett's estimation, the New Right has no alternative but to redress the past, and
sweep away the old political 'consensus'. According to Peter Jenkins,
this has been accomplished at the expense of the Labour party.[32]

The spectrum of political opinion covered by these various interpretations is wide. In the first place, it could be argued that parliamentary
socialism can never be achieved, except within the context of wartime
patriotism. Secondly, it could be argued that Labour declined because
it failed to implement Clause Four in the 1950s or because it has failed
to extend it since. Thirdly, it is possible that the growing affluence of
the electorate and the changing composition of the workforce has
served to undermine and fragment the traditional working-class
support for the party. Fourthly, it may well be that the party's failure
has arisen from its reluctance to develop the socialist, or even
Labourist, policies which might have attracted the political support of
women, the skilled workers, the new middle class and those sections of
society who are not fixed simply on the application and extension of
Clause Four. Fifthly, it could be that the fragmentation of the trade-
union support for Labour and the reaction of workers against some of
the excesses of trade-union power have served to lose Labour support.
The poor record of the Wilson and Callaghan governments within this
context may have simply convinced a substantial majority of the
electorate that the Labour party is simply not fit to govern. Sixthly, it is
possible that the rising support for the views of the New Right has
deprived the Labour party of the backing it gained from being the
party most closely identified with the post-war political 'consensus' in
favour of the welfare state. More than likely it is the conflation of a
number of these factors which offers a comprehensive explanation for
Labour's loss of electoral support – although any answer must look to
the loss of the vote of the skilled worker, the changing attitudes of the
working class and the difficulties which Labour governments have had
in dealing with the trade-union movement. It is, after all, because of
the changes and problems that Labour's vision of building upon the
socialist achievements of the 1940s now seems more distant than ever
and why the philosophy of the New Right and Thatcher's vision of a
property-owning democracy have seemed more attractive.

[31] Op. cit., p. 51.
[32] Jenkins, Mrs Thatcher's Revolution.

Sources

Any interpretation of Labour's recent political decline is fraught with difficulties. Apart from the obvious problems of assessing the changing mood of the electorate, the political record for these years is far from complete. The 30-year rule means that Cabinet records and government papers are not yet available for the Labour governments of the 1960s and the 1970s. This does not mean that there are no strong indications of what went on in Cabinet, or that historians are unaware of the major issues which have convulsed Labour cabinets and divided the Labour party. The problem is the partiality of such evidence.

The diaries and accounts of participating politicians provide one of the most useful, yet also one of the most partial sources. In recent years there have been many instances of the instant revelation, 'sneer and tell all' type of diary. The Crossman diaries, the Castle diaries, and many others, have provided a good indication of what has happened in Labour cabinets since the 1960s. For instance, the real battles, fears and illusions connected with the 'Social Contract', as arranged between the Labour government of 1974–76 and the TUC, are fully explored in *The Castle Diaries 1974–76* and, from another perspective, by Harold Wilson in *Final Term: The Labour Government of 1974–76.*[33] But readers must be sceptical of the big self-serving element of these accounts.

Political diarists are always participants, or close observers, of what they describe. The very nature of their contribution is that of having a very personal interest in the events they cover and of protecting their own reputations. The later publication of diaries often allows the authors the benefits of hindsight, which might well allow them to hide accuracy and truth. Tony Benn, for instance, has recently reflected upon the events of 16 March 1955, when the PLP withdrew the whip from Aneurin Bevan. He noted that there are now five accounts, in books and diaries, of the events of that day by those who were present.

> For accounts of that historical meeting of the Parliamentary Labour Party which expelled Nye, feature in Hugh Dalton's diary, he having hoped to provoke Nye into resigning from the party; and in Michael Foot's book, himself being Nye's closest associate. It was also written about by Hugh Gaitskell who thought Attlee was unduly weak and was already planning his own leadership bid to replace him as Leader, as he did later in the year; by Dick Crossman, who was by then somewhere in the middle, and by me, who sat and wrote copious notes throughout the whole meeting . . .

[33]B. Castle, *The Castle Diaries 1974–76* (London, Weidenfeld & Nicolson, 1980); H. Wilson, *Final Term. The Labour Government of 1974–1976* (London, Weidenfeld & Nicolson, 1979).

Anyone who wished to know what happened that day could, with these five accounts in their hands, acquire a good understanding of the truth. It is not a question of trying to show whose diary is best, but to make the obvious point that the more diary entries there are covering any single event, the greater the chance that the truth will emerge.[34]

On that particular incident, it is clear that accounts and interpretations have varied. Partisan attitudes have emerged and the recollections of Gaitskell are at variance with those of Crossman and Foot. There have been, and will be, similiar disagreements on the role of Labour ministers in government for, as Tony Benn also reflected, the official Cabinet minutes and documents may well hide the truth and the substance of debate.[35]

In addition to the problem of sources, there is also the problem of interpretation. History is constantly being rewritten in the light of changing social, economic and political conditions. Much Labour history has been written within the context of the political consensus established by Beveridge and the Attlee governments. In that framework there has always been the possibility that Labour might win power, even if it might not be able to offer socialism. However, in the climate of the politics of the 1980s, when the New Right has become dominant and the whole policy of welfare politics is under question, it is difficult to perceive how Labour can easily fit into the new age of *laissez-faire* politics. As Thatcherism and the philosophy of the New Right gather support, and the electorate become less willing to reject an attack upon the welfare state as being an obscene gesture, the difficulties for the Labour party increase and perceptions change. Peter Jenkins might well be correct in his assessment that the Thatcher years represent the end of the socialist era.[36] He certainly would not be alone in his assessment. It is an estimation which, as it gathers more popular support, has been forcing Labour to look towards individual, rather than collective, socialism for the 1990s. It is an assessment which has forced Labour to re-examine its relations with the trade-union movement. It is certainly a factor in the continuing debate about Labour's political decline.

Nevertheless, whatever the current problems of the Labour party, and the inadequacy of the public record, it is clear that historians and politicians will continue to debate the root cause of its recent loss of political support. For some, that decline stems from the difficulties which the party faced in the 1950s.

[34]A. Benn, 'Writing our own History', *History Today* 37 (April, 1987), p. 12.
[35]A. Benn, 'Writing our own History', p. 12, which deals with the discussion of the writing of political diaries in a Cabinet meeting in January 1976.
[36]Jenkins, *Mrs Thatcher's Revolution*.

Bevanism v. Gaitskellism

For Miliband the crucial factor in the decline of socialism was the reluctance of the Labour party to fight for socialism between 1951 and 1955. He argues that this was largely a product of the right-wing's commitment to winning wider electoral support via the abandonment of public ownership. But equally it was the weakness of the Labour Left which permitted the Labour leaders to free-wheel on socialism:

> Throughout, parliamentary Bevanism was a mediation between the leadership and the rank and file opposition. But the parliamentary Bevanites, while assuming the leadership of the opposition, also served to blur and blunt both its strength and its extent. Themselves limited by their parliamentary and executive obligations they fell back on the politics of manoeuvre and were regularly outmanoeuvred in the process.[37]

The fact is that the Labour Left was never very effective throughout the 1950s, largely because of three main factors. In the first place, it faced the opposition of trade-union leaders – most notably Deakin of the transport workers, Williamson of the municipal workers, and Lawther of the miners. These union leaders were determined to support the Labour leaders and were opposed to disunity within the party, which they felt might have contributed to the election defeat of 1951. Secondly, the Bevanites were largely concerned with foreign affairs and defence, and neglected the more obvious erosion of socialist principles in domestic policy. Thirdly, Bevan himself, whose name was attached to all those of a critical left-wing stance towards the party, was unable to provide a clear leadership for the Left.

The Bevanites as a group consisted of 32 members in October 1951, though it is suggested that they numbered about 57 by the mid 1950s. Apart from Bevan, the chief figures were Barbara Castle, Tom Driberg, Ian Mikardo, Fenner Brockway, Jennie Lee and Richard Crossman. They had initially emerged from the 'Keep Left' group, which had been formed in 1947. By 1950, when the constituency Labour parties were growing increasingly disenchanted with Attlee's leadership, the 'Keep Left' group won more support for its advocacy of Bevan's case against prescription charges. Further impetus was given when Michael Foot and Jennie Lee, the editors of the left-wing newspaper *Tribune*, published *One Way Only* with an introduction by Aneurin Bevan, demanding a reduction in defence expenditure and the stabilization of the cost of living.

As Richard Crossman made clear in his diaries, the Bevanites met frequently in the wake of the Labour government's defeat of 1951 and, in their early meetings, considered the appeal of Brockway and Lee to

---

[37]Miliband, *Parliamentary Socialism*, p. 327.

widen their membership and not to remain 'a small exclusive group'.[38] They agreed to this, although they decided to remain a group of activists without an executive committee. But, lacking a central and unifying organization, they stood little chance of making a significant impact upon the party's policy – although, as David Howell suggests, it would be a mistake to see them as simply a parliamentary force.[39]

Nevertheless, despite support in the constituencies and within the trade-union movement, the Bevanites were unable to achieve significant success in any department of Labour policy. At the 1952 Labour party conference they managed to pass a resolution committing the party to draw up a list of key industries to be taken into public ownership. But the General Council of the TUC and NEC of the Labour party submerged this demand by advocating the need for further research on the matter.[40] The Bevanites were even less successful on the issues of British and German rearmament. In March 1952, 57 Labour MPs defied the Whips and voted against the government motion demanding reapproval for the rearmament programme in Britain. These Bevanites carried their views at the 1950 Labour party conference, when German rearmament was also opposed 'before further efforts had been made to secure the peaceful reunification of Germany'. Nevertheless, the NEC and the PLP felt confident enough to ignore the reservations of the Bevanites and to support the case for German rearmament in 1954. Thus the Bevanites were defeated and outmanoeuvred on every important principle they stood for.

It is simply not true to maintain that the Bevanites were increasing their strength and influence in the early 1950s. In 1951 they held four of the constituency party seats on the NEC, increasing the number to six between 1952 and 1954, but only at the price of accepting collective responsibility for policies which their position on the NEC did not permit them to shape. The Bevanites on the NEC – Bevan, Castle, Driberg, Mikardo, Crossman and Wilson – were powerless to give a lead to the opponents of Labour's policies and Bevan was further disadvantaged by the fact that he was a member of the Shadow Cabinet between 1952 and 1954, where he was unable to make much headway with his colleagues.

The failures of the Bevanites were further compounded by the restrictions which the party placed upon dissension. When the 57 Labour MPs had defied the party Whips in April 1952, there had been a powerful trade union demand for their expulsion from the PLP, and

[38]R. H. S. Crossman, *The Backbench Diaries of Richard Crossman*, ed., J. Morgan (London, Book Club Association, 1981), pp. 28, 31.
[39]D. Howell, *The Rise and Fall of Bevanism* (n.p., Independent Labour Publications, n.d.), pp. 14–34.
[40]TUC Annual Conference *Report*, 1953, Appendix A, pp. 475–525; Labour Party Annual Conference *Report*, 1953, pp. 61–80.

its Standing Orders, suspended in 1945, were reimposed. These prevented MPs defying the party Whip except where they could invoke a
narrowly defined 'conscience clause', a restriction which was further
strengthened by Attlee's decision to get the PLP to ban all unofficial
groups and insist upon the end of personal attacks.

Bevanism was nipped in the bud, even though Bevan resigned from
the PLP in April 1954 and gave up his seat on the NEC in order to fight
Gaitskell for the Treasuryship of the party. After his expected defeat
he turned to organizing the rank and file trade unionists and was
threatened with possible expulsion from the party in February and
March 1955 for his action of defying the decision of the PLP to support
manufacture of the hydrogen bomb. According to Crossman there was
little real possibility of his being expelled, for Attlee was too intent
upon keeping the party together.[41] But this is not the impression given
in Gaitskell's diary, where it is clear that he was discussing the possibility of making Bevan's expulsion a possible resignation issue.[42] In the
end, although the PLP withdrew the whip from Bevan, the NEC
avoided expelling him from the Labour party by one vote.[43]

By that time Bevan was isolated from the majority of the party and
increasingly at odds with his close colleagues. Bevanism had never
been more than a loose confederation of the Left, whose broad
approach to issues had focused upon one key figure. There was nothing
sacrosanct about Bevan's leadership of this group, which was, in any
case, prevented from meeting on any formal basis by Attlee's ban on
unofficial groups in 1952. In the heat of debate over the H-bomb,
Bevan had clashed with Crossman, who felt that he should declare his
intention not to form a separate party in opposition to Attlee, and with
Barbara Castle, who felt that he was jumping on her bandwagon.[44]
Even his acolytes were beginning to doubt the wisdom of his actions.

Bevan soon became a spent force as the representative of the Left
against the party machine. Following Labour's unsuccessful performance in the 1955 General Election, and the retirement of Attlee, he
was decisively defeated by Gaitskell in the Labour leadership contest
of December 1955. With his leadership hopes dashed, he soon became
reconciled to working within the party, becoming its Treasurer in
October 1956 and returning to the Shadow Cabinet, as 'Shadow'
Foreign Secretary, in November 1956. He effectively divested himself
of the title 'leader of the Left' at the 1957 Labour party conference by
attacking unilateral disarmament. This action was a devastating shock
to those who trusted in Bevan's support for unilateralism. One
Bevanite reflected that it was an 'utter repudiation of everything for

[41]Crossman, *Backbench Diaries*, p. 396.
[42]H. Gaitskell, *The Diary of Hugh Gaitskell*, ed., P. M. Williams (London, Jonathan
Cape, 1983), pp. 383, 385–94.
[43]Crossman, *Backbench Diaries*, pp. 402–5, 411–12.
[44]*Op. cit.*, pp. 396, 402.

which Nye stood for three days before'.[45] Indeed, the 1957 Labour conference as a whole saw the rapid demise of the Left's influence within the party and Crossman reflected that it was a complete victory for Gaitskell: 'After three years he has got his own interpretation of nationalization through without conceding an inch to his opponents and . . . he has maintained his position on nuclear weapons without conceding an inch more than he conceded in the Parliamentary Party'.[46] The impromptu Bevan proved no match for the revisionist Gaitskell.

Miliband is right: the Labour left was never very effective in the early 1950s and the party was certainly moving away from Clause Four and the extension of the socialist policies of the Attlee years. Whether this was the cause of Labour's decline must, however, remain conjecture. What is evident, however, is that the views of the Gaitskellites and Anthony Crossland, on the need to widen the electoral appeal of the party beyond Clause Four, did not appear to stem the tide, though it may be that the dominant presence of the clause prevented the party arresting its general electoral decline.

The Gaitskellites were able to dominate the party throughout the 1950s, though they could never remove Clause Four from the Labour constitution. They were a loose grouping of politicians who hovered around Gaitskell, including Anthony Crosland MP, John Strachey MP, and Dr Rita Hinden, who was largely responsible for editing *Socialist Commentary*, a periodical of right-wing Labour opinion which was founded in 1942. Indeed, the links between the various strands of this grouping were forged by Gaitskell, who was Treasurer of the Friends of *Socialist Commentary* between 1953 and 1955. Through his friends in the trade-union movement, he was able to secure considerable financial support for that journal.

The views of the Gaitskellites were more coherent than those of the Bevanites. On foreign policy they expressed concern about the scale of rearmament in Britain, German rearmament and the development of nuclear weapons, but on the whole approved of these measures and adopted a multilateral attitude to nuclear disarmament. On domestic issues their views tended to stem from the assumption that capitalism had been fundamentally changed as a result of the successes of the Attlee governments. Gaitskell simply accepted that nationalization was no longer vital to socialism, since the controls of government and Keynesian interventionism permitted capitalism to be controlled and since he saw nationalization as the means to the end, not the end in itself.[47] Anthony Crosland, the real intellect behind the Gaitskellite

[45]*Op. cit.*, p. 614.
[46]*Op. cit.*, p. 615.
[47]S. Haseler, *The Gaitskellites: Revisionism in the British Labour Party, 1951–1964* (London, Macmillan, 1969), chapter 5, pp. 99–111.

revisionists, was even more emphatic upon such points. His article in the *New Fabian Essays* (1952) maintained that the power which property owners had wielded had been dissipated due to the fact that industry was now run by professional managers and civil servants. This meant that there was no urgent need to nationalize industry. In addition, the proliferation of social services meant that redistribution of income through direct taxation was no longer essential.[48] Strachey made much the same point in his article.[49]

Crosland's views were further articulated in his book *The Future of Socialism* (1956), the most forceful attempt to reinterpret the meaning of socialism in the light of the changes which had taken place since 1945. He argued that the growth of democratic pressures and the rapid expansion of the economy had invalidated the Marxist theory of the inevitable collapse of capitalism for there was now full employment, a radical welfare programme and a strong trade-union movement. He also accepted that nationalization was no longer vitally important and that in future socialism must turn to the development of socialist ideals for the party could not simply defend the programme it had introduced between 1945 and 1951.

These revisionist views became more important when Gaitskell became party leader in December 1955, though they had won some ground in the early 1950s. By 1953 Labour had more or less dropped the idea of drawing up a shopping list of industries to be nationalized in favour of further research and planning. In 1957 revisionist views were reaching their zenith with the publication, and acceptance by the Labour conference, of *Industry and Society: Labour's Policy on Future Public Ownership*, a document which played down the need for further public ownership and suggested that alternative types of common ownership were possible.

It was now felt that Labour had to offer itself as a moderate and respectable party, free from class bias. According to Gaitskell, the Labour party needed to focus upon the needs of a working class which was being imbued with middle-class values. For that reason it had to play down its socialism. But to do so, as Miliband has stressed, would be to deny what was distinctive about the Labour party. Nonetheless, Gaitskell launched his major assault on the old shibboleths of the party at the Blackpool conference in 1959.

Yet Gaitskell's revisionism could only go as far as the trade unions would allow. On most matters the major trade unions accepted NEC policy but, in 1959 and 1960, they rejected Gaitskell's famous attempt to remove Clause Four from the party constitution.

---

[48]C. A. R. Crosland, 'The Transition from Capitalism', in Crossman, ed., *New Fabian Essays*, p. 38.
[49]J. Strachey, 'Task and Achievements of British Labour', in Crossman, ed., *New Fabian Essays*.

Gaitskell was motivated by Labour's defeat at the general election in 1959, reflecting that the party had performed well in the campaign but had still lost the election by more than 100 seats. He reasoned that this must be the result of the changing social and economic composition of the electorate and presented this view to the Blackpool conference in 1959:

> We may not be far from the frontier of this kind of giant State monopoly [but] . . . I cannot agree that we have reached the frontier of public ownership as a whole.
>   At the same time I disagree equally with the other extreme view that public ownership is the be all and end all, the ultimate first principle and aim of socialism.[50]

The goal to be achieved was not 100 per cent state ownership but the creation of a society in which socialist ideals could be realized.

Gaitskell's speech received a hostile reception from both the left and the right wing of the trade-union movement. Crossman had chronicled the Left's intense hostility to Gaitskell's actions and Frank Cousins, the leader of the Transport and General Workers' Union, was quick to assert that trade unions would not accept the demotion of that clause. The fact is that Clause Four remained a powerful symbol of socialism to most trade-union members, and that many trade unions had similar clauses in their own constitutions. This political defeat for Gaitskell also occurred at a time when the Labour Conference had decided to support a policy of unilateral nuclear disarmament. Though he was able to reverse that decision in favour of multilateral disarmament in 1960, he was unable to achieve much movement on Clause Four. The NEC met in March 1960 to provide a compromise statement which would satisfy both sides but reiterate Labour's attachment to Clause Four.[51] Morgan Phillips, the General Secretary of the Labour party, produced the compromise document, *Labour in the Sixties*, which was presented to, and accepted by, the party conference in 1960. It made no attempt to reject Clause Four, but argued a clear Gaitskellite line throughout:

> In the 1960s Socialism will win more support only when it is recognized that it offers a better way and that it can make a unique contribution to solving the problems of the scientific age. Brute poverty and unemployment can, happily, no longer be expected to act as the recruiting sergeants of the Labour movement. (. . .)
>   In recent years they (the opposition) have tried to present us as an old, backward-looking party – restrictionist and bureaucratic when in office, divided and quarrelling when in opposition. And

[50]Williams, *Gaitskell*, p. 324.
[51]Crossman, *Backbench Diaries*, pp. 828–30.

· we should frankly face the fact that we have sometimes given them, in our own conduct, enough evidence to make such charges stick.[52]

The attempt to revitalize the party remained the preoccupation of Gaitskell and his supporters. The demand was for a young, active and united party which would face up to the changes 'now taking place in the patterns of living, leisure and work'.[53]

The antagonism between the Bevanites and the Gaitskellites had arisen out of the differing perceptions of the way in which the Labour party could recapture power. The Bevanites had opposed what they perceived to be the retreat from socialism, convinced that in some way the development of socialist ideas and policies, firmly supported by the party, would win back Labour's lost votes. This flatly contradicted the view of the Gaitskellites who were adamant that the objective conditions of British society had changed and that Labour had to see beyond Clause Four and the support of the old working class. The problem is that neither strand offered any positive policies for the future other than the defence or the abandonment of Clause Four. In the hands of the Labour party, socialism appeared to be either a static or a waning philosophy – there was little sign of advance. That may well have been, as many of the Left remind us, the reason for Labour's electoral predicament since 1951 but it is also fair to say that society was changing and that the party failed to respond to this fact despite the adumbrations of the Gaitskellites.

A New 'Affluent' Working Class or a Frustrated Working Class?

Since 1951 the social and occupational composition of British society has changed considerably. In 1950 white-collar workers represented about 30 per cent of the workforce; by 1979 the proportion had risen to about 52 per cent.[54] Over the same period the proportion of manual workers fell from 64.2 per cent to about 45 per cent. In consequence, there has been a marked decline in the occupational groups which have traditionally been the bastions of support for the Labour party. In mining and quarrying, employment has fallen from 880,000 in 1948 to 629,000 in 1965 and about 250,000 in 1984. As a result the membership of the National Union of Mineworkers, and related unions, has shrunk. By the same token the expansion in the white-collar section

[52]M. Phillips, *Labour in the Sixties* (London, Labour Party, 1960), p. 15.
[53]Phillips, *Labour in the Sixties*, p. 17.
[54]Cronin, *Labour and Society*, pp. 147–8, 194–6.

has seen the rapid growth of union membership in that sector. The Association of Scientific, Technical and Managerial Staff rose from 123,000 members in 1970 to 427,500 in 1982.[55] The various unions of civil servants experienced a growth of membership of 266,156 between 1970 and 1982.

Some of this growth in the service and white-collar sector has been due to the rise in female employment. The female participation ratio has risen from 34.7 per cent in 1951 to 42.7 per cent in 1971 and 47.4 per cent in 1977.[56] More than one-third of women were employed in part-time work by the end of the 1970s and a large proportion were employed in the low-paid clerical sector and service industries.

Imposed upon a changing structure of employment has been a general increase in real incomes, which rose by about a quarter in the 1950s alone, and the manifestations of greater wealth – the rising demand for consumer items and the strong move towards home ownership which has meant that more than half the families of Britain, 53 per cent in 1976 and about 60 per cent in 1987, are owner-occupiers.[57] It is argued that in such a situation the traditional institutions of working-class life – the trade unions and the clubs – become rather less important and the annealing bond they give to traditional working-class life begins to break down. But does that mean that Dr Rita Hinden is correct to suggest that the Labour party would have to broaden its perspective in order to survive? Is it not possible that consumerism can be absorbed within a working class which is, after all, a multi-layered and evolving social category?

A number of surveys conducted in working-class communities during the early 1960s supported the view that affluence was undermining the class association with Labour.[58] One, based upon a study of working-class life in Luton, suggested that the changed orientation of work and community was leading to political apathy: the workplace did not encourage union collectivism and the more prosperous neighbourhoods lost the traditional communal warmth and associations of working-class communities. Consumerism apparently meant that working families spent more time in front of the television than at the club, the union or in each others' company.

Cronin quite rightly attacked these interpretations on the grounds that whilst the surface characteristics might change the fundamental

[55]Taylor, *Trade Unions and the Labour Party*, pp. 152–4.
[56]Cronin, *Labour and Society*, p. 240.
[57]*Op. cit.*, p. 199.
[58]W. G. Runciman, *Relative Deprivation and Social Injustice* (London, 1966): Goldthorpe, *et al.*, *The Affluent Worker*, 3 vols., (Cambridge, 1968–9), quoted in Cronin, *Labour and Society*, p. 169; M. N. Franklin, *The Decline of Class Voting in Britain: changes in the basis of electoral choice, 1964–1983* (Oxford, OUP, 1985); A. Heath, R. Jowell and J. Curtice, *How Britain Votes* (London, Pergamon, 1985); P. Dunleavy and C. T. Husbands, *British Democracy at the Crossroads: Voting and Party Competition in the 1980s* (London, Allen & Unwin, 1985).

Table 8.1 The trade union electorate, 1974–83

	October 1974 %	1979 %	1983 %
Trade union members (1)			
Conservative	27	33	31
Labour	55	51	29
Liberal/Alliance	16	13	20
ABC1 (upper/middle class) (2)			
Conservative	56	59	55
Labour	19	24	16
Liberal/Alliance	21	15	28
C2s (skilled workers) (3)			
Conservative	26	41	40
Labour	49	41	32
Liberal/Alliance	20	15	26
DE (semi/unskilled) (4)			
Conservative	22	34	33
Labour	57	49	41
Liberal/Alliance	16	13	24

(1) 25% of the total sample (2) 41% of the total sample
(3) 30% of the total sample (4) 29% of the total sample

Source: MORI from A. J. Taylor, *Trade Unions and the Labour Party*, p. 242.

fact remained that the Luton workforce still recognized the value of being a member of a trade union and voting for Labour. In other words, consumerism could be absorbed within working-class communities; it did not necessarily destroy those communities.

There are also other indications that the affluent worker argument is a poor explanation of Labour's decline. The most obvious is that trade-union membership continued to increase, reaching its all-time peak of about 13.5 million in 1979 – although it has since fallen to about 9.5 millions in the face of the hostile Thatcher administrations. Admittedly, the composition of trade unionism altered but the attachment of trade unions to the Labour party remained firm. Indeed, despite the erosion of support, the majority of trade unionists still voted Labour in 1979.

Yet, as Crewe, Taylor and Whiteley have noted, the association between class, union and party was beginning to break down. There has been a continuous decline in working-class and trade-union support for the Labour party since 1951 and this became increasingly obvious from the late 1960s onwards. This appears to have occurred at every level, although Crewe has suggested that it was reversed amongst the semi-skilled and unskilled category in the 1987 General

Table 8.2 Electoral support for Labour, 1964–79

Election	Mana-gerial and profess-ional	Lower middle class	Skilled manual	Semi-skilled and unskilled	Women	Overall Lab.	Con.
1964	9	25	54	59	39	44	43
1966	15	20	58	65	48	48	42
1970	10	30	55	57	45	43	45
1974 (Feb)	10	21	47	54	37	38	39
1974 (Oct)	12	24	49	57	38	39	36
1979	18	21	47	55	39	38	46

Source: Variety of assessments by David Butler and a succession of co-authors on the British general elections 1964 to 1974 and Ivor Crewe, *The Guardian*, 13 June 1983. Taken from J. E. Cronin, *Labour and Society*, p. 205.

Election.[59] Yet why was this occurring? Certainly the underlying and persistent decline may have been due to the changes occasioned by affluence. But, whichever table is taken, it is clear that Labour's dramatic political decline accelerated at all levels from the 1970s onwards – at a time when there was economic depression. It was, perhaps, not so much the positive impact of affluence which accounted for this decline as much as the political events of the late 1960s and 1970s. It is more than mere speculation that the failure of the Labour governments to deliver their promises, especially in matters of industrial relations, damaged the credibility of the party as one of government. It is possible that there were two conflicting developments going on. In the first place, there was a reaction throughout society, and even within the ranks of skilled workers, against what was perceived to be the unchecked and unbridled demands of trade unions. Secondly, trade unionists were annoyed at the inability of the Labour governments to honour promises and to maintain a voluntary pattern of industrial relations.

Labour Governments, Trade Unions and the Collapse of the Post-War Political Consensus

The Beveridge Report of 1942 created a post-war political consensus, a climate of opinion, which favoured the creation of a welfare state. All political parties accepted that the welfare state was essential and, until the 1970s, it would have been considered obscene, unthinkable, to

[59] *The Guardian*, 15 June 1987.

Table 8.3 Party strengths in the House of Commons in general elections, 1945–79

	1945	1950	1951	1955	1959	1964	1966	1970	1974 Feb.	1974 Oct.	1979
Conservative	213	298	321	345	365	303	253	330	296	276	339
Labour	393	315	295	277	258	317	363	287	301	319	268
Liberal	12	9	6	6	9	9	12	6	14	13	11
Independent	14	—	—	—	—	1	—	—	—	—	1
Others	8	3	3	2	—		2	7	24	27	16
Total	640	625	625	630	630	630	630	630	635	635	635

Table 8.4 Percentage of votes given to the major political parties in general elections, 1945–79

General Election	Conservative	Labour	Liberal
	%	%	%
1945	39.8	47.8	9.0
1950	43.5	46.1	9.1
1951	48.0	48.8	2.5
1955	49.7	46.4	2.7
1959	49.4	43.8	5.9
1964	43.4	44.1	11.2
1966	41.9	47.9	8.5
1970	46.4	42.9	7.5
1974 Feb.	38.2	37.2	19.3
1974 Oct.	35.8	39.2	18.3
1979	43.9	36.9	13.8

have even contemplated getting rid of it. But the climate of opinion has changed radically during the last 10 or 15 years as the views of the New Right have gathered support. Correlli Barnett can now quite easily attack Beveridge, and the welfare state which he thrust upon the nation, comfortable in the knowledge that his views will be taken seriously. The fact is that the development of the welfare state has always rested upon the assumption that economic growth would continue to provide the resources essential for its effective operation. The financial crisis of the 1960s, the economic depression of the 1970s and the 1980s, the increased foreign competition have served to sow doubts about whether or not the nation can continue to support the type of universal provisions introduced by Beveridge and the post-war Attlee governments. The experiences of the Wilson and Callaghan Labour governments and the militance of trade unions have also added to these concerns.

The two Wilson administrations of 1964–66 and 1966–70, were pivotal in the process whereby the efficiency of the welfare state was called into question. At first, however, the Labour victory in the general election of 1964 appeared to restore the confidence of a party which had contemplated the possibility of never again holding office.

The transformation came, in part, from the fact that Harold Wilson had become the leader of the party on the death of Gaitskell in 1963. From the outset, he decided that Labour could no longer sustain itself on the old rhetoric of social distribution but that it had to relate its policies to the need to achieve economic growth. For this reason he accepted the need for the modernization of the British economy. There was to be a National Plan for growth by which Labour would release the pent-up forces of 'white-hot' technology. The Labour party conference of 1963 had accepted his proposal and the union agreed that they would also accept a comprehensive incomes policy.

But party programmes, such as *Labour in the Sixties* and, its successor, *Signpost for the Sixties*, offered vague and general support for Wilson's later initiatives. The latter had begun by announcing that 'We live in a scientific revolution' and followed this up by suggesting that Britain needed to harness the forces of science for the community, to supervise the balanced growth of the economy and to ensure the fair distribution of wealth.[60] The document was besotted with the belief that the scientific revolution would make everything possible.

Yet Labour's victory in the general election of 1964 did not permit the transformation which Wilson would have liked. His majority of four was too narrow to allow the initiatives which he had envisaged and, indeed, the government was faced with an economic crisis which forced it to introduce a deflationary package in 1965. Nevertheless, Labour's victory had restored much confidence to a party which was, by the late 1950s, contemplating the prospect of never again achieving office. The tremendous victory which the party achieved in the 1966 General Election, when it secured an overall majority of 96, confirmed it in its rising confidence that it was the party of power and government. It had secured for itself a sense of balance and authority. But this moment of euphoria and confidence was short-lived. By the late 1960s that mood had gone. What went wrong?

Crewe, Taylor and Livingstone have all pointed to the failure of recent Labour governments to deal effectively with the trade unions and to sustain their support amongst the skilled working classes. This was clearly the case in the late 1960s – especially after the devaluation of November 1967, and consequent public spending cuts, forced the Labour government to contemplate methods of improving the efficiency of industry and reducing the disruptive actions of trade unions.

There seems little doubt that the Wilson government of 1966 to 1970 was unable to deal effectively with the unions and that this fact served to undermine the future political prospects of the Labour party.

[60]Labour party, *Signposts for the Sixties* (London, Labour Party, 1960), p. 7.

Labour had secured trade-union support for an income policy in 1963, before it came to power, and had set up a National Board for Prices and Income in 1965. But such policies never worked effectively. Strikes, particularly the Seamen's strike of May 1966, the wage freeze of 1966, and the devaluation of the pound in 1967, destroyed the close links between the Labour government and the trade unions. The unions were in open revolt against the Labour government in 1969 when, in the wake of the Royal Commission on Trade Unions and Employers Organizations (the Donovan Commission), the government published *In Place of Strife*, a White Paper on industrial relations.

Although it offered a number of advantages to trade unions, most notably protection from 'unfair dismissal' for their members, they were sensitive to the suggestion that they would be registered and that their right to strike would be impaired.[61] The White Paper had suggested that the government might be empowered to settle inter-union disputes, that in the case of unofficial strikes the Secretary of State would have the power to issue an Order to impose a 'conciliation pause' of 28 days, and have the right to order secret ballots for official strikes which were considered to 'involve a serious threat to the economy or public interest'.[62] The whole package suggested that trade unions were no longer to be free to conduct industrial relations on the voluntary basis which they had enjoyed for almost a century in peacetime Britain. In consequence, the TUC held a special conference, mobilized its opposition to the White Paper, and even forced the NEC of the Labour party to vote against acceptance. The White Paper had to be withdrawn; the Labour government was humbled by the unions.

In its desire to make British industry more efficient the Labour government had tackled an issue on which it could only lose. If it took action against strikes then it threatened the link between class, union and party which had always been vital to its growth. If, on the other hand, it did not face up to the problem of strikes then, to the electorate at large, it demonstrated its incapacity to govern and its unwillingness to move beyond sectional interests. Was Labour to be the party of the unions or the party of the nation? The events surrounding the White Paper suggested that it might be neither. Its trade-union support certainly began to dip at this point and its credibility as a party of government was greatly diminished as wages rose sharply, to the rate of 13 per cent per annum. In this climate, Labour lost the 1970 General Election to Edward Heath's Conservative party. A Labour majority of 96 was turned into a Conservative majority of 30. The fragility of Labour's hopes and aspirations in the 1960s had been exposed by its failure to achieve significant economic growth and its failure to deal

---

[61]Taylor, *Trade Unions and the Labour Party*, p. 6; Cronin, *Labour and Society*, p. 189.
[62]*In Place of Strife: A Policy for Industrial Relations*, Cmnd 3888, Paragraphs 93–6.

effectively with the trade unions.

These problems remained in February 1974, when Labour was once again returned to office. The party had been returned to power to deal more constructively with industrial relations than the Conservatives, who had been embroiled in industrial conflict following the introduction of the Industrial Relations Act of 1971, with its measures for a 60-day 'cooling-off' period and for pre-strike ballots. But the electorate's judgement had been a negative one, for the party was returned as a minority government faced with an opposition majority against it of 33. Even the October 1974 General Election, which gave Labour an overall majority of three, was hardly evidence of the great confidence of the British electorate in the Labour party. Indeed, in 1977 as by-election defeats took their toll, the Labour government, now under the leadership of James Callaghan, was forced to make a political arrangement with the Liberal party, in order to retain power. Weak Labour governments were therefore faced with the problems of dealing more effectively with the pressing problems of curbing trade-union power, improving industrial relations, and raising the level of economic growth.

The damaging impression that Labour could not deal with the trade unions remained a serious threat to its political future, and a constant worry for Labour leaders. Although the government account of events is not available until early next century, the records of the TUC and the published diaries and books of those ministers who were close to the events provide us with strong, if partial, indications of the pattern of events surrounding the emergence and failure of the 'Social Contract'. They have been used by Cronin, Price, Taylor, Coates and Holmes, to demonstrate the failure of this policy and the bankruptcy of labourism – the reformist policies offered by the Wilson and Callaghan administrations.[63] Despite their wide range of opinions, they all concur upon this point.

The fact is that the Labour governments were never able to sustain economic growth at the rate which was required, partly because of the difficulties it faced in dealing with industrial relations. This was not from a lack of hope and good intent by both the Labour party and the trade-union movement. Wilson had appealed for the unions 'to accept the economic realities and understand the political responsibilities we face in Government'.[64] Trade union leaders were quick to respond and even the normally cautious Hugh Scanlon of the Amalgamated Union of Engineering workers acknowledged the need for unity: 'There had

[63]Cronin, *Labour and Society;* R. F. Price, *Labour in British Society* (London, Croom Helm, 1986); Taylor, *Trade Unions and the Labour Party;* D. Coates, *Labour in Power: A Study of the Labour Government 1974–1979* (London, Longman, 1980); Holmes, *The Labour Government 1974–1979.*

[64]Labour Party Conference *Report,* 1971, p. 165, quoted in Taylor, *Trade Unions and the Labour Party,* p. 9.

been too much blood letting, too much acrimony, too much dissillusionment – and trade unions were not blameless in this – with all the harmful effects that accrued in June 1970, for these mistakes ever to be repeated again.'[65]

The Labour party and the TUC moved towards rapprochment, and *Labour's Programme for Britain*, adopted at the party conference at Blackpool in 1973, recognized the need to establish a balance between full employment, economic growth, a healthy balance of payments and moderate levels of inflation. To make the whole process work effectively, trade unions had to accept a voluntary incomes policy whilst government would redistribute income and resources on an annual basis. The Labour programme recognized that: 'there is need for a far-reaching *social contract* between workers and the government – a contract which can be renewed each year as circumstances change and as new opportunities present themselves'.[66]

Such accord was short-lived once the Labour government came to office. At first it appeared that the government was attempting to make it work when compulsory wage restraint, imposed by Heath's government, was jettisoned in July 1974, a new Ministry of Prices, Consumer Protection and Fair Trading was established, and food subsidies were introduced in Denis Healey's first budget. The Industrial Relations Act was also repealed. As Barbara Castle suggests, in her published diaries, the Cabinet and Wilson were intent upon playing it straight down the line of agreed party policy, at least until the spring of 1975, when inflationary pressures became too great.[67] But Castle, the architect of *In Place of Strife*, perceived that there might be penalties to pay in adopting a voluntary policy at a time of balance of payment difficulties. She was right.

Coates, Taylor, Holmes, and other writers of both the Left and the Right, have traced the decline of the 'Social Contract'. They all agree that it occurred quickly. Taylor suggests that it effectively broke down in July 1975, when the £6 wage rise limit, with a zero increase for those above £8,500 per annum, was imposed. Coates, on the other hand, suggests that it survived a little longer but that it had more or less ceased to be meaningful by 1977:

> When the government had reached the point, as it had in the summer of 1977, of publicly leaving the design of the next stage of the incomes policy to the TUC, only to find the TUC unwilling and unable to cooperate in this way, it is hardly surprising that people like Professor S. E. Finer could begin 'to wonder whether free collective bargaining [was] still compatible with the traditional practices of parliamentary democracy . . . and

[65]Taylor, *Trade Unions and the Labour Party*, pp. 9–10.
[66]*Op. cit.*, p. 25.
[67]Castle, *The Castle Diaries 1974–1976*, pp. 85, 121, 224, 252–6.

to wonder what, if this [was] the case, parliamentary democracy [could] do about it'.[68]

Whichever view is taken, and there are grounds to support both, it is clear that the process of breakdown had begun early in the life of the 1970s Labour governments.

The reasons for the collapse of the voluntary incomes policy are less subject to debate: the Labour government's failure to achieve economic growth against a background of rising unemployment and inflation had forced it to abandon its promises of increasing public control over private industry and of extending and improving social welfare measures. Unemployment rose from 678,000 to 1,129,000 during the course of 1975, at a time of rising inflation. The government panicked and, as early as April 1975, introduced an austerity budget which transferred resources from the public to the private sector and reduced public expenditure spending for 1977–78 by £900 millions, at the expense of about 20,000 jobs. This was followed by the £6 wage limit in July 1975. The Labour government had returned to an old-style incomes policy and matters grew worse when Denis Healey, the Chancellor of the Exchequer, was forced to approach the International Monetary Fund to secure a massive loan. When the deal was struck in December 1975, the Labour government was faced with the necessity of pruning government expenditure by a further £2,500 million in order to secure a loan of £3,000 million. The Labour government was forced to abandon any idea of extending public control, and this view became entrenched once it was forced to come to a political arrangement with the Liberal party in 1977.

Inevitably, industrial relations grew worse, though it was not until the autumn of 1978 that the TUC formally decided to return to free collective bargaining and rejected totally any wage restraint.[69] Amidst a climate of rising unemployment and reduced public expenditure, industrial unrest rocketed in the autumn of 1978 and early 1979. The 'winter of discontent' put paid to any hopes that Labour had of winning the 1979 General Election.

It is Taylor's view that the débâcle of the 'Social Contract', and its obvious failure in the 'winter of discontent' was predictable, and hence avoidable. It happened, nonetheless, because of the failure of both the trade unions and the party to realize the extent to which their fates were inextricably linked up with the need to achieve an understanding which would stimulate economic growth. This seems a realistic assessment of the 1970s Labour governments, especially given the swift abandonment of their commitment to the 'Social Contract'. The Labour governments expected the benefits of trade-union

[68]Coates, *Labour in Power*, p. 202.
[69]Taylor, *Trade Unions and the Labour Party*, pp. 101–3; Holmes, *The Labour Government 1974–1979*, pp. 126–30.

Table 8.5 Industrial conflict, 1974–81

Year	Industrial conflict		Working days lost (000s)	Union organization	
	Strikes	Workers directly involved		Union membership (000s)	Union density %
1974	2,922	1,161	14,750	11,764	50.4
1975	2,282	570	6,012	12,026	51.0
1976	2,016	444	3,284	12,386	51.9
1977	2,703	785	10,142	12,846	53.4
1978	2,471	725	9,405	13,112	54.2
1979	2,080	4,121	29,474	13,447	55.4
1980	1,330	702	11,964	12,947	53.6
1981	1,338	1,326	4,266	12,182	51.0

Source: J. E. Cronin, Labour and Society, p. 242.

co-operation without accepting the responsibilities which that involved. However, their record of default was hardly exceptional.

Indeed, except for the years 1945–51, Labour governments have shown an enormous gap between promise and performance. The major policy failure of the 1960s and 1970s was in the area of economic management. Labour had come to power with policies designed to address this problem but never really came to terms with the changes that had occurred in the class structure and working-class expectation since the 1940s. On the one hand, there were enormous increases in the material well-being of the working class and the demand that they continue. On the other hand, there remained strong opposition to the inequalities of class society. The continued loss of working-class activists and voters appears to have resulted from Labour's failure adequately to address either of these issues.

It may be futile to argue whether more or less radical programmes would have retained or increased the political appeal of Labour, for the primary obstacle to the mobilization of political support for Labour was the contrast between its promise and its achievements in office. This may help to explain the declining support for nationalization as a policy which, in any case, has not substantially altered the position of the worker. Perhaps the most serious failure, though, was the seemingly cynical abandonment of the 1974 programme soon after the Labour party had taken office, when its rapid retreat into conventional and conservative economic and social programmes revealed its ultimate political bankruptcy. The heady optimism of the early 1970s, that the Labour party in power could use its close relationship with the trade-union movement and its declared intention to use state intervention to create a more equal society in which employment was secure and economic growth sustained, had gone by 1979, if not earlier. In 1976, the *Guardian* had detected that the government was having difficulty in financing its growing social expenditure, noting that 'popular expectations about improvements in welfare programmes and public service have not been matched by any willingness to give up improvements in living standards in favour of these programmes'.[70] The issue was quite clear, the Labour government could not sustain its welfare programme without increasing taxation, and thus the cost of living, and threatening the very trade-union members whose voluntary agreement to limit wage increases was vital if industrial costs were to be kept down and if confidence in the pound was to be maintained. In the end, the poor financial position of the Labour government, a weak pound, and slow industrial growth forced the abandonment of the voluntary incomes policy and cutbacks in social and welfare measures. These were actions which the Labour party's most militant ertswhile trade-union supporters found difficult to accept.

The Labour governments of the 1960s and 1970s failed to encourage rapid economic growth, did not deliver their promises and found themselves embroiled in conflict with the unions. Out of these failures emerged support for the views of the New Right – whose policies of cutting state expenditure, shaking out surplus labour, and of unleashing the traditional forces of liberal capitalism did not seem out of tune with the actions of the 1970s Wilson and Callaghan governments, which had presided over welfare cuts and rising unemployment. The unthinkable had happened. The welfare state was no longer sacrosanct. As Price has suggested, it was out of the ashes of the Callaghan government that emerged the political possibilities of the Thatcher era.[71] From 1979 onwards, Margaret Thatcher has been willing to tackle the discredited unions because she does not need them for her economic policies and owing to the fact that many unionists doubted the wisdom of industrial action. She has been able to undermine the welfare state because people of all political persuasions have noted its failings. She has been able to sustain the notion of unfettered *laissez-faire* capitalism as a substitute for the welfare state. The changes in the law she has initiated, such as the legislation of 1980 and 1982 prohibiting the secondary boycott and picket, have helped to remove trade-union immunities. Together with mass unemployment, the anti-welfare state measures, and the privatizing direction of government policy, the attack upon unions represents a radical attempt to alter the basic balance of political power and industrial relations. More fundamentally, it represents an attack upon the political consensus which has hitherto dominated post-war politics, a consensus which has focused upon the maintenance of the welfare

---

[70]*Guardian*, 20 February 1976, quoted in Coates, *Labour in Power*, p. 24.
[71]Price, *Labour and British Society*, p. 245.

state. The policies of the Thatcher government represent an attempt to erect a political economy of power relations between labour, the state and society which will prevent the possibility of the balance of power that came out of the Second World War ever being repeated. The justification for this strategy is that it is the only way to ensure that Britain achieves a new phase of economic growth.

Yet the political triumph of the New Right philosophy is a complex matter and has been dependent upon a deeply divided set of opposition forces, and in the 1983 General Election (for example) on what was virtually a 50/50 split in the popular vote between Labour and the Alliance. The failures of Labour governments in the past, the difficulties posed by trade unions, and the changing aspirations of the working class have also contributed to its success. In future, the entrenchment of a new political consensus based upon *laissez-faire* politics and economics might well help to ensure the Labour party's continued political weakness.

Conclusion

As nemesis threatens the Labour party it is clear that no one explanation can account for the recent decline in its political fortunes. It is hardly fair, as Miliband suggests, to write off Labour's political future on the basis that it did not push strongly enough for the extension of socialism in the early 1950s, but other explanations seem far more plausible. It is obvious that the changing structure of British industry and the contraction of the manufacturing industries have led to the reduction of Labour's traditional working-class support. In addition there has been the loosening of the ties between the trade unions and the Labour party, occasioned by the industrial conflict of the late 1960s and the late 1970s. The economic and political failures of the Wilson and Callaghan governments of the 1970s certainly engendered much frustration at the reformist, or labourist, policies of the party and called into question whether or not economic growth could be sustained through Labour's policies and whether or not a fundamental change in direction was called for. All these factors diminished the Labour party and called into question the political consensus of welfare politics, upon which its post-war successes had been gained. Out of Labour's dismal record in office under Wilson and Callaghan has arisen increasing support for the New Right philosophy which is now attempting to marginalize the politics of the welfare state, thus diminishing the prospects for Labour's political recovery.

Yet the most fundamental reason for Labour's decline, underpinning most other factors, has been the unwillingness of the party to adapt to the changing nature of British society. The old shibboleths, based upon the trade-union objective of a fairer treatment for the working class, have been trotted out at successive general elections, despite the fact that the Labour party is a predominantly middle-class party in Parliament. Gaitskell and the revisionists perceived the need to break the class image of the party in the 1950s and did urge it to offer policies which would attract support from all the social classes. This attempt, just like Bevan's campaign to place socialism at the front of Labour party policies, foundered on the rock of trade unionism. The culmination of Labour's failure to recognize the need for change was the formation of the Social Democratic party in 1981, which saw four of Labour's right-wingers – Shirley Williams, Roy Jenkins, Bill Rodgers and David Owen – form a party which offered policies geared to the needs of the lower middle-class and the professional workers. This has indeed fractured the support which the Labour party enjoyed by stripping it off some of the lower middle-class, and skilled working-class, support it once enjoyed.

The dilemma in which the Labour party now finds itself is that it has been thrust back to its trade-union and working-class base at a time when that base is rapidly contracting. Yet, it cannot abandon its diminishing trade-union base to capture wider support without losing the financial resources upon which it depends.

In order to recapture its former political position the Labour party will have to recognize the essential qualities which led to its initial growth – the continuing relationship with the trade unions and the working class combined with a willingness to compromise. In its early years, the Labour party depended upon its sensitivity to social change and a strong sense of pragmatism. This is what is called for now. In the first place, this may mean offering the type of policies, on taxes and housing, which might appeal to skilled workers and the working class in the South as well as the North. Secondly, it will have to make its peace with the non-union electorate by demoting, though not removing, trade unionism within the party. Taylor believes that only a massive restructuring of the party and the unions offers a prospect of the Labour party ever forming a majority government again.[72] The dilemma for Labour is that, in an increasingly conservative climate, it needs to convince the electorate of the credibility of its remedies at the very moment when the depth of British decline requires that these remedies be very radical indeed. The only hope, according to Taylor, is for the Labour party and the trade unions to strike up a new, revitalizing, relationship – for without it the Labour party will dwindle to the margins of politics.

Neil Kinnock appears to have recognized both necessities in the recent changes he has been making, although his pragmatic rather than overtly socialist approach has already earned him the epithet 'Ramsay McKinnock'. But it is possible that the commitment to change has

[72]Taylor, *Trade Unions and the Labour Party*, concluding section.

come too late. As the hope of building up a socialist state upon the bedrock of the Attlee administrations has faded under the Wilson and Callaghan administrations, we now see an experiment with the policies of the New Right and an attempt to create the Thatcherite property-owning democracy. The Labour party has lost out in this change and, in 1983, the *Economist* gloomily predicted that 'An aspiring Labour member of parliament must now find a decaying city centre with high unemployment, an ageing population and an air of despair. It is not much of a basis for a party of the future.'[73] This is the haunting prospect which faces the Labour party as it wrestles with the *laissez-faire* policy of the New Right, unless it can regain the working-class support it once enjoyed and, at the same time, broaden its appeal. The unfortunate fact for the Labour party is that its failure to respond to social and economic change in the past might yet condemn it to political oblivion. The lack of clear and attractive political policies and the failure fundamentally to change the relationship between the trade unions and the party are not a good basis upon which to sustain and build a dynamic and successful party of government. Yet without such changes, and in the light of its recent difficulties, it may well become only an historical curiosity. Indeed, as Jenkins suggests, the socialist era may have already come to an end.[74]

[73] *The Economist*, 18 June 1983, p. 27, quoted in Taylor, *Trade Unions and the Labour Party*, p. 252.
[74] Jenkins, *Mrs Thatcher's Revolution*.

POSTSCRIPT

The study of British Labour history has come a long way in the course of the twentieth century. Historians no longer accept, without question, the assumptions of the Webbs and Dangerfield, who offered an almost Whiggish interpretation of the inevitable and steady growth of the Labour movement and the Labour party. They now demur at the sweeping statements of national histories which make little concession to the burgeoning evidence of local and regional surveys, and they draw increasingly upon the 'low politics' of the rank and file.

There have been two main stimuli for these changes. The first, and most obvious, is that the records of Labour history are now more readily accessible and available. Numerous manuscript collections have found their way to the PRO, the British Library, the Labour history collection at Warwick University, and similar institutions, during the last two decades. In addition, the Cabinet Minutes and departmental records of the first four Labour governments are now available for consultation at the PRO. The publication of numerous diaries and autobiographies by ex-Labour ministers, and prime ministers, also provide a good indication of what has happened in Labour cabinets since the 1960s. These rich seams of new information mean that historians have had to modify their conception of events – although in Labour history, more than most other forms of history, ideological perspectives tend to override and accommodate new information.

Secondly, there has been an increasing tendency to produce regional and local histories. This began to occur more than a quarter of a century ago when Asa Briggs edited a collection of *Chartist Studies* and appealed for more local research into Chartism. At more or less the same time, E. P. Thompson was encouraging similar work on the early years of the ILP and the Labour party through his observation, in his article 'Homage to Tom Maguire', that the ILP grew from the bottom up. In the wake of this type of stimulus, research degrees, articles and books began to provide regional perspectives of Labour's growth, although no detailed constituency study was published until David Clark's *Colne Valley: Radicalism to Socialism* appeared in 1981.

If the focus of Labour history has changed, however, that does not mean that we have a full understanding, a synthesis, or a generally acceptable account of the changing fortunes of the Labour party. Ideological considerations cut across such a possibility, and many questions remain to be debated and modified in the years to come as local archives, as well as the national archives, are besieged by would-be Labour historians brandishing the historical bibles of their mentors.

There are also many deficiencies in the type and emphasis of research. For instance, whilst a large number of regional and local studies have appeared on Labour history for the pre-1914 period it is only recently that the inter-war years have been subjected to such scrutiny. There is almost a block on such research for the post-1945 years due to the fact that most Labour. party records, where they survive in a continuous form, are restricted from use beyond the 1950s. There is also still very little research on the working class and its relationship to the Labour party and little more than an institutionalized understanding of the relationship between trade unionists and the Labour party.

Despite these deficiencies the cumulative effect of recent research has been to throw doubt on the inevitable and inexorable growth of the Labour party and the wider Labour movement. The parliamentary decline of the Labour party since 1979, the emergence of the SDP and the attack levelled by the Conservative governments against the trade unions have reinforced this view and led historians to ask – has the forward march of Labour been halted? The answers are varied, but it is clear that any future development of the Labour party will be based upon a different relationship with its supporters than has existed in the past. The Liberal Radical strand of the party expired in 1931 and though the trade unions remain a powerful voice they are now subject to both declining numbers and the attempt of Kinnock to redefine their position within the party in favour of the individual membership. Such an adjustment of the power base of the party will not, by itself, revive its fortunes but the image of a party concerned with individual socialism and prepared to develop its policies may yet undermine the increasing notion that capitalism rather than socialism might be the norm in British society. So far, the historiographical debates about British Labour history have been depressingly insular and it may be that future Labour historians and Labour politicians might draw confidence in Labour's future from the history and example of continental socialism. Continental comparisons might at least assist with insight into some of the problems raised. This neglected area of research may encourage further interest in British Labour history. In any case historians will continue to debate the contours of Labour history and discussion will evolve as the views of Gramsci and other writers become embedded in the matrix of argument.

SUGGESTIONS FOR FURTHER READING

Many of the primary and secondary sources are indicated in the footnotes. This list is confined to those works which have become established as essential reading plus some of the more recently published material.

Issues in Labour History

K. D. Brown, *The English Labour Movement* (London, Gill and Macmillan, 1982).

K. Burgess, *The Challenge of Labour* (London, Croom Helm, 1984).

J. E. Cronin, *Labour and Society, 1918–1979* (London, Batsford, 1984).

J. Hinton, *Labour and Socialism: A History of the British Labour Movement 1867–1974* (Brighton, Wheatsheaf, 1983).

R. Miliband, *Parliamentary Socialism* (London, Merlin, 1972 edition).

R. Price, *Labour in British Society* (London, Croom Helm, 1986).

Rise of Labour and Decline of Liberalism, 1890–1918

M. Bentley, *The Climax of Liberal Politics: British Liberalism in Theory and Practice 1868–1918* (London, Edward Arnold, 1987).

K. D. Brown, ed., *The First Labour Party 1906–1914* (London, Croom Helm, 1985).

D. Clark, *Colne Valley: Radicalism to Socialism. The Portrait of a Northern Constituency in the Formative Years of the Labour Party 1890–1910* (London, Longman, 1981).

P. F. Clarke, *Lancashire and the New Liberalism* (Cambridge, CUP, 1971).

G. Dangerfield, *The Strange Death of Liberal England*, with preface by Paul Johnson (London, MacGibbon & Kee, 1966). This classic study, which first appeared in 1935, has been subject to several editions.

M. Hart, 'The Liberals, the War, and the Franchise', *English Historical Review* XLVIII (1982).

J. Hill, 'Manchester and Salford Politics and the early development of the Independent Labour Party', *International Review of Social*

History, XXXVI (1981).

D. Howell, *British Workers and the Independent Labour Party 1888–1906* (Manchester, Manchester University Press, 1983).

K. Laybourn and J. Reynolds, *Liberalism and the Rise of Labour 1890–1918* (London, Croom Helm, 1984).

H. C. Matthew, R. I. McKibbin and J. A. Kay, 'The franchise factor in the rise of the Labour Party', *English Historical Review*, XCI (1976).

K. O Morgan, 'The New Liberalism and the Challenge of Labour: The Welsh Experience 1885–1929', in K. D. Brown, ed., *Essays in Anti-Labour History* (London, Macmillan, 1974).

H. Pelling, *The Origins of the Labour Party* (London, Macmillan, 1954).

D. Powell, 'The New Liberalism and the Rise of Labour, 1886–1906', *Historical Journal*, 29, 2 (1986).

A. W. Purdue, 'The Liberal and the Labour Party in North East Politics', *International Review of Social History*, XXXVI (1981).

J. Reynolds and K. Laybourn, 'The Emergence of the Independent Labour Party in Bradford', *International Review of Social History*, XX (1975).

D. Tanner, 'The Parliamentary Electoral Reform System, the Fourth Reform Act and the Rise of Labour in England and Wales, *Bulletin of the Institute of Historical Research*, LVI (1983).

P. Thane, 'The Working Class and State "Welfare" in Britain 1880–1914', *Historical Journal*, vol. 27, 4 (1984).

E. P. Thompson, 'Homage to Tom Maguire', in A. Briggs and J. Saville, eds., *Essays in Labour History* (London, Macmillan, 1960). This article stimulated research into the regional and local study of the ILP and the local Labour Party.

P. Thompson, *Socialists, Liberals and Labour: The Struggle for London 1885–1914* (London, Routledge & Kegan Paul, 1967).

T. Wilson, *The Downfall of the Liberal Party 1914–1935* (London, Collins, 1966).

The Impact of War

R. Harrison, 'The War Emergency: Workers' National Committee 1914–1920', in A. Briggs and J. Saville, eds., *Essays in Labour History* (London, Macmillan, 1971). This is an excellent and balanced account of the work of the committee.

R. I. McKibbin, *The Evolution of the Labour Party, 1910–1924* (Oxford, OUP, 1974).

J. M. Winter, *Socialism and the Challenge of War: Ideas and Politics in Britain*, 1912–1918 (London, Routledge & Kegan Paul, 1974).

'Expectations born to death': The Labour Party 1918–1929

M. Bentley, *The Liberal Mind, 1914–1929* (Cambridge, CUP, 1977).
M. Cowling, *The Impact of Labour* (London, CUP, 1971).
C. Howard, 'Expectations born to death: the local Labour Party
   expansion in the 1920s', in J. Winter, ed., *The Working Class in
   Modern British History: Essays in Honour of Henry Pelling* (Cam-
   bridge, CUP, 1983).
G. A. Phillips, *The General Strike: The Politics of Industrial Conflict*
   (London, Weidenfeld & Nicolson, 1976).
P. Renshaw, *The General Strike* (London, Eyre Methuen, 1975).
J. Skelley, ed., 1926: The General Strike (London, Lawrence &
   Wishart, 1976).

'Lucifer of the Left': Ramsay MacDonald and the Collapse of the Second Labour Government 1929–1931

S. Ball, 'The Conservative Party and the formation of the National
   Government: August 1931', *Historical Journal*, 29, I (1986).
H. Berkeley, *The Myth that will not die* (London, Croom Helm, 1978).
A. Bullock, *The Life and Times of Ernest Bevin: Trade Union Leader*
   (London, Heineman, 1960).
K. Laybourn, *Philip Snowden* (Aldershot, Gower Publications, 1988).
R. MacDonald, *Ramsay MacDonald's Political Writings*, ed., B.
   Barker (London, Allen Lane, Penguin, 1972). This offers a good
   selection of MacDonald's writings and contains an excellent
   introduction by Barker.
D. Marquand, *Ramsay MacDonald* (London, Jonathan Cape, 1977).
   This book attempted to offer a more balanced biography of
   MacDonald than the accepted Labour mythology would permit.
R. Skidelsky, *Politicians and the Slump: The Labour Government of
   1929–1931* (London, Macmillan, 1967). This is an excellent and
   critical analysis of the reasons for the failure of MacDonald's second
   government.
P. Williamson, 'A 'Bankers' Ramp'? Financiers and the British
   political crisis of August 1931', *English Historical Review*, XCIX
   (October 1984).
L. MacNeill Weir, *The Tragedy of Ramsay MacDonald* (London,
   Secker & Warburg, 1938). This was the book which captured the
   hostility to MacDonald in the 1930s and which provided the basis for
   the mythology surrounding MacDonald's actions for almost forty
   years.

The Review and Triumph of Labour 1931–45

P. Addison, *The Road to 1945: British Politics and the Second World War* (London, Jonathan Cape, 1975).

C. Barnett, *The Audit of War: The Illusion and Reality of Britain as a Great Nation* (London, Macmillan, 1986).

M. Beloff, *Wars and Welfare* (London, Edward Arnold, 1984).

R. Blake, *The Decline of Power 1915–1964* (London, Granada, 1985).

F. Brockway, *Towards Tomorrow* (London, Hart-Davis, MacGibbon, 1977).

A. Bullock, *The Life and Times of Ernest Bevin: Vol II, Minister of Labour* (London, Heinemann, 1967).

H. Dalton, *The Second World War Diary of Hugh Dalton 1940–45* (London, Jonathan Cape, 1986).

R. Dore, 'British Labour, the National government and the National interest, 1931', *Historical Studies* (September 1979).

C. Fleay and M. Saunders, 'The Labour Spain Committee: the Labour Party Policy and the Spanish Civil War', *Historical Journal*, xxviii (1985).

M. Newman, Democracy versus Dictatorship', *History Workshop*, 5 (Spring, 1978).

B. Pimlott, *Labour and the Left in the 1930s* (London, CUP, 1977).

J. Reynolds and K. Laybourn, *Labour Heartland* (Bradford, Bradford University Press, 1987).

J. Stevenson and C. Cook, *The Slump* (London, Jonathan Cape, 1977).

K. W. Watkins, *Britain Divided* (London, Nelson, 1963).

Labour in Office, 1945–51

A. Bullock, *Ernest Bevin: Foreign Secretary 1945–51* (London, Heinemann, 1983).

A. Cairncross, *Years of Recovery: British Economic Policy 1945–51* (London, Methuen, 1985).

J. Campbell, *Nye Bevan and the Mirage of British Socialism* (London, Weidenfeld & Nicolson, 1987).

H. Dalton, *The Political Diary of Hugh Dalton, 1918–1940 and 1945–1960*, ed., B. Pimlott (London, Jonathan Cape, 1987).

B. Donoghue and G. W. Jones, *Herbert Morrison* (London, Weidenfeld & Nicolson, 1973).

R. Eatwell, *The 1945–1951 Labour Governments* (London, Batsford, 1979).

M. Foot, *Aneurin Bevan, 1945–1960* (London, Davis Poynter, 1973).

H. Gaitskell, *The Diary of Hugh Gaitskell*, ed., P. M. Williams (London, Jonathan Cape, 1983).

K. Harris, *Attlee* (London, Weidenfeld & Nicolson, 1982).

K. O. Morgan, *Labour in Power 1945–1951* (Oxford, Clarendon Press, 1984). This is much the best study of the two Attlee governments revealing the fundamental way in which they attempted to change society despite their many failings.

H. Pelling, *The Labour Government 1945–1951* (London, Macmillan, 1984).

B. Pimlott, *Hugh Dalton* (London, Jonathan Cape, 1985).

P. M. Williams, *Hugh Gaitskell* (Oxford, OUP, 1982).

The Crisis in the Labour Party, 1951–79

A. Benn, *Out of the Wilderness: diary 1963–67* (London, Hutchinson, 1987).

B. Castle, *The Castle Diaries 1974–76* (London, Weidenfeld & Nicolson, 1980).

J. Clarke, A. Cochrane and C. Smart, *Ideologies of Welfare: From Dreams to Disillusion* (London, Hutchinson, 1987).

Ivor Crewe, Bo Sarlvik and James Alt, 'Partisan Dealignment in Britain 1964–1974', *British Journal of Political Science*, vol. 7, part 2 (April 1977).

C.A.R. Crosland, *The Future of Socialism* (London, Jonathan Cape, 1956).

R. H. S. Crossman, ed., *New Fabian Essays* (London, 1952).

R. H. S. Crossman, *The Backbench Diaries of Richard Crossman*, ed., J. Morgan (London, Book Club Associates, 1981).

M. Holmes, *The Labour Government 1974–79: Political Aims and Economic Reality* (New York, St Martin's Press, 1985).

D. Kavanagh, ed., *The Politics of the Labour Party* (London, George Allen & Unwin, 1982).

A. J. Taylor, *The Trade Unions and the Labour Party* (London, Croom Helm, 1987).

P. Whiteley, *The Labour Party in Crisis* (London, Methuen, 1983).

H. Wilson, *The Labour Government 1964–70* (London, Penguin, 1974).

H. Wilson, *Final Term. The Labour Government of 1974–1976* (London, Weidenfeld & Nicolson, 1979).

INDEX